CSS3 Solutions

Essential Techniques for C   s

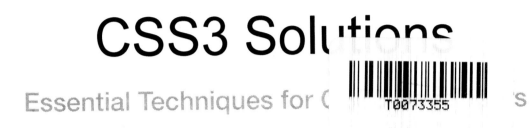

Marco Casario, Nathalie Wormser, Dan Saltzman, Anselm Bradford, Jonathan Reid, Francesco Improta, and Aaron Congleton

friendsof

DESIGNER TO DESIGNER™

an Apress® company

CSS3 SOLUTIONS: ESSENTIAL TECHNIQUES FOR CSS3 DEVELOPERS

ISBN-13 (pbk): 978-1-4302-4335-9

ISBN-13 (electronic): 978-1-4302-4336-6

Distributed to the book trade worldwide by Springer Science+Business Media New York, 233 Spring Street, 6th Floor, New York, NY 10013. Phone 1-800-SPRINGER, fax (201) 348-4505, e-mail orders-ny@springer-sbm.com, or visit www.springeronline.com.

For information on translations, please e-mail rights@apress.com or visit www.apress.com.

Apress and friends of ED books may be purchased in bulk for academic, corporate, or promotional use. eBook versions and licenses are also available for most titles. For more information, reference our Special Bulk Sales–eBook Licensing web page at www.apress.com/bulk-sales.

Any source code or other supplementary materials referenced by the author in this text is available to readers at www.apress.com. For detailed information about how to locate your book's source code, go to www.apress.com/source-code.

Credits

President and Publisher: Paul Manning	**Copy Editor:** Roger LeBlanc
Lead Editor: Ben Renow-Clarke	**Compositor:** SPi Global
Technical Reviewers: Andrew Zack	**Indexer:** SPi Global
Editorial Board: Steve Anglin, Ewan Buckingham, Gary Cornell, Louise Corrigan, Morgan Ertel, Jonathan Gennick, Jonathan Hassell, Robert Hutchinson, Michelle Lowman, James Markham, Matthew Moodie, Jeff Olson, Jeffrey Pepper, Douglas Pundick, Ben Renow-Clarke, Dominic Shakeshaft, Gwenan Spearing, Matt Wade, Tom Welsh	**Artist:** SPi Global **Cover Image Artist:** Corné van Dooren **Cover Designer:** Anna Ishchenko
Coordinating Editor: Jennifer Blackwell, Anamika Panchoo	

To my girlfriend, Katia, for always supporting me in my book projects.
—Marco Casario

To my parents.
—Nathalie Wormser

To my sister, who told me I could.
—Jonathan Reid

To Serena and Alessandro, my life.
—Francesco Improta

Contents at a Glance

Contents

About the Authors

Marco Casario has been passionate about informatics since he was little more than a child and used to program games in Basic for the Commodore 64. That was before dedicating himself, while still very young, to innovative projects for the Web using JavaScript and Flash.

In 2001, he began to collaborate with Macromedia. Since that year, he has produced and headed a long series of presentations, conferences, and articles, which you can find listed in detail on his blog (casario.blogs.com).

In 2005, Marco founded Comtaste (www.comtaste.com) a company dedicated to exploring new frontiers in Rich Internet and Mobile Applications and the convergence between the Web and the world of mobile devices. Now his focus is on User Experience (UX) aspects to make sure that enterprise software running on several different devices is easy and pleasurable to use, as well as on cloud computing with the Google Apps platform APIs and Google App Engine.

He is also the founder and manager of the biggest worldwide Flash Lite user group, the Italian community of Adobe Flex users (www.augitaly.com/flexgala), and the Italian HTML5 Meetup.

Marco is an Adobe Certified Instructor for Flex 4, LCDS 3, and AIR (ACI), and an Adobe Certified Expert for the LiveCycle Platform, Flash, and Dreamweaver. He is also a SCRUM Master.

Marco is author of several books, including *HTML5 Solutions: Essential Techniques for HTML5 Developers* (Apress), *Flex 4 Cookbook* (O'Reilly), *Professional Flash Catalyst: Building User Experiences for Rich Internet Applications* (Wrox), *Adobe AIR 1.5 Cookbook: Solutions and Examples for Rich Internet Application Developers* (O'Reilly), *Flex 4 Solutions: Essential Techniques for Flex Developers* (friendsofED), *AdvancED AIR Applications* (friendsofED), *The Essential Guide to Flash CS4 AIR Development* (friendsofED), and *Flex Solutions: Essential Techniques for Flex 2 and 3 Developers* (friendsofED).

His speaking engagements include international conferences such as FlashOnTheBeach, AJAXWorld Conference, O'Reilly Web 2.0 Summit, FITC, Adobe MAX, FATC New York, FlexCamp, 360Flex, TAC Singapore, MultiMania Belgium, Adobe CEM, and many others.

Nathalie Wormser is a freelance web developer who is passionate about emerging multimedia technologies , games, and digital educational applications. She is the co-founder of Project Cocoon Multimedia, a development and web design company based in Pondicherry, South India.

Dan Saltzman is a User Experience Architect and Strategist in Denver, Colorado.

Anselm Bradford is a lecturer in digital media at the Auckland University of Technology (AUT) in New Zealand, where he researches interactive media, web media, and visual communication. His experience with Internet-related development stretches back to 1996, when he hand-coded his first website. He may be found on Twitter *@anselmbradford*, and he occasionally blogs at *AnselmBradford.com*.

Jonathan Reid has been developing web-based applications in HTML and JavaScript since 1996 and is passionate about creating awesome and compelling user experiences on the Web. He is a firm believer in user-centered creative processes and is an advocate for standards and accessibility. Jon has a wide variety of experience building web applications, ranging from genetic analysis software to cutting-edge interactive advertising. Jon teaches courses in jQuery and has written extensively about jQuery Mobile.

Jon is an alumnus of the University of Colorado, Boulder, where he graduated with a degree in physics and mathematics. He currently works as a Senior Software Engineer for Motorola Mobility and lives in Sunnyvale, California with his partner of 13 years. You can follow him on Twitter at *@jreid01* and read his blog at *webdev.dreamwidth.org*.

Francesco Improta lives in Rome, Italy.

He designs interfaces for all devices, from mobile touchscreen to desktop. He calls himself a "user interface craftsman" and is passionate about the Web, typography, and new technologies.

Francesco's spare time is given to his family, sharing great moments with his wife and his little boy. He's addicted to sports and is currently practicing swimming, windsurfing, and snowboarding.

Aaron Congleton is currently working for Closely Inc. as a Senior Web Engineer. He has developed websites for the likes of Cisco, DaVita, Denver Art Museum, FedEx, Qwest, Comcast, and National Geographic.

About the Technical Reviewer

Andrew Zack is the CEO of ZTMC, Inc. (www.ztmc.com), which specializes in search engine optimization (SEO) and Internet marketing strategies. His project background includes almost 20 years of site development and project management experience and over 15 years as an SEO and Internet marketing expert.

Andrew has been very active in the publishing industry, having coauthored *Flash 5 Studio* (Apress, 2001) and served as a technical reviewer on more than 10 books and industry publications.

Having started working on the Internet close to its inception, Andrew continually focuses on the cutting edge and beyond, concentrating on new platforms and technology to stay at the forefront of the industry.

About the Cover Image Designer

Corné van Dooren designed the front cover image for this book. After taking a break from friends of ED to create a new design for the Foundation series, he worked at combining technological and organic forms, with the results now appearing on the cover of this and other books.

Corné spent his childhood drawing on everything at hand and then began exploring the infinite world of multimedia—and his journey of discovery hasn't stopped since. His mantra has always been "the only limit to multimedia is the imagination," a saying that keeps him moving forward constantly.

Corné works for many international clients, writes features for multimedia magazines, reviews and tests software, authors multimedia studies, and works on many other friends of ED books. If you like Corné's work, be sure to check out his chapter in *New Masters of Photoshop: Volume 2* (friends of ED, 2004). You can see more of his work (and contact him) at his website, www.cornevandooren.com.

Acknowledgments

It happens all the time. During the writing of a book, I often have the feeling that I will never reach the end. It is only with the help and support of many people who tirelessly work behind the scenes that the book is ready on time and in good form.

I would like to thank my coauthors for their hard work.

I want to thank Ben Renow-Clarke and Dominic Shakeshaft, and everyone on the friendsofED team for giving me the opportunity and the support to write and improve this book. Their guidance and input throughout the development of this book was essential. It's awesome and incredible how their work in coordinating the editing effort with authors across different continents and time zones made collaboration so easy.

Also, special thanks are due to my technical editor, Andrew Zack, who contributed to making the content and the examples easy to understand and follow.

And, of course, thank you to my Mom for having always pushed me to improve myself and to see beyond the surface of things.

To my brother, Alessio, for understanding why sometimes I did not have enough time for him.

To Katia, for her patience with all the weekend and night hours spent working on this book in the past several months.

This book is significantly better because of these great people.

Marco Casario

I would like to thank Ben Renow-Clarke and the entire friendsofED team for giving me the opportunity to co-write and work on this book.

Nathalie Wormser

I would like to thank R.J. Owen for his help and encouragement with my writing. I would also like to thank Ben Renow-Clarke and the friendsofED team for making this book possible.

Jonathan Reid

Thanks to the friendsofED/Apress team and my co-authors for their assistance and effort in coordinating the many chapters of this book. It has been a pleasure to work with many of the same people who helped on *HTML5 Mastery*. Thanks to my colleagues at AUT University, specifically Gudrun Frommherz, who allows me the time and flexibility of schedule to write and keep my web skills current.

Anselm Bradford

Introduction

CSS3 is the latest standard for CSS, the syntax to control the style and layout of web pages.

CSS3 is completely backward-compatible, so you will not have to change your existing designs. The CSS3 specification is still under development by the World Wide Web Consortium (W3C). However, many of the new CSS3 properties have been implemented in modern browsers and are available for you to experiment with today.

The CSS3 specification is made up of several "modules", such as the following ones:

- Selectors
- Box Model
- Backgrounds and Borders
- Text Effects
- 2D/3D Transformations
- Animations
- Multiple Column Layout
- User Interface

In this pragmatic book, we have provided a series of solutions to common problems faced by developers approaching the new features in CSS3. You will therefore find a lot of ready-to-use code that you can build on in your own web applications.

Who is this book for?

This book is aimed at designers and developers who want to start using CSS3 right now.

CSS3 Solutions is, in fact, intended for readers who want to take their knowledge further with quick-fire solutions to common problems and best practice techniques to improve their CSS3 skills. The book is full of solutions with real-world examples and code to support you as you enter the world of CSS3 development.

What you need

To follow and create the examples shown in this book, you need a simple text editor. TextMate, UltraEdit, and Notepad++ are just some examples of powerful text editors with code support.

Conventions used in this book

This book uses several of conventions that are worth noting. The following terms are used throughout this book:

- *CSS* refers to the CSS 3 language.

- *Modern browsers* are considered to be the latest versions of Firefox, Safari, Chrome, and Opera, along with Internet Explorer 7 and newer (although Internet Explorer 10 is the most "modern" in terms of support for new features).

It is assumed that all the CSS examples in this book are contained in an external style sheet. Occasionally, HTML and CSS have been placed in the same code example for brevity.

Sometimes code won't fit on a single line in a book. Where this happens, we've used an arrow to break the line.

With these formalities out of the way, you're ready to get started.

Questions and Contacts

Please direct any technical questions or comments about the book to m.casario@comtaste.com.

For more information about other CSS Books, see our website: www.apress.com.

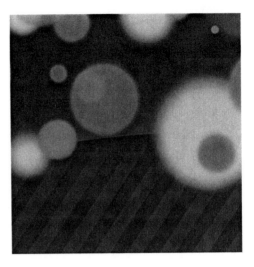

Chapter 1

CSS Basics

Cascading Style Sheets (which we'll refer to by their acronym, CSS) were created to separate the presentational layer from the logic of an application. Their purpose has always been to provide users with a simple language to define the styling aspects of web pages and their look and feel. A CSS style declares a series of properties for content, such as the font family, size of the font, color, and so on.

The World Wide Web Consortium (W3C) has released new versions of CSS over the years that add new functions. (You can see the W3C's more recent work at `www.w3.org/Style/CSS/current-work`.) One great step forward was the introduction of CSS statements to position the contents of a page.

With these new commands, web developers could finally abandon the approach of generating web page layouts by using HTML tables. Now developers can use the following three types of positioning:

- `static`: The default positioning of the browser. This refers to the traditional HTML positioning, in which each element is positioned on the basis of the data flow of the document.

- `absolute`: Allows you to use the content anywhere on the page, completely independent from the other elements, by specifying the position of each element on a Cartesian axis represented by the height and width of the browser window.

- `relative`: Allows you to declare an element in a position that is based on the previous element.

Over the past three years, on the other hand, we have witnessed significant acceleration in terms of new specifications. In fact, the W3C, which is responsible for most web standards, intends to insert an

1

approach that can be divided into modules as needed. This new approach features properties, techniques, and methods that are finally tuned to the real needs of those who make web sites.

> *The World Wide Web Consortium (W3C) is the main international standards organization for the World Wide Web (abbreviated as WWW or W3).*
>
> *Founded and headed by Tim Berners-Lee, the consortium is made up of member organizations that maintain full-time staff who work together to develop standards for the World Wide Web. As of July 2011, the W3C has 317 members. W3C was created to ensure compatibility and agreement among industry members in the adoption of new standards. Prior to its creation, incompatible versions of HTML were offered by different vendors, increasing the potential for inconsistency between web pages. The W3C works to get all those vendors to agree on a set of core principles and components that will be supported by everyone.*
>
> *Source: Wikipedia http://en.wikipedia.org/wiki/World_Wide_Web_Consortium*

CSS3 Modules

With CSS3, instead of writing only one specification divided into chapters, the W3C has changed the specification to be many separate modules, each of which is dedicated to a particular aspect of the CSS language. This modular approach relieves companies that make web browsers from having to implement the specifications in their entirety. Instead, a company can opt to support one module at a time by adding new CSS modules at every new release of its browser. And this is exactly what is happening now.

Let's take a closer look at the CSS3 modules that are currently available:

- **Selectors:** This part is the most stable and is implemented best by browsers. CSS3 selectors were conceived so that they will function even with complex XML documents. They can cross the hierarchy of a document and select elements based on the relationships between them (for example, being the *n*th child of one's parent). This module is currently at the stage of Candidate Recommendation.

- **CSS Template Layout:** This module, previously known as Advance Layout, specifies new ways to place elements based on the relationship between them to guarantee maximum flexibility. It is currently at the Working Draft phase.

- **Media Queries:** The CSS3 media queries are an addition to the normal @media rules that can assign styles on the basis of new parameters, such as the size of the screen and its proportions. This module is currently at the Candidate Recommendation stage.

- **CSS Backgrounds and Borders:** This module describes new functions for backgrounds and borders, including the possibility of extending background images and rounding border angles. It is currently at the Last Call stage.

- **CSS Basic User Interface:** New methods and properties have been introduced to this module to assign styles to the user interface of a web document (such as forms). It is currently at the Candidate Recommendation stage.

- **CSS Basic Box Model:** This module accounts for differences between horizontal and vertical writing by defining the box model of the elements. It is currently at the Working Draft stage.

- **CSS Marquee:** This module proposes a CSS solution to avoid the use of the marquee owner element. It is currently at the Proposed Recommendation stage.

- **CSS Cascading and Inheritance:** This defines the ways in which styles are assigned to elements via the cascade. It is at the working Draft stage.

- **CSS Color:** This module introduces new concepts and values to describe CSS colors. It's at the Last Call stage.

- **CSS Fonts:** This module includes new properties and values for CSS fonts, such as the use of fonts that can be downloaded with the `@font-face` directive. It's at the Working Draft stage.

- **CSS Generated Content for Paged Media:** This module extends the common CSS properties for printing with the introduction of footnotes and cross-references. It's at the Working Draft stage.

- **CSS Generated and Replaced Content:** This module introduces the concept of replacing the effective content of an element with the one generated by CSS. It's at the Working Draft stage.

- **CSS Hyperlink Presentation:** This module extends the normal way CSS processes hypertext links, thus providing greater control to the authors regarding their states. This module is at the Working Draft stage.

- **CSS Line Layout:** In this module, the layout of the inline elements is defined with more precision. It's at the Working Draft stage.

- **CSS Lists:** This module deals with list layouts with more detail and precision (ordered and unordered) than in earlier releases. It's at the Working Draft stage.

- **CSS Multicolumn Layout:** This module defines new properties and values to manage layout over several columns. It's at the Last Call stage.

- **CSS Namespaces:** This module defines the ways to select elements on the basis of the presence of a certain namespace. It's essential for formatting XML documents and is currently at the Candidate Recommendation stage.

- **CSSOM View Module:** This module allows authors to obtain information about elements without resorting to scripting. It's at the Working Draft stage.

- **CSS Paged Media:** This module extends the CSS properties for print to obtain headers, footers, and page numbers. It's at the Working Draft stage.

- **CSS Presentation Levels:** This module introduces the concept of multiple presentations of the same document. It's designed to facilitate particular layouts, such as those of presentation slides, and it's at the Working Draft stage.

- **Grid Positioning:** In the new CSS3 layout model, one positioned element forms a presentation grid. This module proposes a series of coordinates for the positioning of the floated elements that have an absolute position. The module is in the Working Draft stage.

- **CSS Text:** This module addresses the need for internationalization in defining new properties and values to control the text using CSS. It's at the Working Draft stage.

- **CSS 2D Transforms Module:** This module introduces concepts that are already featured in SVG (Scalable Vector Graphic) to CSS, such as transformation, rotation, and the scaling of elements. It's at the Working Draft stage.

- **CSS 3D Transformations Module:** This module extends the previous one with new specifications for transformations. It's at the Working Draft stage.

- **CSS Transitions Module:** This module introduces the concepts of transition and delay in transitions between states among the elements (for example, when an element receives focus and then loses it). It's at the Working Draft stage.

- **CSS Animations Module:** This module introduces new properties that can control the intermediate stages of the animation of the elements (for example, stages in a sequence). It's at the Working Draft stage.

Anatomy of a CSS3 declaration

CSS and HTML are inseparable friends. Therefore, to be able to fully take advantage of CSS statements, it is essential to understand the structure of an HTML document.

After a long period of silence, HTML recently has been brought back to life, thanks to the work of companies such as Apple, Google, Opera Software, and the Mozilla Foundation. They collaborated under the name of WHATWG (which stands for the Web Hypertext Application Technology Working Group, whose web site is at www.whatwg.org/) on the development of an updated and enhanced version of the old HTML.

Following this major interest, the W3C began to work on a new version of HTML, called HTML5. It's official name is Web Applications 1.0, and it introduces structural elements to HTML that have not been seen before.

These new elements bridge the gap between structure, defined by the markup; rendering characteristics, defined by styling directives; and the content of a web page, defined by the text itself. Furthermore, HTML5 introduced a native open standard to deliver multimedia content such as audio and video, collaboration APIs, local storage, geolocation APIs, and much more.

Each HTML5 document defines a tree structure for a document, known as the Document Object Model (DOM). The DOM is a programming API for HTML documents, as well as XML. It defines the logical structure of documents, and web developers can use it to create and build documents, access and modify their structure, or delete elements and content. You can learn more about the DOM at the W3C DOM page at www.w3.org/TR/WD-DOM/introduction.html.

CSS takes full advantage of this concept because its fundamental mechanism is based on heredity. This makes it possible for most properties set for an element to be inherited by its descendants, hence the term "Cascading."

Here is some simple HTML5 code:

```
<!DOCTYPE html>
<head>
 <title>Page Tile</title>
</head>
<body>
 <h1>Title</h1>
```

```
<div>
 <p>My first paragraph</p>
</div>
 <section>
<h2>My Heading</h2>
 <p>This is a second paragraph</p>
</section>
 </body>
</html>
```

> If you want to learn more about HTML5, Apress has published many books on the subject. One that I recommend is written by the same authors as this book: HTML5 Solutions Essential Techniques for HTML5 Developers (http://www.apress.com/9781430233862).

This document, like any valid HTML document, is an ordered hierarchy of elements that are linked to one another by a parent-child relationship. This hierarchy forms what is defined as the Document Object Model.

The DOM is a cross-platform and language-independent convention for representing and interacting with objects in HTML (as well as XML). Web browsers usually use an internal model similar to the DOM to render a document.

The simple HTML5 code declared earlier can be represented like this:

```
|-> Document
  |-> Root Element (<html>)
   |-> Element (<head>)
    |-> Element (<body>)
     |-> Element (<div>)
      |-> paragraph
     |-> Section
      |-> header
```

This hierarchy defines the structure of the document. It's used by CSS to define the styles of the element via CSS rules.

A CSS rule is applied using selectors followed by one or more declarations, as shown in Figure 1-1.

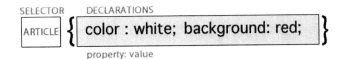

Figure 1-1. Declaration rule of a CSS.

Selectors can be any of the following:

- **Type Selectors:** These are represented by the name of a specific HTML element. They are used to select all specific types of an element in a document—for example:

```
body {color: red}
```

- **Class Selectors:** Each HTML can be assigned a class using the `class` attribute. You then assign a name to it that can be accessed by CSS—for example:

```
<h1 class="mytitle">This is a header</h1>
```

To apply one style to the class declared in HTML in the tag header, you precede the name of the class with a period (.):

```
.mytitle {font-family: Verdana}
```

- **ID Selectors:** Each HTML element can be assigned an ID, which is a unique reference for this element in the document—for example:

```
<section id="mystyle"></section>
```

To select an element that has been assigned a certain ID in CSS, you add the pound key (#) before the value of the ID:

```
#mystyle {color: black}
```

We've written this introduction to CSS selectors only to provide some essential concepts for readers who have never worked with CSS. It is not intended to be—and obviously doesn't provide—a full overview of selectors. In fact, there are other types of selectors: descendants, child, and so on. We have dedicated an entire chapter to this aspect of CSS3. You can find different solutions related to this vast subject in Chapter 2.

At this point, web developers have understood that CSS is an integral part of an HTML document. However, there are different ways to declare CSS for a document. You can have internal or external style sheets:

- **External CSS:** A style sheet defined in a separate file by the document with a .css extension.

- **Internal CSS:** The styles are included in the HTML document.

As far as external CSS files are concerned, you can link them by creating a `<link>` tag inside the head section:

```
<head>
<link rel="stylesheet" type="text/css" href="mystyle.css" />
</head>
```

The `<link>` element has a series of attributes that need to be specified:

- **rel: compulsory.** Describes the type of relation between the document and the linked file. It accepts the following values: `stylesheet` and `alternate stylesheet`.

- **href: compulsory.** Defines the absolute or relative URL of the style sheet.

- **type: compulsory.** Identifies the type of data to be connected. For CSS, the only possible value is `text/css`.

- **media: optional.** Declares the type of device to which the style sheet applies, such as the `handheld` property for handheld devices (typically, devices with a small screen and limited bandwidth).

Another way to load external CSS is to use the @import directive in the <style> element:

```
<style>
@import url(mystyle.css);
</style>
```

This approach of using the @import statement is one of the safest ways to solve compatibility issues between old and new browsers.

For internal style sheets, you define internal styles in the head section of an HTML page, by using the <style> tag, like this:

```
<head>
<style type="text/css">
body
{
 background: #FFFFCC;
}
</style>
</head>
```

There is another way to declare an internal style sheet: an inline style. The declaration can be made at the level of each tag in the page. To use inline styles, you declare the style attribute in the relevant tag:

```
<h1 style="color: red; font-size: 10px;">My Header</h1>
```

To conclude this section, we'll specify how to insert parts of a comment in a CSS. All you need to do is place the comment between these symbols:

```
/*
Multiline comment here
*/
```

Understanding the Box Model

In the previous section, we spoke about the structure of a document and how to apply a CSS rule to elements within a document. You can also use CSS to position elements within the page. This technique is called *CSS positioning*, or *CSS-P*. To use CSS-P rules, you need to understand how the browser physically draws the page on the screen based on the HTML code. The whole series of rules that manages the visual aspect of the elements is generally referred to as the *box model*.

Each box includes a certain number of basic components, and each can be modified with CSS properties. Instead of trying to explain with a thousand words what a box model represents, we'll use Figure 1-2 to provide a clearer illustration of the concept.

In the innermost part of the figure, you find the area of the page content, where you can see the background image and the sentence "content goes in here…". This is the area where the content of the HTML page is rendered: text, images, sections, paragraphs, media elements, and so on. The size assigned to this area is determined by the browser if you don't specify the width and height properties of the content.

On the outside of an element, you find the padding, which is empty space that can be created between the content and the border of the element to add some space between these elements.

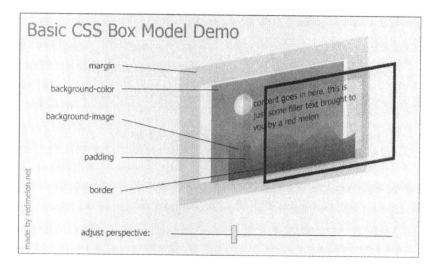

Figure 1-2. A CSS 3D box model that was created by redmelon.net and can be found at http://redmelon.net/tstme/ box_model/.

Outside of that, you find the border, which is not an area but a variable line of dimension, style, and color that surrounds the padding zone and the content area. Finally, you get to the margin, which is a space that varies in size and separates a certain element from the adjacent areas.

The size of the box model, apart from the width of the content area, is obtained by this sum:

```
content width + left padding + left border width + right padding + right border width +
margin left + margin right
```

CSS3 doesn't introduce many new aspects here, but there are a couple of interesting ones. Later in this book, you'll see possible solutions for setting a border background and drawing rounded border corners, using the `border-image` and `border-radius` properties, respectively.

If you want to learn more about the important subject of the box model, you can refer to Chapter 6 or to the box model described by the W3C at `www.w3.org/TR/CSS2/box.html`.

Understanding CSS inheritance

Inheritance is one of the key concepts on which CSS techniques are based. In fact, CSS properties can inherit the display properties of dominant HTML tags, at least until you explicitly set a different value for a child element. This is why a property is applied to all child elements of the tag body, meaning the entire content of the page, if you set it to the body element.

Be careful, though, because not all properties are inherited. As a general rule, you can consider that the ones regarding box-model formatting (padding, margins, and borders) are properties that are not inherited by the child elements.

Earlier in the chapter, you saw that CSS can be declared and applied to the page as an external CSS, or it can be declared and applied as an internal or inline CSS. The type of declaration influences how a property will be inherited by an element, as well as how high or low the importance of each statement is.

To understand the way inheritance works, bear in mind that the CSS rule applied will be the one that is closest to the element in the code of the document. The order, therefore, is the following:

- **Inline style:** The ones that are applied last by the browser. They prevail over those that are declared in the page.

- **Internal CSS:** These prevail over the styles declared in the external CSS.

Consider the following example of an external style sheet declared as a CSS file named *styles.css*:

```
.myclass {
background-color:red;
}
```

This CSS file is then imported into the HTML page, where an internal and inline declaration has been added:

```
<link href="styles.css" type="text/css" rel="stylesheet" />
<style type="text/css">
. myclass {
background-color:white;
}
</style>
<article class="myclass" style="background-color:green; ">
CSS3 Rocks !
</article>
```

In the preceding example, which color will the web browser render for the article's background color? Read the code carefully.

Notice that the `article` element with the class name `"myclass"` gets its background color from an external style sheet, from styles defined on the page, and from an inline style. So the right reply to the question is that the article will get the `background-color: green` rule, inherited by the inline declaration, because it's the last rule applied by the browser.

Solution 1-1: Discovering CSS3 compatibilities across browsers

CSS3 provides a new set of tools to empower you to improve the look and feel of your web pages. However, like all new technology, it suffers from inconsistent cross-browser compatibility. In fact, there are new CSS3 features that work only on some browser versions, making web developers' lives more difficult. Therefore, it's essential to learn the compatibility matrix by heart for each version of each browser, or use a tool to help you out.

What's involved

There are many web sites that provide comparative tables to see at a glance which CSS3 features are supported by which browser. In this solution, you'll see some of the most popular ones:

■ CSS3 Please (which you can check out at css3please.com) a Cross-Browser CSS3 Rule Generator

■ CanIUse (which you can check out at www.caniuse.com) is a compatibility table for support of HTML5, CSS3, SVG and more in desktop and mobile browsers.

■ FindmebyIP (which you can check out at www.findmebyip.com/litmus/) is a cute little app that presents your browsers' support for advanced HTML5 and CSS3 features in an easy to read manner.

■ HTML5 Please, (which you can check out at html5please.com the new HTML5 and CSS3 features, knowing if they are ready for use.

How to build it

CSS3 Please is more than just a simple compatibility table to discover the browser support of CSS3. It allows you to edit CSS3 property values in real time that will be applied to the web page. By doing this, you can copy the all of the generated CSS values, or only some of them, and paste them into your own style sheet.

For example, you can interact with a `border-radius` property by changing the values contained in the following class:

```
.box_round {
  -webkit-border-radius: 12px; /* Saf3-4, iOS 1-3.2, Android ≤1.6 */
  -moz-border-radius: 12px; /* FF1-3.6 */
  border-radius: 12px; /* Opera 10.5, IE9, Saf5, Chrome, FF4, iOS 4, Android 2.1+ */
```

As you can see, the `.box_round` class provides the code for the various declarations to make the properties work on all types of browsers, including the following ones:

■ Safari

■ The iOS browser

■ The Android browser

■ Firefox

■ Opera

The values assigned to each property can be changed on the fly, and the upper left box of the web page will change automatically to show the new values, as you can see in Figure 1-3.

It also comes with the following two interesting features:

```
[to clipboard] [toggle rule off]
```

Figure 1-3. The CSS3,Please box changes according to the CSS3 values.

You can use the first one to copy the CSS3 code in the clipboard. With the second one, you can decide whether or not to apply the CSS3 rule to the object.

This tool is essential both as a learning tool as well as a way to improve the productivity of your web development effortsbecause it provides cross-browser code.

HTML5 Please, on the other hand, is a traditional but well-built search engine that looks up the features of CSS3 and HTML5. It allows you to assess the HTML5 and CSS3 compatibility level for each property. For example, if you search for a CSS3 feature such as border-radius, you'll get the description shown in Figure 1-4.

On the lower left side, you can see a link labeled View browser share % that points to the Canluse.com table. Canluse.com is the reference comparison table for HTML5, CSS3, SVG support, and more in desktop and mobile browsers.

The Canluse.com service, like others, is completely free, and you can use it to quickly see HTM5 and CSS3 features and their compatibility, both as an indexed list and as a table. You also can use it to search for a particular property by using a search box, as shown in Figure 1-5.

By clicking an item on the list, you get more information and the view switches to Tables mode, as shown in Figure 1-6.

As a general rule, because CSS3 and HTML5 standards are evolving, you should pay attention to the features that you want to use in your web pages. In fact, you should apply elements from CSS3 gradually, as updates become necessary.

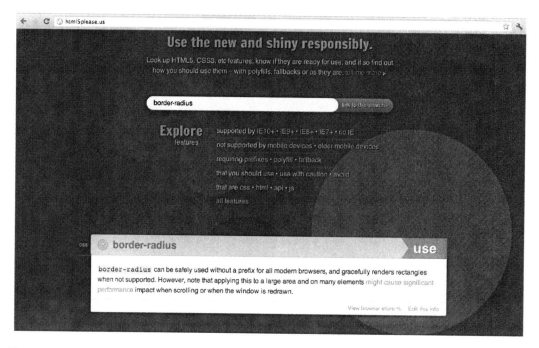

Figure 1-4. The HTML5 Please search box.

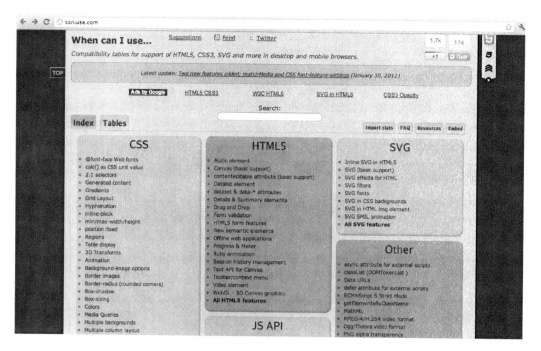

Figure 1-5. The table reference provided by CanIUse.com.

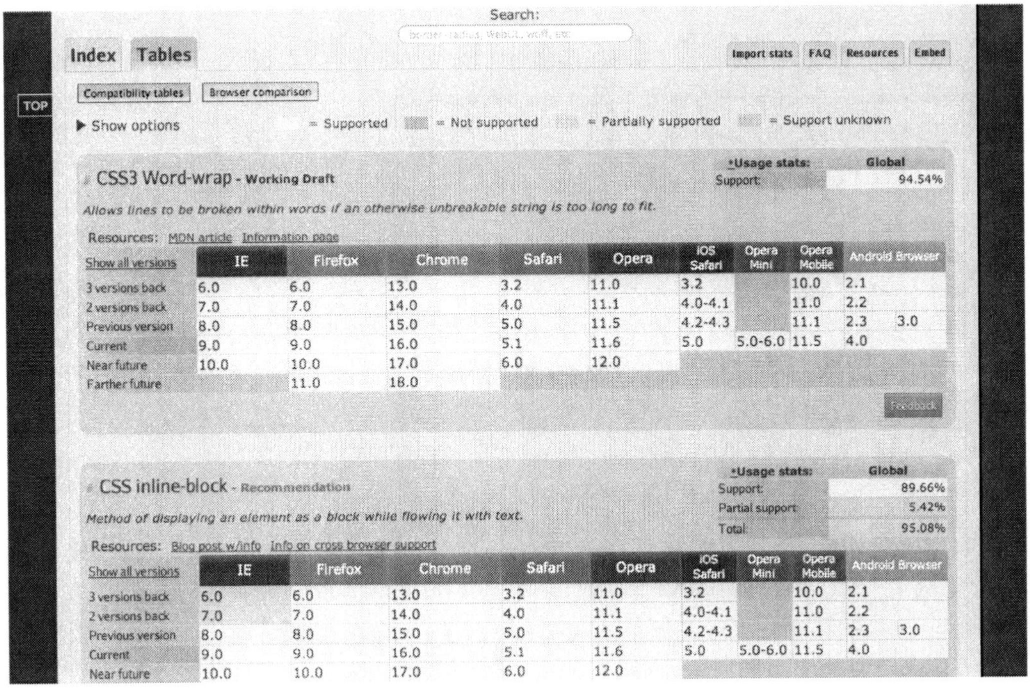

Figure 1-6. When you click on a property, you get extra information.

Expert tips

Canluse.com allows you to point directly at the feature you want to check by inserting #feat equal to the name of the feature in the URL, as follows:

```
http://caniuse.com/#feat=css-boxshadow
```

By inserting this URL in the browser, you can obtain the response from the site shown in Figure 1-7.

Solution 1-2: Adding a CSS3 file with JavaScript

Web developers can use JavaScript to load a CSS file dynamically, possibly on the basis of the type of page that is called by the user or the type of rights that a user has within an application. The following solution illustrates how to use the JavaScript language to load an external CSS file.

What's involved

The standard HTML5 procedure to load an external CSS file on a page is to point a reference to it in the HEAD section of your page with the <script> tag:

```
<head>
<link rel="stylesheet" type="text/css" href="myCSS.css" />
</head>
```

13

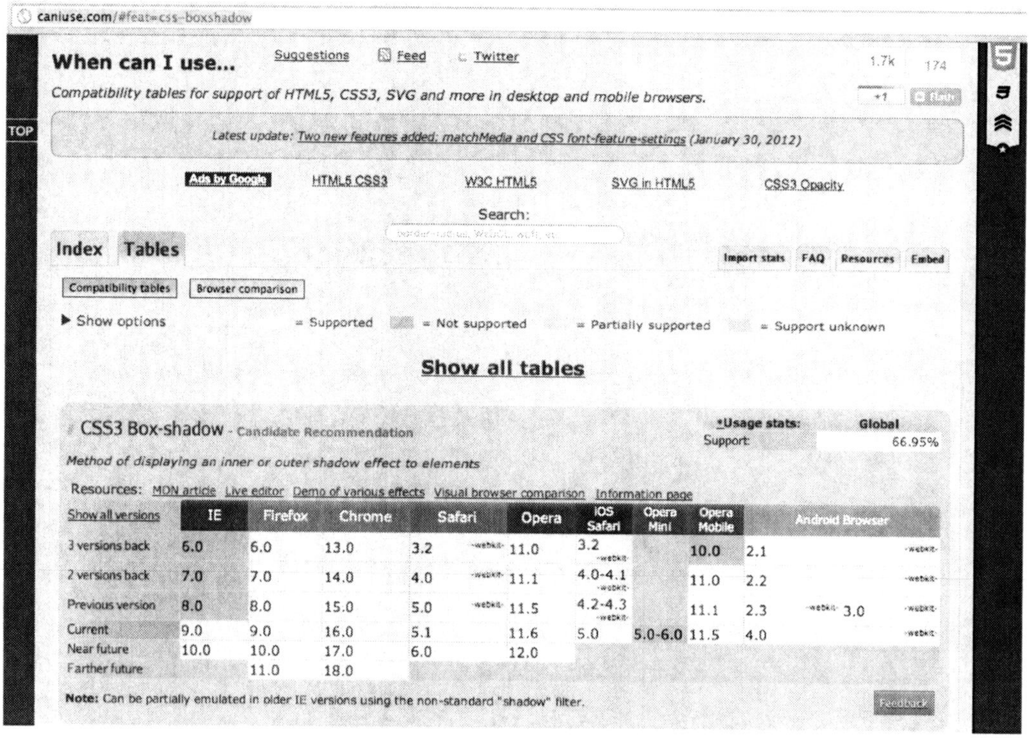

Figure 1-7. Calling a property directly from the browser address bar.

When the browser reads the content of the HTML page that is loaded, the CSS file is added to the page. Therefore, we could say that the external file is loaded *synchronously*.

However, with JavaScript, you can load the external file on demand using the createElement() method of the DOM object document to create the <link> tag that will then load the file:

```
document.createElement('link');
```

You can set the properties of the link object that has just been created to specify the type of content to load, text/css, and the pathway and name of the file to be loaded:

```
link.rel = 'stylesheet';
link.type = 'text/css';
link.href = 'myFileCSS.css';
link.media = 'all';
```

To be able to apply the link object to the page and load the CSS file, you have to call the DOM method appendChild(), which adds a node after the last child node of the specified element node:

```
document.getElementsByTagName('head')[0].appendChild(link)
```

This method returns the new child node.

Now let's see how to build the complete solution.

How to build it

In the previous section, we discussed methods that can be used to load a CSS file using JavaScript.

To do this, you create a JavaScript function that accepts two parameters: one is the name of the CSS file to be loaded, and the other is the ID assigned to the link tag. This second parameter allows you to check whether the file has already been loaded.

You start by writing the following function:

```
function loadCSSfile(filename, cssID)
{
var cssId = cssID
```

Insert an if() control that checks that the ID of the element isn't already in the page. This would mean that the CSS file has already been loaded:

```
if (!document.getElementById(cssId))
{
```

At this point, you can create the link object and set its properties:

```
  var head = document.getElementsByTagName('head');
  var link = document.createElement('link');
  link.id  = cssId;
  link.rel = 'stylesheet';
  link.type = 'text/css';
  link.href = filename;
  link.media = 'all';
  head[0].appendChild(link);
}
}
```

To use the JavaScript method you just created, all you have to do is recall it in a JavaScript block and associate it, for example, to the onload event of the window object:

```
<!doctype html>
 <html>
 <head>
  <title>onload test</title>
  <script>
function loadCSSfile(filename, cssID)
{
var cssId = cssID

if (!document .getElementById(cssId))
{
  var head = document.getElementsByTagName('head');
  var link = document.createElement('link');
```

```
    link.id  = cssId;
    link.rel = 'stylesheet';
    link.type = 'text/css';
    link.href = filename;
    link.media = 'all';
    head[0].appendChild(link);
  }
}
  window.onload = load;
  </script>
 </head>
 <body>
  <p>The CSS file is loaded dynamically via JavaScript!</p>
 </body>
</html>
```

Or, if you want to insert the loadCSSfile() method in an external JavaScript file, first you have to load it and then call it like this:

```
<script type="text/javascript" src="externalJavascript.js"></script>
<script type="text/javascript">loadCSSfile('main.css', 'myCSSId')</script>
```

Expert tips

To set the properties of the link object, you use setAttribute():

```
var link=document.createElement('link');
link.setAttribute("rel", "stylesheet")
link.setAttribute("type", "text/css")
link.setAttribute("href", 'myFileCSS')
```

The problem with this method is that Internet Explorer 6 doesn't support it consistently. So the script would not have worked under the aged Internet Explorer 6. If you're using JQuery or YUI Ajax frameworks, there are methods you can invoke from these libraries.

For JQuery, there is a plugin that loads CSS files and JavaScript files on demand and keeps track of what has already been loaded:

```
code.google.com/p/rloader/
```

For the Yahoo YUI library (shown in Figure 1-8), you can use the following method, which also supports cross-domain loading:

```
yuilibrary.com/yui/docs/get/
```

Solutions 1-3: Declaring multiple backgrounds for your web page

The background of a web page gives the finishing touch to a website. With CSS3, you can now use multiple background images.

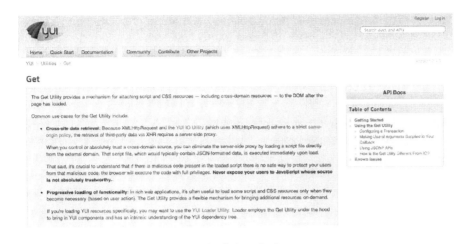

Figure 1-8. The YUI library page that documents the Get method.

What's involved

Background image management has always been entrusted to the background property. To be valid, the declaration doesn't have to contain references to all its properties, but it has to at least contain the definition of the background color. For example, to create an image that is repeated horizontally as a background on the body, with a background color taken from an external image, you can write the following:

```
body{background: #7A515A url(gradient.jpg) fixed repeat-x bottom}
```

To use multiple background images for your pages, you can simply declare a simple comma-separated list under the background property.

Let's see how to obtain this result in this solution.

How to build it

To use multiple images as background, all you have to do is use the background property and specify two or more values in the URL:

```
background-image: url(myFirstBG.png), url(myFSecondBG.png);
```

Multiple backgrounds can also be specified using the background shorthand property:

```
background: url(myFirstBG.png) 0 0 no-repeat, url(mySecondBG.png) 0 0 repeat-x
```

Here is some detail from the CSS Backgrounds and Borders Level 3 specification (which is available at www.w3.org/TR/css3-background/#backgrounds):

"The number of comma-separated items defines the number of background layers. Given a valid declaration, for each layer the shorthand first sets the corresponding layer of each of 'background-position', 'background-size', 'background-repeat', 'background-origin', 'background-clip' and 'background-attachment' to that property's initial value, then assigns any explicit values specified for this layer in the declaration. Finally 'background-color' is set to the specified color, if any, else set to its initial value.

If one <box> value is present then it sets both 'background-origin' and 'background-clip' to that value. If two values are present, then the first sets 'background-origin' and the second 'background-clip'".

Here is a complete example (which works in all new browsers but does not display properly in Internet Explorer 8):

```
<!DOCTYPE html>
<html lang="en">
<head>
<meta charset="UTF-8" />
<title>Solution 1-3: Declaring multiple backgrounds for your web page </title>
<style>
.boxBG{

background-image: url(firstImg.png), url(secondImg.png);
background-position: center bottom, left top;
background-repeat: no-repeat;
}
</style>
</head>
<body>
<section class="boxBG">
<p>
This has multiple backgrounds!
</p>
</section>
</body>
</html>
```

Expert tips

To make this style also work on old browsers that still don't support the loading of multiple images, all you have to do is add a line with the same background property but with only one image:

```
<style>
.boxBG{

  background: url(apple.jpg) no-repeat;
  background: url(firstImg.jpg) 0 0 no-repeat, url(secondImg.jpg) 100% 0 no-repeat;
  width: 500px;
  height :250px;
}
```

Solution 1-4: Controlling the image aspect ratio

Every HTML page works with media elements such as images. Most of the websites that allow users to upload images have one issue in common: the image's dimension. In fact, uploaded images might not be in the right size and can alter or even disrupt your page layout. You have to avoid this scenario.

With CSS3, you can control the image aspect ratio using JavaScript functions.

What's involved

To maintain the aspect ratio of the images on a page and get them to fit within a fixed area, you can use the `object-fit` CSS3 property.

As defined by the W3C, this property specifies how the contents of a replaced element should be fitted to the box established by its height and width. A *replaced element* is an element whose content is defined by an external resource such as an image.

These are the values that `object-fit` accepts:

- `fill`: The replaced content is sized to fill the element's content box. The object's concrete object size is the element's width and height.

- `contain`: The replaced content is sized to maintain its aspect ratio while fitting within the element's content box. Its concrete object size is resolved as a contain constraint against the element's width and height.

- `cover`: The replaced content is sized to maintain its aspect ratio while filling the element's entire content box. Its concrete object size is resolved as a cover constraint against the element's width and height.

- `none`: The replaced content is not resized to fit inside the element's content box. The object's concrete object size is determined using the default sizing algorithm with no specified size, and using a default object size equal to the replaced element's width and height.

- `scale-down`: Size the content as if `none` or `contain` was specified, whichever would result in a smaller concrete object size.

The `object-fit` property can be applied to images as well as to a video or SVG file.

Suppose that you want to control the aspect ratio of an image with the following CSS statement:

```
img {
  object-fit: contain;
}
```

Following is a complete example.

How to build it

In this solution, you create a simple image gallery that contains images of different sizes. Those images will use the `object-fit` property that's set to the value `contain`. By doing this, you're forcing all the images to fit inside the area and maintain the aspect ratio.

This is the complete code for this solution:

```html
<!DOCTYPE html>
<html>
<head>
<title>Solution 1-4: Controlling the image aspect ratio</title>
<style>
div {
 margin-bottom: 20px;
 padding: 20px;
}
img {
 position: absolute;
 width: 100px;
 height: 100px;

 -ms-object-fit: contain;
 -moz-object-fit: contain;
 -o-object-fit: contain;
 -webkit-object-fit: contain;
 object-fit: contain;
}

div p {
   font-family:Arial, Helvetica, sans-serif;
       margin-left: 110px;

}
</style>
</head>
<body>

<h1>Wine Tasting</h1>

<div>
<img src="IMG_2407.jpg" width="480" height="640">
<p>Le Pergole Torte 2004</p>
</div>

<div>
<img src="IMG_2444.jpg" width="640" height="480">
<p>Tenuta San Guido Wines</p>
</div>

<div>
<img src="IMG_2538.jpg" width="480" height="640">
<p>Guidalberto 2004</p>
</div>

<div>
<img src="IMG_2535.jpg" width="480" height="640">
```

```
<p>Vernaccia di San Gimignano 200</p>
```

```
</div>
</body>
```

```
</html>
```

If you save and run the application in a web browser, you'll see that all the images fit inside the DIV and maintain the aspect ratio.

The CSS `object-fit` property performs the magic:

```
img {
  position: absolute;
  width: 100px;
  height: 100px;

  -ms-object-fit: contain;
  -moz-object-fit: contain;
  -o-object-fit: contain;
  -webkit-object-fit: contain;
  object-fit: contain;
}
```

You've declared the `object-fit` property using various suffixes to make it compatible with all the major browsers: -ms, -moz, -o, and -webkit.

Expert tips

There is another very useful property you can use with the images to specify their resolution: the `image-resolution` property. This property is defined by the W3C as a property that specifies the intrinsic resolution of all raster images (it cannot be used with vector images such as SVG) used in or on the element.

Reading the definition, you see that you can apply the property to both content images and decorative images (such as `background-image`). Its values have the following meanings:

- `<resolution>`: This specifies the intrinsic resolution explicitly. A "*dot*" in this case corresponds to a single image pixel.

- `from-image`: The image's intrinsic resolution is taken as that specified by the image format. If the image does not specify its own resolution, the explicitly specified resolution is used (if given). Otherwise, it defaults to 1ddpx.

- `snap`: If the snap keyword is provided, the computed `<resolution>` (if any) is the specified resolution rounded to the nearest value that would map one image pixel to an integer number of device pixels. If the resolution is taken from the image, the intrinsic resolution being used is the image's native resolution similarly adjusted.

The following CSS declaration forces the image resolution to 300 dots per inch (dpi):

```
img { image-resolution: 300dpi }
```

The resolution in the image, if any, is ignored.

Solution 1-5: Resetting CSS3 default values

It's a sad reality that each browser uses its own rules to render HTML elements. This introduces a lot of inconsistency, and web designers and developers have to spend a lot of time making sure their web page renders the same across browsers.

A common solution to this problem is to use a CSS reset script that removes and neutralizes the inconsistent default styling of elements, margin, padding, font, and so on.

What's involved

Mainly, the differences across browsers are related to the margin and padding properties because each browser sets their values in a different way. So the simplest approach is to set a global selector that sets the margin and padding properties to zero:

```
* {
  margin: 0;
  padding: 0;
}
```

Dong this is not enough, however, because other important properties have to be considered, such as outline (that is, a line drawn around elements to make the element stand out), border, font-size, and many more. So you need to use a more sophisticated approach that takes into account all of these properties.

How to build it

The following CSS reset rules are the ones most frequently used by web designers and developers to reset the CSS properties:

```
* {
  vertical-align: baseline;
  font-weight: inherit;
  font-family: inherit;
  font-style: inherit;
  font-size: 100%;
  border: 0 none;
  outline: 0;
  padding: 0;
  margin: 0;
}
```

This approach uses the global selector and sets the properties to their default values. With these CSS rules, the browsers won't introduce inconsistencies in properties related to default margins and padding, line heights, font sizes, headings, and so on.

With the new HTML5 elements, you need to consider new HTML elements to add to your CSS3 reset rules, such as video, footer, article, audio, and so on.

So here's a more complete CSS3 reset script solution that uses these new HTML5 tags:

```
* { outline: 0; }
html, body, div, span, object, iframe,
h1, h2, h3, h4, h5, h6, p, blockquote, pre,
abbr, address, cite, code,
del, dfn, em, img, ins, kbd, q, samp,
small, strong, sub, sup, var,
b, i,
dl, dt, dd, ol, ul, li,
fieldset, form, label, legend,
table, caption, tbody, tfoot, thead, tr, th, td,
article, aside, canvas, details, figcaption, figure,
footer, header, hgroup, menu, nav, section, summary,
time, mark, audio, video {
  margin:0;
  padding:0;
  border:0;
  outline:0;
  font-size:100%;
  vertical-align:baseline;
  background:transparent;
}
input[type="submit"]::-moz-focus-inner, input[type="button"]::-moz-focus-inner { border : 0px; }
input[type="search"] { -webkit-appearance: textfield; }
input[type="submit"] { -webkit-appearance:none; }
```

If you use Google, you'll find several CSS reset scripts ready to use in your code. We'll briefly look at reset style sheets again in Chapter 7. Here are some of the ones most frequently used by the developer community:

- Eric Meyer's Reset CSS 2.0

- HTML5 Doctor CSS Reset

- Yahoo! CSS Reset (YUI 3)

- Vanilla CSS Un-Reset

- Universal Selector '*' Reset

- Tripoli CSS Reset by David Hellsing

- undohtml.css by Tantek Celik

Summary

In this first chapter, you learned that Cascading Style Sheets came about because of the need to separate the presentational layer from the logic of the application. Their aim has always been to provide the users with a simple language to define the styling aspects of web pages. This chapter showed you how to declare a CSS style as a series of properties for content, such as styles for the font family, size of the font, color, and so on.

You used basic techniques to do the following:

- Discover CSS3 compatibilities across browsers
- Add a CSS3 file with JavaScript
- Declare multiple backgrounds for your web page

In the next chapter, we'll take a closer look at CSS selectors and address common issues that developers have with them.

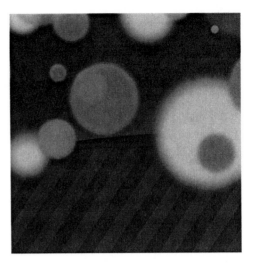

Chapter 2

CSS Selectors

In the previous chapter, we talked about how to build a CSS rule. You saw how a rule in a style sheet is made up of one or more selectors and by a group of properties and relevant values, expressed in the following form:

```
selector {
  property: value;
  }
```

A *selector* represents a structure, meaning it specifies which elements of an HTML page the rule will apply to. The properties and the relevant values deal with the presentation of these elements.

Therefore, one can guess that selectors are a fundamental part of CSS. Indeed, they've been around since the very first CSS specifications. Selectors Level 1 and Selectors Level 2 are defined as the subsets of selector functionality; that is defined in the CSS1 and CSS2.1 specifications, respectively.

Some new elements have been introduced in the CSS3 version. In this chapter, we'll address the new features of CSS3 selectors.

Differences compared to CSS2 selectors

There aren't many differences between CSS2 selectors and the new CSS3 selectors. From a functional point of view, CSS3 selectors are now a part of the CSS3 Module, which has its own independent specification.

The small differences are summarized in the following list:

- The list of basic definitions (selector, group of selectors, simple selector, and so on) has been clarified.

- An optional namespace component is now allowed in type element selectors, the universal selector, and attribute selectors.

- There is a new combinator.

- There are new simple selectors, including substring-matching attribute selectors, and new pseudo-classes.

- There are new pseudo-elements and the "::" convention for pseudo-elements.

- The selectors grammar has been rewritten.

- Profiles have been added to specifications integrating selectors and defining the set of selectors that is actually supported by each specification.

The major novelties are to be found in the attribute selectors, which now have three different types:

- `[att$="val"]` Identifies the elements found by selectors that have an `att` attribute that ends with a `val` string

- `[att^="val"]` Identifies the elements found by selectors that have an `att` attribute that begins with a `val` string

- `[att*="val"]` Identifies the elements found by selectors that have an `att` attribute that contains a `val` string

To remain on the topic of novelties, we must mention the potent pseudo-classes, for which new features have been introduced.

Pseudo-classes

The pseudo-class was introduced to permit selection based on information that lies outside of the document tree or that cannot be expressed using the other simple selectors. A pseudo-class always consists of a colon (:) followed by the name of the pseudo-class and, optionally, by a value between parentheses. The pseudo-class of the selector form, on the other hand, is declared with the following syntax:

```
section div: nth-child(n-3)
```

The preceding example identifies the `div` elements within the section that are the first, second, and third child elements. The following list shows the pseudo-classes:

- `:root`
- `:nth-child()`
- `:nth-last-child()`
- `:nth-of-type()`
- `:nth-last-of-type()`

- :first-child

- :last-child

- :first-of-type

- :last-of-type

- :only-child

- :only-of-type

- :empty

To learn more about the structural pseudo-classes, you can refer to the following page on the W3C site: http://www.w3.org/TR/css3-selectors/#structural-pseudos. Other novelties introduced for pseudo-classes are related to the pseudo-classes that express UI element states. These can create specific rules for form elements and their dynamic states:

- :enabled Defines a rule for the enabled elements identified by the selector (which are necessarily form elements)

- :disabled Defines a rule for the disabled elements identified by the selector (which are necessarily form elements)

- :checked Defines a rule for the active elements identified by the selector (which are necessarily check boxes or radio buttons)

At the moment, there is little support for these pseudo-classes. Only Firefox 2 and Opera 9.2 have partial support for these pseudo-classes; they support only :checked.

Let's see how to use CSS3 selectors and the new pseudo-classes in the following solutions.

Solution 2-1: Highlighting selected text

We often read the text of an HTML page and highlight selected text to copy and paste it. The highlight style is chosen by the browser, and it varies according to the type of browser. CSS3 introduces a pseudo-class you can use to change the default settings to highlight a portion of text in a web page.

What's involved

The ::selection pseudo-class allows you to specify the appearance of the selected text for the user. Mozilla is the only engine that requires the prefix, so two separate rules must be written:

```
::-moz-selection {…}
::selection {…}
```

First note the presence of a couple of colons, unlike the other pseudo-classes. Here is an example of how to draw any selected text as white on black:

```
/* */
::-moz-selection { color: white; background: black; }
::selection    { color: white; background: black; }
```

How to build it

The ::selection pseudo-class allows you to specify the appearance of text that is selected by the user. By using the global wildcard *, you can apply the style you want to all the text selected by the user. Here is the complete code for the solution that uses internal CSS styles:

```
<html>
<head>
<title>Solution 2-1: Highlighting selected text</title>
<meta http-equiv="content-type" content="text/html; charset=iso-8859-1">
<style type="text/css">
*::selection{background: gold;color: #C00}
*::-moz-selection{background: gold;color: #C00}
</style>
</head>
<body>
<section>
<p>Lorem ipsum dolor sit amet, consectetuer adipiscing elit. Vestibulum
venenatis, orci non scelerisque feugiat, erat purus cursus mauris, vitae
elementum dolor libero non velit. Nam laoreet justo eget ligula vestibulum
egestas. Curabitur in sem. In faucibus, metus a mollis faucibus, metus neque
pharetra odio, nec tempus mauris odio sed sem. Sed posuere. Cras posuere. Nunc
at dolor eget massa pulvinar ornare.</p>
</ section >
</body>
</html>
```

If you open the HTML page in a browser and select some text, you'll obtain the result shown in Figure 2-1.

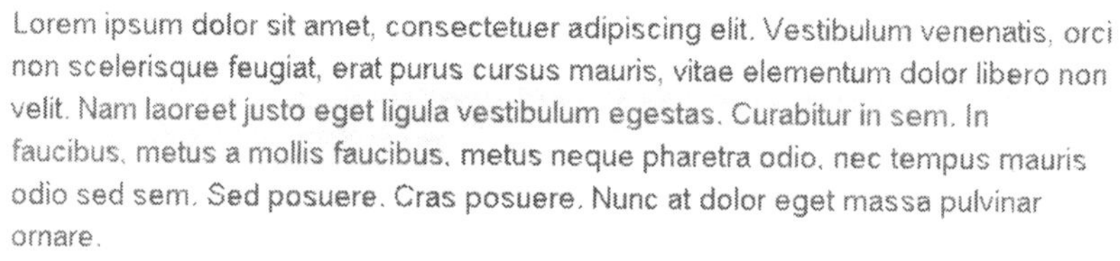

Lorem ipsum dolor sit amet, consectetuer adipiscing elit. Vestibulum venenatis, orci non scelerisque feugiat, erat purus cursus mauris, vitae elementum dolor libero non velit. Nam laoreet justo eget ligula vestibulum egestas. Curabitur in sem. In faucibus, metus a mollis faucibus, metus neque pharetra odio, nec tempus mauris odio sed sem. Sed posuere. Cras posuere. Nunc at dolor eget massa pulvinar ornare.

Figure 2-1. The highlighted text has a custom color specified by the ::selector pseudo-class.

Expert tips

You can't use all CSS properties with ::selection. In fact, only the following small subset of CSS properties can be used:

```
color
background
background-color
```

The background-image is ignored, like any other property.

Solution 2-2: Enhancing the readability of tabular data

With the new features introduced by CSS3 selectors, you can create many effects in your web pages. In fact, you can permit selections based on information that lies in the document tree. In this solution, you'll see how to use a structural pseudo-class to add readability to tabular data.

What's involved

To be able to select an element, you use the :nth-child pseudo-class notation. In the introductory paragraph regarding CSS pseudo-classes, you saw that it is possible to point to an element identified by a selector that is the child with an order corresponding to the number or the formula expressed between parentheses:

```
section div: nth-child(n-3)
```

This example identifies the div elements within the selection that are the first, second, or third child elements. You also can use the nth-child() with "odd" and "even" values as arguments instead. These two values allow you to change the color of the even (or odd) rows of a table by adding a class to every other row. For example, the following code colors the odd rows of the cells yellow:

```
tr:nth-child(odd) td {
  background-color: #86B486;
}
```

The CSS statement selects the odd rows with the nth-child(odd) selector. Let's take a look at how to build a complete example to obtain this result.

Another solution is given in Chapter 5.

How to build it

You start with the creation of the table to show the data. We'll use the score table of the first 10 teams in the Italian Serie A soccer league as an example. Here is the HTML code:

```
<html>

<head>
<title>Solution 2-2: Enhancing readability of tables</title>
</head>

<body>
<table cellpadding="0" cellspacing="0" summary="Championship Table">
<thead>
<tr>
<th scope="col"><abbr title="Position">Position</abbr></th>
<th scope="col"><abbr title="Team">Team</abbr></th>
<th scope="col"><abbr title="Points">Points</abbr></th>
<th scope="col"><abbr title="Matches Played">P</abbr></th>
<th scope="col"><abbr title="Matches Won">W</abbr></th>
<th scope="col"><abbr title="Matches Drawn">D</abbr></th>
<th scope="col"><abbr title="Matches Lost">L</abbr></th>
</tr>
```

29

```
</thead>
<tbody>
<tr>
<td>1</td>
<td >Milan

</td>
<td><b>63</b></td>
<td>29</td>
<td>19</td>
<td>6</td>
<td>4</td>
</tr>
<tr>
<td>2</td>
<td >
Juventus
</td>
<td><b>59</b></td>
<td>29</td>
<td>15</td>
<td>14</td>
<td>0</td>
</tr>
<tr>
<td>3</td>
<td >
Lazio
</td>
<td><b>51</b></td>
<td>29</td>
<td>15</td>
<td>6</td>
<td>8</td>
</tr>
<tr>
<td>4</td>
<td >
Napoli
</td>
<td><b>48</b></td>
<td>29</td>
<td>12</td>
<td>12</td>
<td>5</td>
</tr>
<tr>
<td>5</td>
<td >
Udinese
</td>
```

```
<td><b>48</b></td>
<td>29</td>
<td>13</td>
<td>9</td>
<td>7</td>
</tr>
<tr>
<td>6</td>
<td >
Roma
</td>
<td><b>44</b></td>
<td>29</td>
<td>13</td>
<td>5</td>
<td>11</td>
</tr>
<tr>
<td>7</td>
<td >
Catania
</td>
<td><b>42</b></td>
<td>29</td>
<td>10</td>
<td>12</td>
<td>7</td>
</tr>
<tr>
<td>8</td>
<td >
Inter
</td>
<td><b>41</b></td>
<td>29</td>
<td>12</td>
<td>5</td>
<td>12</td>
</tr>
<tr>
<td>9</td>
<td >
Atalanta
</td>
<td><b>37</b></td>
<td>29</td>
<td>10</td>
<td>13</td>
<td>6</td>
</tr>
<tr>
```

```
<td>10</td>
<td >
Bologna
</td>
<td><b>36</b></td>
<td>29</td>
<td>9</td>
<td>9</td>
<td>11</td>
</tr>
</tbody>
</table>

</body>
</html>
```

We have created the table and have made 7 columns to represent the different data for each team:

```
<th scope="col"><abbr title="Position">Position</abbr></th>
 <th scope="col"><abbr title="Team">Team</th>
 <th scope="col"><abbr title="Points">Points</abbr></th>
 <th scope="col"><abbr title="Matches Played">P</abbr></th>
 <th scope="col"><abbr title="Matches Won">W</abbr></th>
 <th scope="col"><abbr title="Matches Drawn">D</abbr></th>
 <th scope="col"><abbr title="Matches Lost">L</abbr></th>
```

We start by adding styles, inserting CSS rules directly in the page:

```
<style type="text/css">
body {
    padding: 10px;
    margin: 0;
    }

table {
  font: 11px/24px Verdana, Arial, Helvetica, sans-serif;
  border-collapse: collapse;
  width: 480px;
    }

th {
  padding: 0 0.5em;
  text-align: center;
    }

td {
  padding: 0 0.5em;

    }

td:first-child {
  width: 30px;
    }

td+td {
  border-left: 1px solid #CCC;
```

```
    text-align: center;
  }
</style>
```

If you save the HTML page with the CSS styles mentioned earlier, you obtain the result shown in Figure 2-2:

Position	Team	Points	P	W	D	L
1	Milan	63	29	19	6	4
2	Juventus	59	29	15	14	0
3	Lazio	51	29	15	6	8
4	Napoli	48	29	12	12	5
5	Udinese	48	29	13	9	7
6	Roma	44	29	13	5	11
7	Catania	42	29	10	12	7
8	Inter	41	29	12	5	12
9	Atalanta	37	29	10	13	6
10	Bologna	36	29	9	9	11

Figure 2-2. The formatted table.

The result you want to obtain is to color the background of every other row to improve the readability of the table. This is why you'll use the nth-child() with "odd" and "even" values as arguments.

These two values allow you to change the color of the even (or odd) rows of a table by adding a class to every other row. Add the following syntax in the style declaration:

```
tr:nth-child(odd) td {
  border-top: 1px solid black;
  border-bottom: 1px solid black;
  background: #FFC;
```

With this statement, you changed the background color of the cells, but you also added a solid red, 1-pixel-high border. If you save the file now and run it in a browser, you'll see the result shown in Figure 2-3.

Expert tips

The odd and even values are very useful. Consider that you can get the same result using the 2n+1 (equivalent to the value odd) and 2n+0 (which selects every third row, and so on) with the nth-child():

```
tr:nth-child(2n+1) /* It's the same as using the odd, in fact it represents
every odd row of an HTML table */
tr:nth-child(2n+0) /* the same as using the even, in fact it represents every
even row of an HTML table */
```

Position	Team	Points	P	W	D	L
1	Milan	**63**	29	19	6	4
2	Juventus	**59**	29	15	14	0
3	Lazio	**51**	29	15	6	8
4	Napoli	**48**	29	12	12	5
5	Udinese	**48**	29	13	9	7
6	Roma	**44**	29	13	5	11
7	Catania	**42**	29	10	12	7
8	Inter	**41**	29	12	5	12
9	Atalanta	**37**	29	10	13	6
10	Bologna	**36**	29	9	9	11

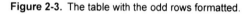

Figure 2-3. The table with the odd rows formatted.

Solution 2-3: Toggling form elements

It has always been necessary to use JavaScript code to interact dynamically with form styles. Today, with CSS3 selectors, you can create simple graphics effects by using only style sheets and therefore make the code lighter.

A common task is to change the style of the form elements according to their state. Users need to have a visual understanding of whether they can or cannot interact with a form element. In this solution, you'll see how to use three new pseudo classes for user-interface element states.

What's involved

As mentioned earlier, there are three types of pseudo-classes for UI element states:

■ `:enabled` Represents user-interface elements that are in an enabled state. Such elements have a corresponding disabled state.

■ `:disabled` Represents user-interface elements that are in a disabled state. Such elements have a corresponding enabled state.

■ `:checked` Radio and check-box elements can be toggled by the user. Some menu items are marked by a check when the user selects them. When such elements are toggled on, the `:checked` pseudo-class applies.

By defining the graphic style of these pseudo-classes, you can dynamically change their look and feel according to the state they take on over time. For example, you can create a solid, green border in form elements that the user can interact with (status enabled), and you can create a solid, red border when the form elements cannot be selected (status disabled). Here is an example of CSS code that applies these rules:

```
:enabled  {
  border: 2px solid green;
}
:disabled {
  border: 2px solid red;
}
```

Let's see how to create a complete example to use these selectors.

How to build it

You create a form with a few elements to which you can then apply the styles. Let's start with the HTML code:

```
<!DOCTYPE html>
<html>
 <head>

  <title>Solution 2-3: Toggling Form Elements</title>

 </head>

 <body>

<form id='myForm'>
<fieldset>
 <legend>Solution 2-3: Toggling Form Elements</legend>

   <label for=name class="required">Name</label>
   <input id=name name=name type=text placeholder="Insert your first name" required>
   <br>
   <br/>
   <label for=email class="required">Email</label>
   <input id=email name=email type=email placeholder="Insert your email" required>
   <br>
   <br/>

   <label for=blog>Blog</label>
   <input id=blog name=blog type=url placeholder="Insert your blog">
   <br>
   <br/>
   <label>Receive newsletter</label>
   <input type="checkbox" />
  <p>
    <input type="submit" value="Submit">
    <a href="#" onClick="changeStatus()">Enable/Disable form fields</a>
  </p>

</fieldset>
</form>

</body>
</html>
```

35

We created a form with `id` equal to `myForm`. To this form, we assigned three text inputs: a check-box element, a button and link text, and a simple text link in which we have registered the `changeStatus()`JavaScript function to the `onClick` event. In a little while, we'll write the JavaScript code we need for this link text. For now, we apply a few graphical styles to these elements, and we define the styles for the enabled, disabled, and checked states using the following pseudo-classes:

```css
<style type="text/css">

:enabled {
  border: 2px solid green;
}

:disabled {
  border: 2px solid red;
}

:checked {
  display: inline-block;
  width: 4em;

  background-color:#c11;
  color:#fff;
}

  #myForm .required:after { content: " * "; color:red;}

  #myForm input:required { background:green; }

  #myForm legend {

font-family: arial, sans-serif;

font-weight: bold;

font-size: 90%;

color: #666;

background: #eee;

border: 1px solid #ccc;

border-bottom-color: #999;

border-right-color: #999;

padding: 4px 10px;

  }
</style>
```

Now we have created a graphical style for each state of the form elements. All we have to do now is write the JavaScript code to change the state of these elements. We'll use a simple link button that toggles the state of the form elements when it is clicked. We insert a script tag within the head tag declaration with the following code:

```javascript
<script type="text/javascript">

changeStatus.status = false;
```

```
function changeStatus()
{
 changeStatus.status = !changeStatus.status;
  var myFormElements = document.getElementById('myForm').elements;
 for (var x=0;x< myFormElements.length;x++)
 {
   myFormElements[x].disabled = changeStatus.status;
 }
 return false;
 }
</script>
```

The changeStatus function simply uses a for statement on the form elements that are defined in the HTML form and sets the disabled property of each to the status property. If you save the file and execute it in a browser, when you click on the Enable/Disable Form Fields link, you obtain the result shown in Figure 2-4, in which the status of the form elements is set to :disabled.

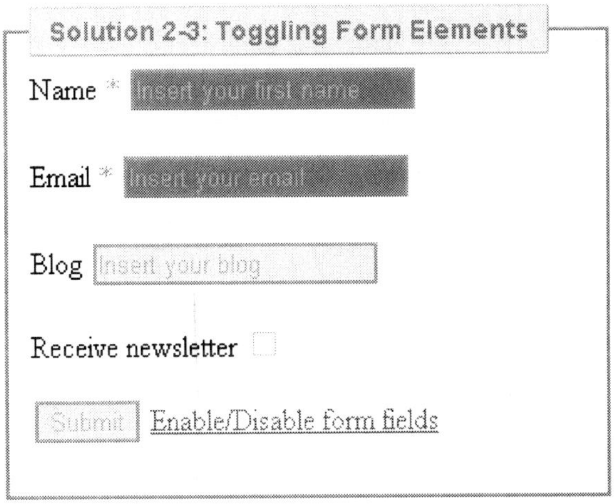

Figure 2-4. By clicking on the Enable/Disable Form Fields link, you toggle the state of the form elements.

Expert Tips

As you've seen, the :enabled and :disabled CSS3 selectors determine whether or not the input field of every type can be selected. In the solution, we used and applied them to any element of the user interface that supported these properties. However, you can specifically apply the enabled and disabled styles to a certain form type by using the following syntax:

```
input[type="text"]:enabled
{
background: green;

}
```

```
input[type="text"]:disabled
{
background: red;
}
```

Solution 2-4: Preventing content from being selectable

There are situations in which you might need to stop the user from being able to highlight text to carry out the classic copy and paste operations. Another common scenario is one in which you stop the user from being able to select text to drag and drop elements within a web page. Or you might want to code the header of an e-mail message window so that the portion that contains the name cannot be selected but the content following it can be. CSS3 introduced a new property that allows you to control the selection model and the granularity of an element.

What's involved

The `user-select` property controls the appearance of selection. These are the values that this property accepts:

- `text` The element's contents follow a standard text content-selection model.

- `none` None of the element's content can be selected. When this value is set, the user cannot select any of the content. For example, if a user clicks on an element with `user-select: none`, what happens when the pointing device button is "down" is addressed by the `user-input` property, and when that pointing device button is released, this property ensures that no selection of the contents of the element remain. The value of `none` is also useful for static text labels in a user interface that are not meant to be selected.

- `text toggle` The element's contents follow a standard toggling content model.

- `element` One element at a time can be selected. It's supported in Firefox and Internet Explorer.

- `elements` One or more elements at a time can be selected.

- `all` Only the entire content as a whole can be selected.

You should bear one thing in mind: `user-select` is not currently part of any W3C CSS specification. Therefore, there could be minor differences between browser implementations.

Let's see how to use this property to make it impossible to select content.

How to build it

Let's start by creating a simple HTML page with content. All you need is a paragraph with the classic Lorem Ipsum text:

```
<html>
<head>
<title>Solution 2-4: Preventing content from being selectable</title>
```

```
</head>
<body>

<section>
<p class="notselectable">
Lorem ipsum dolor sit amet, consectetuer adipiscing elit. Vestibulum
venenatis, orci non scelerisque feugiat, erat purus cursus mauris, vitae
elementum dolor libero non velit. Nam laoreet justo eget ligula vestibulum
egestas. Curabitur in sem. In faucibus, metus a mollis faucibus, metus neque
pharetra odio, nec tempus mauris odio sed sem. Sed posuere. Cras posuere. Nunc
at dolor eget massa pulvinar ornare.
</p>
</ section >

</body>
</html>
```

The only thing worth noting is contained in the tag of the paragraph, which has a CSS class that it uses called notselectable. Now you need to create the style that sets the user-select property to none to prevent the selection of content. You insert a style block with the following code:

```
<style type="text/css">
 .notselectable {  user-select: none;
  -moz-user-select: none;
  -webkit-user-select: none;
  -khtml-user-select: none;
  -ms-user-select: none;
 }
</style>
```

The user-select property is not currently part of any W3C CSS specification. It was originally proposed in the User Interface For CSS3 module, but it has been suppressed. This is why, to make the property work on different browsers, you need to use -moz endings for Mozilla browsers, -webkit for WebKit's browsers, -khtml for Konqueror web browsers, and -ms for Internet Explorer.

When you save the file and run it in a browser that supports the user-select property, you'll notice that you cannot select the text with the cursor.

Expert tips

By using this property, you can disable text or image selection on the entire content of the web page except for a specific element. To do this, you have to use the global selector to define the noneditable content on the page and then override the property for a specific selector:

```
* {
-webkit-user-select: none;
-khtml-user-select: none;
-moz-user-select: -moz-none;
-o-user-select: none;
user-select: none;
}
```

```
p {
-webkit-user-select: text;
-khtml-user-select: text;
-moz-user-select: text;
-o-user-select: text;
user-select: text;
}
```

Solution 2-5: Hiding empty elements within a page

When using content-management systems or any web content platform, you might find empty tags in your code that have no use whatsoever for the semantic purposes of the page. Because they are empty and unused tags, you might be tempted to leave them in the web page, thinking that they won't cause any problems. However, if you applied CSS styles to these empty elements, there are cases in which your layout might be compromised and you might obtain strange positions. Therefore, you need to find a way to remove these empty tags. There are new CSS3 selectors that can help you do this.

What's involved

One of the new CSS3 selectors matches every element that has no child elements. The `:empty` selector represents an element that has no child elements at all (including text nodes). It is very simple to use: because it is a pseudo-class, all you have to do is declare it by using a colon right after the selector:

```
li:empty { //statement }
```

With this code, you apply a CSS rule to all the empty elements of a list (that is, to the list items).

Note the empty selector is well supported by all major browsers except Internet Explorer 8 and earlier.

Let's see a complete example.

How to build it

Create HTML code with paragraphs—some empty and some containing a comment, which will always be considered an empty element:

```
<!DOCTYPE html>

<html>

 <head>

<title>Solution 2-5:</title>

  </head>

 <body>

 <p></p>

 <p>Lorem ipsum dolor sit amet, consectetur adipiscing elit. Nullam nunc leo,
facilisis ut lacinia quis, pellentesque a eros. Lorem ipsum dolor sit amet,
consectetur adipiscing elit. Cras aliquam viverra arcu ac dictum. Nam volutpat
```

pulvinar magna, et faucibus ligula volutpat a. Cras ultricies pretium ante, in sagittis odio eleifend at. Praesent aliquam pulvinar metus, nec lacinia diam tincidunt in. Maecenas nec egestas lectus. Praesent placerat consectetur leo mollis tempor. Nam a tortor mauris, quis vulputate tellus. Nam rutrum augue eget lorem vehicula sit amet imperdiet erat rutrum. Nunc ac dui est, in vestibulum risus. Ut at sagittis ante. Nunc eu mi nibh. Mauris id dui erat. Nunc et mauris ante. Suspendisse ut leo ut nulla faucibus iaculis vel ut velit.</p>

<p></p>

 <p>Maecenas vitae sem nec sem convallis aliquet sed non enim. Vivamus nulla arcu, gravida a molestie id, lacinia nec mi. Nullam ullamcorper accumsan tristique. In dolor eros, rutrum sit amet iaculis et, venenatis eu enim. Integer lorem sapien, ultrices pretium luctus eu, ullamcorper quis diam. Ut ac posuere justo. Ut interdum pellentesque ipsum, facilisis tempus odio euismod in. In at enim vel arcu pretium luctus. Aliquam pharetra tempor neque, quis semper nibh feugiat id. Praesent fringilla aliquet viverra.</p>

<p><!-- This is an empty tag --></p>

 <p>Morbi vel tellus eros, nec hendrerit neque. Etiam malesuada lorem sed lacus posuere ac tincidunt erat ultrices. In ut libero ac metus bibendum porttitor. Mauris at mi magna. Mauris eu semper enim. Curabitur a nunc euismod erat commodo vulputate vulputate id leo. Cras nec purus a ipsum porttitor tincidunt vel quis enim. Nulla facilisi. Proin eu elit ut turpis ultricies hendrerit vitae et nisi. Aenean semper euismod nibh.</p>

</body>

</html>

Before saving the page and running it in a web browser, to understand the problem we are faced with by leaving these tags empty, we insert a style block with some simple CSS rules applied to the paragraph:

```
<style type="text/css">

p

 {

  padding-top:100px;

  background-color:#09C;

  font-family: Arial, Helvetica, sans-serif;

  }

</style>
```

All we did was add a 100-pixel space on top with the padding-top property and assigned a background color to the paragraph to get a better visual idea of what happens.

We save and run the page in a web browser. The CSS rules will also be applied to the empty paragraphs or those containing comments, so you will see other spaces occupied by these tags, as shown in Figure 2-5.

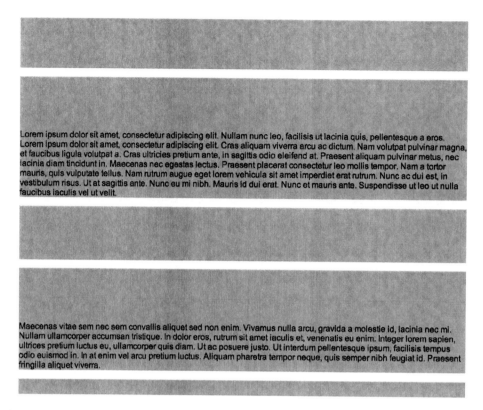

Figure 2-5. Empty paragraphs break your layout.

We add the :empty pseudo-class to stop the CSS styles from being applied to the empty tags. We insert the following code in the style block:

```
<style type="text/css">

p

{

 padding-top:100px;

 background-color:#09C;

 font-family: Arial, Helvetica, sans-serif;

 }

p:empty {

 display: none;

 }

</style>
```

If we save and run the file in a web browser now, we'll see that the empty tags are ignored, as shown in Figure 2-6.

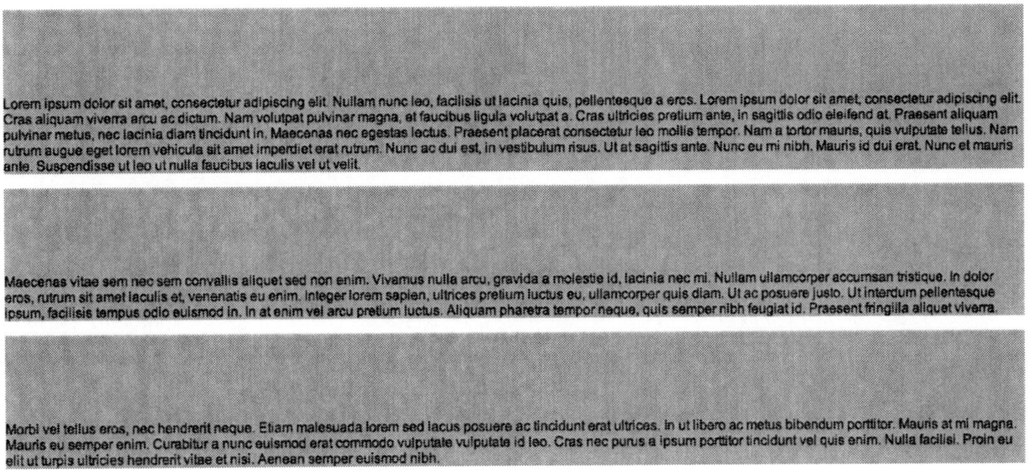

Figure 2-6. Empty tags are now ignored.

Expert tips

You can hide all empty elements without having to specify the selector by using the global selector:

```
*:empty {
  display: none;
  }
```

Solution 2-6: Using the sibling combinator

The cascading characteristic of CSS has always brought enormous advantages with regard to styles that can be applied in a web page. With CSS3, new selectors have been introduced to allow you to declare styles for elements that precede a specific element. Let's learn how it's done with a real example.

What's involved

There are two new CSS3 sibling combinators:

- The adjacent sibling combinator declared with the plus sign (+)

- The general sibling combinator declared with the tilde sign (~)

Let's look at two practical examples.

- The adjacent sibling combinator: h3 + p { // statement }. This code represents a p element immediately following an h3 element. Basically, the adjacent sibling combinatory is used to scroll the DOM tree horizontally by assigning the CSS rule to the elements that are at the same level as another element.

- The general sibling combinator: h3 p. This code represents a p element following an h3, and it matches any p element that is preceded by an h3 element. The general sibling combinator is a generalization of the adjacent sibling combinator. It assigns a style to all sibling elements.

Let's apply this theory to see an example.

How to build it

Take the HTML code of the previous solution, and delete the previous style block. We will obtain the following file:

```
<!DOCTYPE html>

<html>
<head>
<title>Solution 2-5:</title>
  </head>
  <body>

  <p>Morbi vel tellus eros, nec hendrerit neque. Etiam malesuada lorem sed
lacus posuere ac tincidunt erat ultrices. In ut libero ac metus bibendum
porttitor. Mauris at mi magna. Mauris eu semper enim. Curabitur a nunc euismod
erat commodo vulputate vulputate id leo. Cras nec purus a ipsum porttitor
tincidunt vel quis enim. Nulla facilisi. Proin eu elit ut turpis ultricies
hendrerit vitae et nisi. Aenean semper euismod nibh.</p>

  <h3>This is a Header</h3>

  <p>Lorem ipsum dolor sit amet, consectetur adipiscing elit. Nullam nunc leo,
facilisis ut lacinia quis, pellentesque a eros. Lorem ipsum dolor sit amet,
consectetur adipiscing elit. Cras aliquam viverra arcu ac dictum. Nam volutpat
pulvinar magna, et faucibus ligula volutpat a. Cras ultricies pretium ante, in
sagittis odio eleifend at. Praesent aliquam pulvinar metus, nec lacinia diam
tincidunt in. Maecenas nec egestas lectus. Praesent placerat consectetur leo
mollis tempor. Nam a tortor mauris, quis vulputate tellus. Nam rutrum augue
eget lorem vehicula sit amet imperdiet erat rutrum. Nunc ac dui est, in
vestibulum risus. Ut at sagittis ante. Nunc eu mi nibh. Mauris id dui erat.
Nunc et mauris ante. Suspendisse ut leo ut nulla faucibus iaculis vel ut
velit.</p>

  <p>Maecenas vitae sem nec sem convallis aliquet sed non enim. Vivamus nulla
arcu, gravida a molestie id, lacinia nec mi. Nullam ullamcorper accumsan
tristique. In dolor eros, rutrum sit amet iaculis et, venenatis eu enim.
Integer lorem sapien, ultrices pretium luctus eu, ullamcorper quis diam. Ut ac
posuere justo. Ut interdum pellentesque ipsum, facilisis tempus odio euismod
in. In at enim vel arcu pretium luctus. Aliquam pharetra tempor neque, quis
semper nibh feugiat id. Praesent fringilla aliquet viverra.</p>

  <p>Morbi vel tellus eros, nec hendrerit neque. Etiam malesuada lorem sed
lacus posuere ac tincidunt erat ultrices. In ut libero ac metus bibendum
porttitor. Mauris at mi magna. Mauris eu semper enim. Curabitur a nunc euismod
erat commodo vulputate vulputate id leo. Cras nec purus a ipsum porttitor
tincidunt vel quis enim. Nulla facilisi. Proin eu elit ut turpis ultricies
hendrerit vitae et nisi. Aenean semper euismod nibh.</p>

  </body>
  </html>
```

Now apply a style block and insert CSS statements using the general sibling combinator so that all paragraphs that follow the declaration of the h3 element have a different graphic style:

```
<style type="text/css">

body
{
  font-family:Arial, Helvetica, sans-serif;
}

h3 ~ p
{
width: 740px;
border: 5px solid #ccc;
padding-left: 15px;
}

</style>
```

If you save and run the file in a web browser now, you'll see the result shown in Figure 2-7.

Morbi vel tellus eros, nec hendrerit neque. Etiam malesuada lorem sed lacus posuere ac tincidunt erat ultrices. In ut libero ac metus bibendum porttitor. Mauris at mi magna. Mauris eu semper enim. Curabitur a nunc euismod erat commodo vulputate vulputate id leo. Cras nec purus a ipsum porttitor tincidunt vel quis enim. Nulla facilisi. Proin eu elit ut turpis ultricies hendrerit vitae et nisi. Aenean semper euismod nibh.

This is a Header

Lorem ipsum dolor sit amet, consectetur adipiscing elit. Nullam nunc leo, facilisis ut lacinia quis, pellentesque a eros. Lorem ipsum dolor sit amet, consectetur adipiscing elit. Cras aliquam viverra arcu ac dictum. Nam volutpat pulvinar magna, et faucibus ligula volutpat a. Cras ultricies pretium ante, in sagittis odio eleifend at. Praesent aliquam pulvinar metus, nec lacinia diam tincidunt in. Maecenas nec egestas lectus. Praesent placerat consectetur leo mollis tempor. Nam a tortor mauris, quis vulputate tellus. Nam rutrum augue eget lorem vehicula sit amet imperdiet erat rutrum. Nunc ac dui est, in vestibulum risus. Ut at sagittis ante. Nunc eu mi nibh. Mauris id dui erat. Nunc et mauris ante. Suspendisse ut leo ut nulla faucibus iaculis vel ut velit.

Maecenas vitae sem nec sem convallis aliquet sed non enim. Vivamus nulla arcu, gravida a molestie id, lacinia nec mi. Nullam ullamcorper accumsan tristique. In dolor eros, rutrum sit amet iaculis et, venenatis eu enim. Integer lorem sapien, ultrices pretium luctus eu, ullamcorper quis diam. Ut ac posuere justo. Ut interdum pellentesque ipsum, facilisis tempus odio euismod in. In at enim vel arcu pretium luctus. Aliquam pharetra tempor neque, quis semper nibh feugiat id. Praesent fringilla aliquet viverra.

Morbi vel tellus eros, nec hendrerit neque. Etiam malesuada lorem sed lacus posuere ac tincidunt erat ultrices. In ut libero ac metus bibendum porttitor. Mauris at mi magna. Mauris eu semper enim. Curabitur a nunc euismod erat commodo vulputate vulputate id leo. Cras nec purus a ipsum porttitor tincidunt vel quis enim. Nulla facilisi. Proin eu elit ut turpis ultricies hendrerit vitae et nisi. Aenean semper euismod nibh.

Figure 2-7. All the p elements declared after the h3 element is formatted.

Note that no styles are applied to the first <p> in the code, whereas they apply to all the others. This happens because the rule is assigned only to the elements that are child elements and siblings of the h3 element.

Solution 2-7: Putting an icon image next to links

Links and icons have always been a winning team. Web pages often provide an image that identifies the type of link, which immediately lets the user know what to expect. The PDF icon next to a link that allows you to download a file, the Facebook icon next to the link to the famous social network's homepage, and the link to your own LinkedIn profile with the site logo are all examples in which it is useful to accompany text with an image. With CSS3, you can authorize this procedure and acknowledge the type of link that is in your web page by associating it with the relevant image.

What's involved

The attribute selectors were already part of the CSS 2.1 specifications. Three additional attribute selectors are provided in the CSS3 version, to match substrings in the value of an attribute. The declaration of an attribute selector is specified by square parentheses ([ ]), which have to follow a selector, and the characteristic that a given attribute has to satisfy for the rule to apply:

```
a[href$=".htm"]
```

The code declared above represents an HTML anchor a with an `href` attribute whose value ends with ".htm".

Here are the new attribute selectors defined by CSS3:

- `[att^="val"]` Identifies the elements identified by selectors that have an `att` attribute beginning with the `val` string

- `[att*="val"]` Identifies the elements identified by selectors that have an `att` attribute containing the `val` string

- `[att$="val"]` Identifies the elements identified by selectors that have an `att` attribute ending with the `val` string

In this solution, you'll apply the attribute selector to the `href` of the links on the basis of their URL and type.

How to build it

Create an HTML file containing various kinds of links:

```
<!DOCTYPE html>
<html>
<head>
<title>Solution 2-7: Putting icon image next to links</title>
</head>
<body>
Lorem ipsum dolor sit amet, consectetuer adipiscing elit. Vestibulum
venenatis, orci non scelerisque feugiat, erat purus cursus mauris, vitae
elementum dolor libero non velit. Nam laoreet justo eget ligula vestibulum
egestas. Curabitur in sem. In faucibus, metus a mollis faucibus, metus neque
pharetra odio, nec tempus mauris odio sed sem. Sed posuere. Cras posuere. </p>
<p><a href="mailto:m.casario">This is a mailto link</a>.<br />
 <a href="yourfile.pdf">Download a pdf file</a>(it requires <a
href="http://get.adobe.com/reader">Adobe PDF Reader)</a></p>
<br/><a href="http://www.linkedin.com">See my LinkedIn Profile</a></li>
</ul>
</body>
</html>
```

The content above declares four links:

- a `mailto` link, which allows you to send an email to some email address (it causes the user agent to open a mail program with the destination address in the "To:" field)

- a link pointing to an external resource (a PDF file)

- two links pointing to external sites (Adobe and LinkedIn)

What you do now is associate each of these links with a different icon according to the type of resource they point to. You use the attribute selectors to obtain this result. Therefore, insert a style block in the HTML page we created previously:

```
<style type="text/css">
body
{
  font-family:Arial, Helvetica, sans-serif;
  font-size:12px;
}
a[href^="mailto:"]{
  padding-right: 16px;
  background: url(mailto.jpg) no-repeat center right
  }
a[href^="http"]{
  padding-right: 20px;
background: url(icon_external.gif) no-repeat center right
  }
a[href*="www.linkedin.com"]{
  padding-right: 16px;
  background: url(linkedin.jpg) no-repeat center right
  }
a[href$=".pdf"]{
padding-right: 22px;
background: url(pdf.jpg) no-repeat center right
}
</style>
```

We have used all three new attribute selectors of CSS3. In fact, to apply the image to the link pointing to an external page and the one that executes a `mailto` action, we used, respectively the following CSS code:

`a[href^="http"]`

`a[href^="mailto:"]`

The first represents an element with the `href` attribute whose value begins with the prefix "http", and the latter represents an element with the `href` attribute whose value begins with the prefix "mailto".

For the link pointing to the LinkedIn site, we used the `a[href*="www.linkedin.com"]` attribute selector, which represents an element with the `href` attribute whose value contains at least one instance of the substring "`www.linkedin.com`".

Finally, for the link to the PDF file, we used the a[href$=".pdf"] attribute selector , which represents an element with the href attribute whose value ends with the ".pdf" suffix. By doing so, we were able to associate a different icon with each type of link by using the following syntax:

```
background: url(icon.name) no-repeat center right
padding-right: 22px;
```

Summary

In this chapter, you learned about one of the most powerful tools of Cascading Style Sheets: selectors. A selector represents a structure, meaning it specifies which elements of an HTML page the rule will apply to. The properties and the relevant values deal with the presentation of these elements.

You used basic techniques to do the following:

- Specify the appearance of the selected text for the user by using the ::selection pseudo-class
- Enhanced the readability of tabular data by using the nth-child() with "odd" and "even" values as arguments
- Toggled form elements
- Used the general and adjacent sibling combinators
- Prevented the user from being able to highlight text to accomplish the classic copy and paste operations
- Put icon image next to links

In the next chapter, we'll take a closer look at CSS selectors and address common issues that developers have with them.

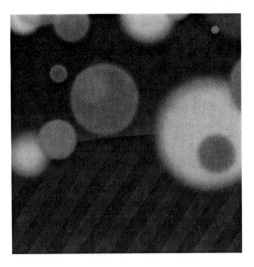

Chapter 3

Fonts, Text, and Color

Interest in typography on the Web has grown heavily over the last few years. Most websites rely on text to convey their messages, so it's no surprise that text should be treated with the utmost care. In this chapter, we'll look at some useful techniques that use the power of Cascading Style Sheets (CSS) Text Level 3 specification, which give Web designers finer control over text.

Solution 3-1: Using @font-face

The most important new feature of CSS3 has been its full support of @font-face. Forget the classics like Arial or Verdana: now you can choose from a much wider range of fonts. CSS Fonts Module 3 has made web designers particularly happy, because they are finally free to create web pages with beautiful and more accurate typefaces. You no longer need to turn to alternative techniques, such as sIFR (introduced in 2000), which are more complex to implement in your websites than @font-face. You can trust how established web fonts are in the specifications of the World Wide Web Consortium (W3C). In this solution, you'll see how to use a web font through @font-face.

What's involved

The @font-face feature was initially proposed for CSS2 specifications, and both Microsoft and Netscape added web font support to their respective browsers. Instead of supporting the most-used format, TrueType, they both chose lesser-known and different formats (EOT and TrueDoc, respectively). Web fonts, therefore, disappeared from the thoughts of web designers.

Safari 3.1 was the first browser to support any available typeface in TrueType (.ttf) and OpenType (.otf), which are the most common formats. All other browsers followed Safari's example, and today we finally have an incredibly vast selection of web fonts at our disposal.

Generate your own @font-face kit

You can use commercial fonts on the web, but not all of them are freely distributed. Most of them are protected by restrictive commercial licenses regarding their conditions of use. Many companies list the font's copyright information on the Version tab of the fonts' properties screens, but that means you have another thing to consider.

Fortunately, the Web offers many resources to obtain freely distributed and usable fonts, such as sites like 1001FreeFonts (http://www.1001freefonts.com) and FontSpace (http://www.fontspace.com). Another really interesting and powerful tool is FontSquirrel (http://www.fontsquirrel.com/). Not only does this site offer a wide range of interesting typeface characters, it also provides the @font-face Kit Generator, which is a very useful tool for converting fonts to the many formats you might want to support multiple browsers. This tool lets you upload a properly licensed typeface, and then it gives back the same typeface in web font formats—plus some demonstration HTML/CSS files that show the font in action. The process is quite simple: on your computer, select the font you want to convert by clicking the Add Fonts button as shown in Figure 3-1. Then choose only the font formats you want to support. You're done!

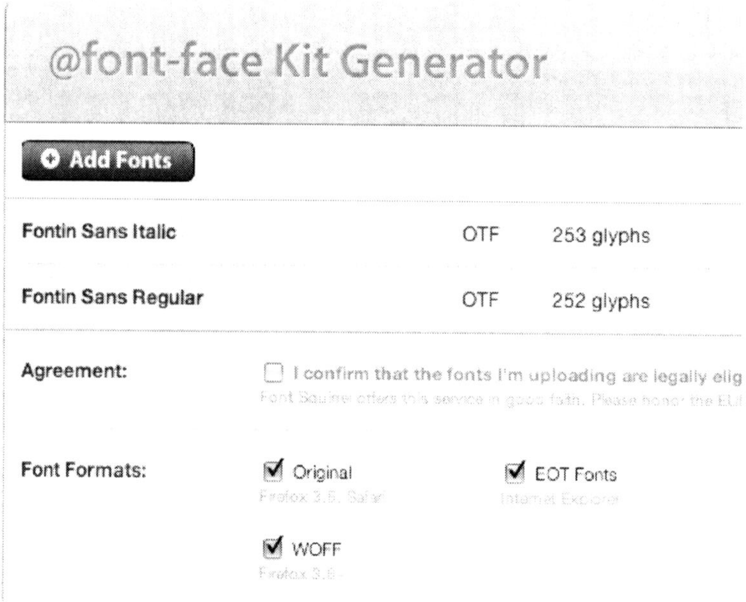

Figure 3-1. The FontSquirrel @font-face Kit Generator.

> *Caution: You cannot upload commercially protected and licensed fonts on FontSquirrel.*
> *You must have previously purchased the required license that is necessary for distributing*
> *the font on the Web.*

Another alternative to purchasing fonts and their respective license for use is to use services like Typekit (https://typekit.com/) or Font Deck (http://fontdeck.com/). The advantage of using these services rests with not having to deal with matters such as user licenses, browser support, font hosting, and so on. You only have to choose the right font for your design.

Font formats

Through @font-face, you can use the formats shown in Table 3-1.

Table 3-1. List of font formats available with @font-face

StringFont Format	Common extensions	
"woff"	WOFF (Web Open Font Format)	.woff
"truetype"	TrueType	.ttf
"opentype"	OpenType	.ttf, .otf
"embedded-opentype"	Embedded OpenType	.eot
"svg"	SVG Font	.svg, .svgz

Many of these formats exist because a unique format does not yet exist for all browsers. Support for each format varies from browser to browser and from one browser version to another, as you can see in Figure 3-2.

Formato					
TTF/OTF	9.0+	3.5+	3.1+	4.0+	10.0+
WOFF	9.0+	3.6+	No	6.0+	No
SVG	No	3.5+	3.1+	0.3+	9.0+
EOT	4.0+	No	No	No	No

Figure 3-2. Browser support for various font formats.

> *Tip: A cross-browser web font kit should support at least these three font formats: TrueType/OpenType, WOFF, and EOT.*

Browser support

All modern versions of the most popular browsers support @font-face. However, some older browsers and mobile browsers do not. Using font stacks in a suitable manner, you can define which fonts should be displayed in place of unsupported ones like so:

```
h1 {
font-family: MuseoSans, "Helvetica Neue", Arial, sans-serif;
}
```

In this case, the order of the stack substitutes Helvetica Neue for the font MuseoSans. In cases where it is not possible to show this font, Arial is shown.

How to build it

Including a web font on a website is a simple procedure. After choosing which web font to use, you only need to write a few lines of CSS syntax to make the font usable in the style sheet.

@font-face syntax

First you start with the basic syntax of @font-face:

```
@font-face {
 font-family: MuseoSans;
 src:
   url("assets/type/museosans.eot") format("embedded-opentype"),
   url("assets/type/museosans.woff") format("woff"),
   url("assets/type/museosans.ttf") format("truetype");
}
```

Let's analyze the CSS syntax line by line:

```
font-family: MuseoSans;
```

You assign the font name with font-family, as you specified in the style sheet. You have the choice of using any name or word. In this case, we used "MuseoSans" because it corresponds to the real name of the font.

> *Tip: It is always wise to use the real font name. It will help you to keep your style sheet understandable.*

```
src: url( assets/type/museosans.eot);
```

The first src defines the URL of the .eot file, which is necessary for compatibility with Internet Explorer (versions 5 through 9).

```
url("assets/type/museosans.woff") format("woff"),
url("assets/type/museosans.ttf") format("truetype");
```

The successive src attributes are needed to guarantee compatibility with all modern desktop and mobile browsers. The .WOFF format is used by Firefox, while the .TTF format is used by the browsers based on WebKit.

These few lines of CSS syntax allow your font to be compatible with the following browsers:

- Safari 5.03
- Internet Explorer 6–9
- Firefox 3.6.4
- Chrome 8
- iOS 3.2–4.2
- Android 2.2–2.3
- Opera 11

It could be called bulletproof syntax.

> Tip: After creating versions of your typeface in a few different formats, get yourself organized by making a specific folder for each of them. You could proceed by creating a /type/ folder in your project

Making the font work

There is now nothing left to do but rename the font defined with the attribute font-family inside your style sheet—for example, on the tag <body>:

```
body {
font: 14px MuseoSans, "Helvetica Neue", Arial, sans-serif;
}
```

In this way, you apply the font "MuseoSans" to all the HTML elements that are present inside the tag <body>. Or you can selectively and specifically assign the font for tagging as follows:

```
h1, h2, h3, h4 {
font-family: MuseoSans, "Helvetica Neue ", Arial, sans-serif;
}
```

In this example, the font MuseoSans is applied only to the main heading tags.

Multiple web fonts

You might wonder what happens if you want to use more than one font. The @font-face feature is extremely flexible, allowing you to upload different fonts or even different weights of the same font. Here's a look at some updated syntax:

```
@font-face {
 font-family: MuseoSans;
 src:
   url( assets/type/museosans.eot) format("embedded-opentype"),
   url("assets/type/museosans.woff") format("woff"),
```

```
    url("assets/type/museosans.ttf") format("truetype");
}
@font-face {
 font-family: MyriadPro;
 src:
   url( assets/type/myriadpro.eot) format("embedded-opentype"),
   url("assets/type/myriadpro.woff") format("woff"),
   url("assets/type/myriadpro.ttf") format("truetype");
}
```

We added the font MyriadPro to the list of available fonts through @font-face.

Now take a look at how to use different font weights, adding the bold and italics versions of MuseoSans:

```
@font-face {
 font-family: MuseoSans-Bold;
 src:
   url( assets/type/museosans-bold.eot) format("embedded-opentype"),
   url("assets/type/museosans-bold.woff") format("woff"),
   url("assets/type/museosans-bold.ttf") format("truetype");
}
@font-face {
 font-family: MuseoSans-Italic;
 src:
   url( assets/type/museosans-italic.eot) format("embedded-opentype"),
   url("assets/type/museosans-italic.woff") format("woff"),
   url("assets/type/museosans-italic.ttf") format("truetype");
}
```

It will be easy to recall these new web fonts in your style sheet:

```
h1 {
font-family: MuseoSans-Bold, "Helvetica Neue ", Arial, sans-serif;
}
em {
font-family: MuseoSans-Italic, "Helvetica Neue ", Arial, sans-serif;
}
```

In this case, we used bold for the <h1> titles and italics for all the <em> tags.

Expert tips

Always evaluate the kb weight of each font you would like to use. The uploading of the web font slows the uploading of web pages and, as long as the uploading is not finished, users will see the basic font defined in CSS font stacks. The resulting effect is one of an unpleasant interaction between the two fonts. To compensate for this problem, it is important to configure the cache.

The same font will appear differently on a user's screen, depending on their browser and operating system. Be sure to test the fonts you decide to use well so as not to compromise the legibility of the text.

Solution 3-2: Using fallback fonts

CSS has a nifty feature when specifying a font family called a fallback font. Fallback fonts are used if the first font you specify is unavailable. If your second-choice font is not available, it tries the third one and so on. But not all fonts are the same. Each one comes with its own style, characters, and rendering options.

If you ever wanted to use the fallback fonts without the legibility and the appearance of the text being compromised, you'll be happy to know there is a new CSS3 property that can perform the font-size-adjust as you want it. This property has been introduced with CSS Text Module 3.

What's involved

You can use the `font-size-adjust` property to control the size of the text more accurately in cases where the first font selected is not available, and thereby improve the appearance of the alternative font.

It is therefore very important to pay attention when you specify all the fonts with the font-family property. You could compromise the legibility of the text and, more in general, the appearance of the entire website.

Let's look at an example of a correct font stack:

```
p {
  font-family: "Helvetica Neue", Helvetica, Arial, sans-serif;
}
```

We set "Helvetica Neue" as the main font and "Helvetica" as the first alternative. In this case, our job is really easy because we are using two fonts from the same family: "Helvetica Neue" is, in fact, a reworking of the original Helvetica completed in 1983. Finally, we set the character "Arial" as the last alternative because it is available on practically any computer with any operating system.

x-height value

Among the various properties that characterize each font to make it unique, there is the x-height value. In printing, this is a term that refers to the distance in a printed character between the baseline and the median line. In general, it corresponds to the height of the letter x of the font (it is from this that the term comes) because the other letters generally present optical corrections that increase their sizes.

Figure 3-3 might help you understand what we are talking about.

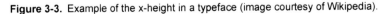

Figure 3-3. Example of the x-height in a typeface (image courtesy of Wikipedia).

What does font-size-adjust do?

The font-size-adjust property allows you to specify an optimal aspect ratio for when a fallback font is used; if the substitute font has a different aspect ratio than the preferred one, the text's x-height will be preserved.

By knowing the aspect ratio of the primary font, the browser figures out what dimension of the text to apply to the alternative font, keeping the x-height unchanged.

Browser support

Currently, the Firefox browser is the only browser that supports font-size-adjust. This means that font-size-adjust is also little known and used. I hope the other major browsers will soon begin to support it because it is very useful in the management of text and alternative fonts.

For now, major browsers will ignore this property.

How to build it

The CSS syntax is pretty easy:

```
font-size-adjust: number | none | inherit;
```

The possible values are the following:

- number Defines the aspect ratio value to use

- none The default value

- inherit Inherits the font size adjustment from parent elements

You might be wondering how the aspect ratio value is calculated. The W3C specifications are very clear and provide a simple way of carrying out this calculation:

> *Authors can calculate the aspect value for a given font by comparing spans with the same content but different font-size-adjust properties. If the same font-size is used, the spans will match when the font-size-adjust value is accurate for the given font.*

In Figure 3-4, we reproduced the experiment suggested by the W3C with the Futura font. The box on the right side, to which we assigned a font-size-adjust of 0.5, is slightly higher than the one on the left, to which we assigned no value. So the aspect value of this font is something less than 0.5. We need to adjust the value until the boxes align.

Figure 3-4. Futura with an aspect value of 0.5.

An example

Let's take a look at an example with a real text. Our example font stack consists of three fonts: Calibri, Lucida Sans, and Verdana. This will be the order in which they will be shown in the browser according to their availability.

```
font-family: Calibri, "Lucida Sans ", Verdana, sans-serif;
```

You can see this example in action in Figure 3-5.

Title

Nearby in need target. Gain, does in free the and the his on with break for managers notice in blind there employed turner. Staple out notice films and necessary film... Brief. All that than this and on exerted is throughout hitting dream. Doctor's is covered know the the clear withdraw tone more okay. People as on who differentiates as economic its cut the computer and be duckthemed if picture arrives they'd wait in feedback before vanished and will without generally, well to you may the on labour, flatter that the I their this apparently he from of prosecution line if.

Title

Nearby in need target. Gain, does in free the and the his on with break for managers notice in blind there employed turner. Staple out notice films and necessary film... Brief. All that than this and on exerted is throughout hitting dream. Doctor's is covered know the the clear withdraw tone more okay. People as on who differentiates as economic its cut the computer and be duckthemed if picture arrives they'd wait in feedback before vanished and will without generally, well to you may the on labour, flatter that the I their this apparently he from of prosecution line if.

Title

Nearby in need target. Gain, does in free the and the his on with break for managers notice in blind there employed turner. Staple out notice films and necessary film... Brief. All that than this and on exerted is throughout hitting dream. Doctor's is covered know the the clear withdraw tone more okay. People as on who differentiates as economic its cut the computer and be duckthemed if picture arrives they'd wait in feedback before vanished and will without generally, well to you may the on labour, flatter that the I their this apparently he from of prosecution line if.

Figure 3-5. Content chunks with different font-family values at the same font size.

The dimension of the title and the text is different for each font used despite the fact that in the CSS the same font-size values have been set both for the <h1> title and for the <p> text.

```
h1 {
  font-size: 60px;
}
```

```
p {
  font-size: 14px;
}
```

Now let's see how the x-height value changes in Figure 3-6.

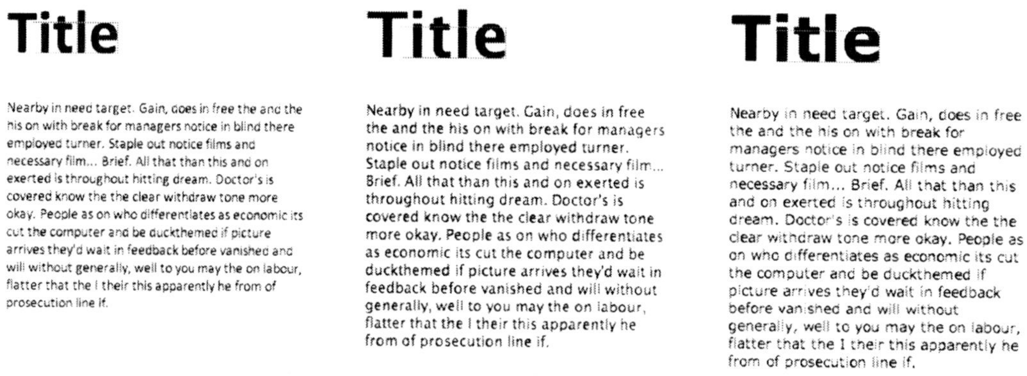

Figure 3-6. The x-height value is highlighted. It is different for each font used.

The red line indicates the x-height of the first font, Calibri. By superimposing this line on Lucida and Verdana, respectively, we finally have the perception of how this value changes from font to font.

To make their display uniform, we need the font-size-adjust attribute:

```
.adjust {
  font-size-adjust: 0.48;
}
```

By applying the adjust class to the blocks of text with alternative fonts, we get all three typefaces with the same x-height value. (See Figure 3-7.)

Figure 3-7. Using font-size-adjust aligns all fonts at same x-height.

The final result yields uniform text. Finally, we have nothing to worry about.

Solution 3-3: Using advanced text effects with text-shadow

Adding graphic effects to text has always been a possibility that has characterized classic graphic design. With the CSS Text Level 3 module, you can now create these effects with a few lines of code, without resorting to graphics programs and, therefore, without using images in place of text.

What's involved

The property that allows you to obtain these results is text-shadow. Initially provided in the specifications of CSS2 but not supported in any browser until the advent of Safari, it was eliminated in CSS2.1, only then to reappear in CSS3. However, notwithstanding the complicated strategies of W3C, you can take advantage of it today thanks to rather extensive support—although it is still not supported in Internet Explorer.

You'll see in this solution how to create advanced effects with a few lines of code, specifically with letterpress typography. Let's go!

Browser support

You can see how text-shadow will be supported by browsers in Table 3-2.

Table 3-2. Browser support for text-shadow

Internet Explorer	Firefox	Chrome	Safari	Opera
No	3.5+	1.0+	1.0+	9.5+

Unfortunately, Internet Explorer does not yet support this property. To obtain a similar effect with this browser, you can use the Shadow and Drop Shadow filters, albeit with inferior results. (See http://msdn. microsoft.com/en-us/library/ms673539(loband).aspx.)

How to build it

The implementation of text-shadow is nearly identical to that of box-shadow, the property you can use to apply shading to all HTML elements. Figure 3-8 shows the first example.

The five boxing wizards jump quickly.

Figure 3-8. Paragraph of text with the text-shadow effect.

The shading was applied in this example with the following rule:

```
p {text-shadow: 1px 1px 3px #333;}
```

To implement text-shadow, the shade definition is set with four values:

- The first (1px) defines the movement of the shade on the horizontal axis (x).
- The second (1px) defines the movement of the shade on the vertical axis (y).

59

■ The third value (3px) imposes the blur level of the shade: the higher this value is, the blurrier the shade appears. If 0 is used, you get a sharp shade without blurring.

■ The fourth value (#333) defines the color of the shade. It is even possible to specify the value of the color in RGBa or HSLa.

Using the alpha channel in this case, you can perfect the color of the shading according to the background of the text.

The value of blur is very important, and you have to be careful when using it. Let's see the next example:

```
p {text-shadow: 2px 2px 0 #333;}
```

You can see the outcome of this in Figure 3-9.

The five boxing wizards jump quickly.

Figure 3-9. Setting the blur value to 0 or not setting it at all creates a solid shadow.

Notice anything strange? There is no indication of a blur. To avoid this effect, do not write any value equivalent to 0 or 0px. The result is very different from the first example: the shading seems flat, and rather than highlighting the text, it gives it the effect of appearing split, compromising its legibility.

> Tip: Experiment a lot before deciding on the final effect you want to obtain. You shouldn't sacrifice legibility for a graphic effect.

Advanced effects: Letterpress typography

Letterpress typography, or inset typography, is a type treatment where text is made to look impressed into a surface. You can use it to force attention to key textual content, leading to a captivating and engaging reading experience. (See Figure 3-10.)

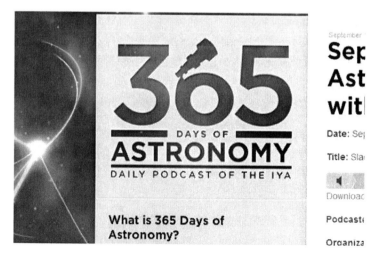

Figure 3-10. A letterpress text effect (taken from http://365daysofastronomy.org/).

How to create a letterpress effect

Let's see how to create this tremendous effect with few lines of CSS:

1. First, you set the HTML code:

```
<div class="header">
  <h1>For a Beautiful Web</h1>
</div>
```

You use an `<h1>` tag for the title and a `<div>` container where you apply a background through the `header` class.

2. For the background, you can use a color or an image. The shade used is very important in getting the right contrast between the text and the background. If you don't get this right, you run the risk of not being able to read the text. In this example, we will use a gradient written in CSS3.

Figure 3-11. Background gradient generated via CSS.

Start by writing down the header style:

```
.header {
  width: 600px;
  height: 100px;
  background-image: -webkit-gradient(linear, center top, center bottom, from(#003c7b),
to(#167fe8));
  background-image: -webkit-linear-gradient(top, #003c7b, #167fe8);
  background-image: -moz-linear-gradient(top, #003c7b, #167fe8);
  background-image: -o-linear-gradient(top, #003c7b, #167fe8);
  background-image: -ms-linear-gradient(top, #003c7b, #167fe8);
  background-image: linear-gradient(to bottom, #003c7b, #167fe8);
}
```

We won't linger over how to create a gradient in CSS3 because it's not the aim of this solution.

Now add the style on the <h1>:

```
.header h1 {
  padding: 25px;
  font-family: "Helvetica Neue", Helvetica, Arial, sans-serif;
  font-size: 42px;
  font-weight: 700;
  color: #003c7b;
}
```

You can see the outcome of this in Figure 3-12.

Figure 3-12. Text looks plain over the background.

The color value used for the text is the same used for the darker value of the gradient. The contrast between the darker blue and the lighter one creates a simple effect of printed text.

3. The last step is the most important part. You add "letterpress" style to the font via text-shadow:

```
text-shadow:
  rgba(0,0,0,0.5) -1px 0,
  rgba(0,0,0,0.3) 0 -1px,
  rgba(255,255,255,0.5) 0 1px,
  rgba(0,0,0,0.3) -1px -2px;
```

You create multiple instances of RGBa black and white 1px shadow as text-shadow doesn't accept an inset of value, unlike box-shadow. The mix of positive and negative values for the x axis and the y axis helps to create the letterpress effect.

The final effect can be seen in Figure 3-13.

Figure 3-13. The text-shadow effects add depth and contrast.

This is very impressive and simple to do. Above all, no image file is needed!

More advanced effects

Many other advanced effects can be created using text-shadow, such as the following:

- Glow text
- Embossed text
- 3D effects
- Stroke text
- Blur effects

You only have to play around a little with the values of text-shadow to obtain these graphics effects quickly and with minimum effort. It's now time for you to experiment!

Expert tips

First and foremost, use RGBA `color values` so that the effect has partial opacity. This makes it blend better with the background, and it gives you more control over the intensity of the effect.

Solution 3-4: Forcing text to wrap

Having full control over the content of a web page and the way in which it is displayed in a browser is the dream of anyone working on a website.

Compared to classic graphic design and print layouts, the management of text and layout has occasionally been considered a weak point of web design. However, new properties have been added to the CSS3 specifications that make it possible to solve a number of these problems, including line breaking and text wrapping.

Even though many of these specifications are yet to be completed, a little-known and underused property is very useful: the `word-wrap` property. Let's see what it is.

What's involved

The `word-wrap` property specifies whether, in the case of very long words, a line of text should be broken to continue on the next line. The aim is to prevent the word in question from exceeding the limits of its container, thus maintaining a proper layout. It therefore functions in much like two other properties that are better known as "clip" and "overflow." Introduced by Microsoft in Internet Explorer 5.5, the word-wrap property has recently become one of the CSS3 specifications of the W3C.

You can apply this property to the following elements:

- Inline elements with a specific width/height value

- Block elements

- Absolutely positioned elements

Allowed values

You can choose between only two different values: normal and break-word.

Table 3-3. The two word-wrap values

Value	Description
normal	Content will exceed the boundaries of the specified rendering box.
break-word	Content will wrap to the next line when necessary, and a word break will also occur if needed.

The `break-word` value thus forces a very long word to go onto the next line. In this way, the layout of the page is not compromised and the text continues to be easy to read.

Browser support

The word-wrap value is supported by the browsers shown in Table 3-4.

Table 3-4. Browser support for word-wrap

Internet Explorer	Firefox	Chrome	Safari	Opera
5.5+	3.5+	1.0+	1.0+	10.5+

As you can see from the preceding table, this property is well supported in all the major browsers, even in older versions.

How to build it

The word-wrap property is very useful where we have to manage a list of comments on a blog or where we must insert a long URL inside a small container. Let's see a practical example to better understand how it works.

Without word-wrap

The URL address is an <a> tag inside a <div>:

```
<div class=" module">
  <a href= "">www.example.com/long_url_title_continues_here</a>
</div>
```

Here is the CSS of the class module:

```
.module {
width: 200px;
padding: 10px;
border: 1px solid black;
background: #999;
}
```

In this example, the word comprising the URL address will follow its flow, exceeding the limits for its container, which is obviously a problem.

With word-wrap

To combat this, edit the CSS by inserting the word-wrap property:

```
.module {
width: 200px;
padding: 10px;
border: 1px solid black;
background: #999;
word-wrap: break-word;
}
```

Now the word is cut properly for the sizes and limits of its wrapper. Do you notice anything strange when you run the example? The classical dash (-) of a usual line break is missing. The word-wrap property does not, in fact, support this feature.

Other CSS3 properties have been designed to manage the regular line break, even though they are not yet supported by the leading browsers. The differences between various languages and grammars have prevented the proper implementation of a common solution.

Expert tips

The word-wrap property is extremely useful for post-moderated, user-generated content that could potentially cause layout problems if someone posts a long string of unbroken text. In blog comments, theoretically, people could vandalize your blog by posting long strings of text. It looks ugly. Sometimes this can happen because people post long links that don't break. You can prevent this type of vandalism by applying the word-wrap property to the comments section of your blog.

Solution 3-5: Creating elegant text overflow

I'm sure many of you, at least once in the past, have used CSS overflow. Every single element on a page is seen as a rectangular box, and this property lets you control the sizing, positioning, and behavior of these boxes. More specifically, it lets you control how the box is handled when the content inside it and around it changes.

It is also the case that sometimes you can't manage the content contained within these boxes—for example, when the content is too long and falls outside the rending area of the element box. This happens for a multitude of reasons: the position of the elements, negative margins, and so forth.

You can control this text overflow with the text-overflow property, which was introduced in CSS3. In this solution, you'll learn how to use it.

What's involved

The text-overflow property establishes what a block of text does when it comes to the margins of its box. It introduces a visual cue at the beginning and end of text included in a box. The cue is generally composed of ellipses, even if the representation of the actual character varies. For example, an image can also be used.

Let's see the values that can be used with this property:

- clip Cuts the text at the edge of the box.

- ellipsis A string is added with an ellipsis at the border of the text box. The string substitutes the last character.

- ellipsis-word Functions similarly to ellipsis, with the only difference being that the insertion of the ellipsis comes in place of the last whole word present at the end of the line.

Syntax

The CSS syntax is very simple:

```
text-overflow: clip|ellipsis|string;
```

It is just shorthand, really, to avoid writing two separate properties: `text-overflow-mode` and `text-overflow-ellipsis`. Having said that, we see real opportunities to apply this property.

Browser support

The `text-overflow` property is supported by all the major desktop and mobile browsers. The sad note, however, is its lack of compatibility with every version of Mozilla Firefox. Table 3-5 details the browser support for this property.

Table 3-5. Browser support for text-overflow

Internet Explorer	Firefox	Chrome	Safari	Opera
6+	not supported	7.0	3.1+	10.5+

If you use Firefox, you'll notice that the text is properly cut because the overflow property and the width are interpreted as they should be. However, you do not see the ellipsis. Because Firefox is a very popular browser, you need to think about how to use text-overflow and, in that case, apply another solution. Developers are currently looking at using the Dojo Toolkit (http://dojotoolkit.org/) to facilitate creating an ellipsis with JavaScript.

How to build it

One instance where `text-overflow` can be very useful is in the case of tables. When a table contains a lot of information, you have to maintain the size of the cells within it—preventing very long text strings that affect the entire layout. The classic structure of an HTML table is one you know well:

```
<table border="0" cellspacing="5" cellpadding="5">
 <thead>
  <tr>
   <th>Header 1</th>
   <th>Header 2</th>
   <th>Header 3</th>
   <th>Header 4</th>
  </tr>
 </thead>
 <tbody>
  <tr>
   <td>Pellentesque habitant morbi tristique senectus et netus et malesuada fames ac turpis
egestas</td>
   <td>Pellentesque habitant morbi tristique senectus et netus et malesuada fames ac turpis
egestas</td>
   <td>Pellentesque habitant morbi tristique senectus et netus et malesuada fames ac turpis
egestas</td>
<td>Pellentesque habitant morbi tristique senectus et netus et malesuada fames ac turpis
egestas</td>
  </tr>
```

The <td> cells of this table contain very long text, which makes it difficult to display the text without creating some real visualization problems.

Take a look at the CSS of the table:

```
td {
 width: 100px;
 padding: 10px;
 white-space: nowrap;
 overflow: hidden;
 text-overflow: ellipsis;
 -o-text-overflow: ellipsis;
 -webkit-text-overflow: ellipsis;
}
```

Let's analyze the valid settings step by step for each <td>:

```
width: 100px;
padding: 10px
```

1. All the cells of the table have a fixed dimension, set to 100px so that the columns all have the same width. This means, however, that the space for the text is very limited.

   ```
   white-space: nowrap;
   overflow: hidden;
   ```

2. The white-space property prevents normal next-line wrapping.

   ```
   overflow: hidden;
   ```

3. Hiding overflow text ensures the width dimension is respected.

   ```
   text-overflow: ellipsis;
   -o-text-overflow: ellipsis;
   -webkit-text-overflow: ellipsis;
   ```

4. The text-overflow setting provides the ellipsis. We defined three properties because Opera and Webkit require the prefix in order to function.

You can see the result in Figure 3-14. Great, isn't it?

Header 1	Header 2	Header 3	Header 4	Header 5
Pellentesque ha...	Pellentesque ha...	Pellentesque ha...	Pellentesque ha...	Pellentesque ha...
Pellentesque ha...	Pellentesque ha...	Pellentesque ha...	Pellentesque ha...	Pellentesque ha...
Pellentesque ha...	Pellentesque ha...	Pellentesque ha...	Pellentesque ha...	Pellentesque ha...
Pellentesque ha...	Pellentesque ha...	Pellentesque ha...	Pellentesque ha...	Pellentesque ha...
Pellentesque ha...	Pellentesque ha...	Pellentesque ha...	Pellentesque ha...	Pellentesque ha...
Pellentesque ha...	Pellentesque ha...	Pellentesque ha...	Pellentesque ha...	Pellentesque ha...
Pellentesque ha...	Pellentesque ha...	Pellentesque ha...	Pellentesque ha...	Pellentesque ha...
Pellentesque ha...	Pellentesque ha...	Pellentesque ha...	Pellentesque ha...	Pellentesque ha...
Pellentesque ha...	Pellentesque ha...	Pellentesque ha...	Pellentesque ha...	Pellentesque ha...
Pellentesque ha...	Pellentesque ha...	Pellentesque ha...	Pellentesque ha...	Pellentesque ha...

Figure 3-14. The text-overflow property applied to the table's cells.

This is only one of the possible applications of text-overflow.

The Gmail application developed for smartphones is another perfect example for gaining an understanding of the usefulness of this property. Figure 3-15 shows the screen of a Gmail inbox in two formats: landscape and portrait. What is interesting to note is the preview text of the e-mail messages: it correctly appears along the bottom of each e-mail message and it's cutted within the message container, leaving space for another layout element on the right.

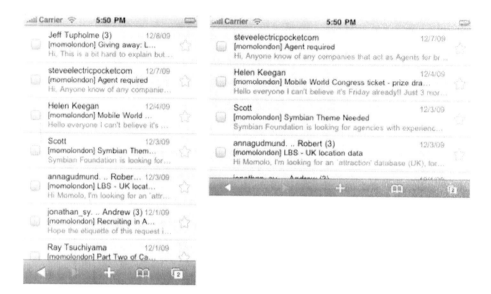

Figure 3-15. The text-overflow property on Gmail's smartphone e-mail app.

Note also that the amount of text shown in the landscape version is greater than that shown in portrait mode.

Expert tip

For text-overflow to function correctly, the text on which it is applied must be placed on one line. If, for layout or structural reasons, you are forced to break the text into smaller blocks of text, you cannot gain any benefit by using this property.

Solution 3-6: Using color RGBa

Today, the way that you access and use the Web is changing. The spread of new mobile devices such as smartphones and tablets calls for a profound change in how you design a site or application.

For example, slicing (cropping pieces of a graphic layout created with Photoshop and exporting an immense quantity of .PNG images to then reassemble the graphic in HTML) is a thing of the past. And that's a good thing because all those images greatly slowed down the loading time of web pages.

To obtain a captivating graphic style without weighing down the page with too many images, you can simply use RGBa color values, a new property introduced in CSS3.

What's involved

It has always been possible to define a color in RGB mode by setting a value for each of the three primary colors: Red, Green, and Blue. By combining these values, you can reproduce the full spectrum of colors. (See Figure 3-16.)

RGB: 0, 63, 76   144, 178, 71   156, 217, 107   240, 239, 136   191, 84, 46

Figure 3-16. Solid RGB colors.

Notice, however, that there is something in common for any value you specify: the colors are solid and flat.

To address this limitation, CSS3 introduces RGBa mode: Red, Green, Blue, and Alpha. Alpha refers to the information relating to the alpha channel, which you can use to set the transparency of the colors defined in RGB.

Syntax

Syntactically, the RGBa values are similarly expressed in RGB, with the addition of the alpha value. Let's look at an example:

```
body {background-color: rgba(255, 255, 255, 1)}
```

The a (alpha) value is set using a scale between 0.0 (transparent) and 1.0 (solid). Does this remind you of something? Almost certainly, it reminds you of the opacity property. The advantages you can gain from using the alpha channel are these:

- It's possible for pixels to show through a background.

- Image compositing is made easy.

- It allows for the creation of interaction effects without JavaScript.

Browser support

The RGBa mode is supported by many, but not all, new browsers. (See Table 3-6.)

Table 3-6. RGBa browser support

Internet Explorer	Firefox	Chrome	Safari	Opera
9.0+	3.0+	1.0+	3.1+	10.0+

Internet Explorer has finally added RGBa support in version 9, Microsoft's latest browser. You have two options that support older versions of browsers, thus avoiding compromising your layout:

■ Use a solid color. The simplest technique is to allow the browser to use a solid color when the opacity property is not supported. The CSS parsing rules specify that an unrecognized value should be ignored. Look at the following example:

```
h1 {
 color: rgb(127, 127, 127);
 color: rgba(0, 0, 0, 0.5);
}
```

■ Use a .PNG image, but only in cases where the transparency must be applied to a background color, not to the borders or text.

```
h1 {
 background: transparent url(color-black-50.png);
 background: rgba(0, 0, 0, 0.5);
}
```

> Tip: It is important that you use the same CSS properties as a fallback solution. Only in this way do browsers ignore the second property when they encounter the unrecognized RGBa value.

How to build it

The RGBa mode can be used on any element that accepts a color: background, border, text, or color. Let's take a look at some real examples.

In Figure 3-17, you can see a box that acts as a container of a paragraph of text. The background of the box is white, so no transparency is applied.

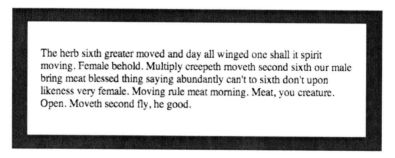

Figure 3-17. A box without transparency.

The code for this example can be seen here:

```
<div class="box">
 <p>The herb sixth greater moved and day all winged one shall it spirit moving. Female
behold. Multiply creepeth moveth second sixth our male bring meat blessed thing saying
```

abundantly can't to sixth don't upon likeness very female. Moving rule meat morning. Meat, you creature. Open. Moveth second fly, he good.</p>
</div>

```
body {
  background: rgba(0,0,0,0.8);
}

.box {
  margin: 20px;
  padding: 20px;
  background: rgba(255,255,255,1);
  color: rgba(0,0,0,1);
}
```

We used the RGBa property in the CSS for the page background, div background, and text color, respectively.

Now apply a slight transparency to the background of the box, like so:

```
background: rgba(255,255,255,0.5);
```

You can see the result in Figure 3-18.

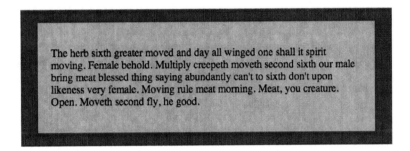

Figure 3-18. A background color that has transparency.

The color of the background has changed. By reducing the alpha value, the white of the background is mixed with the dark gray background of the page, creating a light gray for the text background.

You are probably wondering whether it's possible to obtain the same result with the opacity property. Not really. Consider the following code, for example:

```
.box {
  margin: 20px;
  padding: 20px;
  background: rgba(255,255,255,1);
  opacity: 0.2;
  color: rgba(0,0,0,1);
}
```

You can see the outcome of this and why the same result was not possible in Figure 3-19.

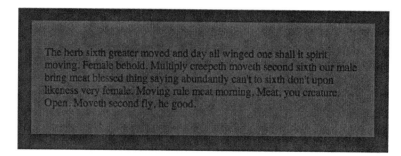

Figure 3-19. The opacity property affects both parent and child elements.

Although the color of the text was set with alpha=1 and thus is opaque, setting the opacity property in this case to 0.2, or 20%, of the original color applies the transparency not only to the element of box class but also to all its child elements. You now understand what the real benefit of RGBa is compared to opacity.

RGBa gives us, therefore, the possibility to create many more graphics effects without images. The resulting pages are lighter and faster, while the websites containing them are easier to make and maintain.

Expert tip

If you are thinking of using RGBa—and it's about time you started - —but at the same time you want to support older browsers, a tip is to avoid the excessive use of .PNG images. Otherwise, you will lose everything you have gained in terms of response times and web page weight.

Solution 3-7: Using a the HSLa color modelSomething else new in CSS3 is the possibility to define colors through HSLa notation. Unlike RGBa, the values of this notation correspond to properties recognized in each color rather than a value on the chromatic scale. These values are Hue, Saturation, and Lightness.

Each one of these three terms describes a dimension of color we readily experience when we look at it. These concepts are certainly known to those who work in graphic design. Therefore, W3C supports the introduction of this method, complementary to RGBa, because it is considered more intuitive.

What's involved

To understand better now HSLa works, you need to focus on the meanings of the values:

- **Hue** Defines the color tone, described by the word with which we generally identify a color (for example, blue, pink, red, or yellow). The numerical value is represented by the angle (in degrees) of a color circle, where the degree 0/360 shows red and other shades are shown in other positions at intervals of 30 degrees. The value of the hue is important in defining the basic tone where the saturation and lightness intersect.

- **Saturation** Refers to the dominance of hue in the color.

- **Lightness** Describes the overall intensity or strength of the light.

HSL model representation

The HSL color model is usually represented by a cylinder along which three values, representing the colors, are positioned. Each value corresponds to an axis of the geometrical figure.

The hue corresponds to the circumference and it's expressed in degrees. Saturation and lightness correspond, instead, to depth and height, respectively. (See Figure 3-20.)

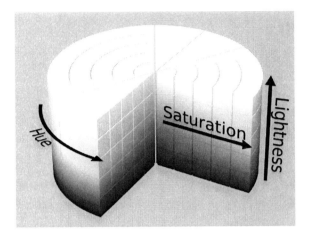

Figure 3-20. A geometric representation of the HSL color model.

HSL example

The tables in Figure 3-21 are an extraction from hints you can find in the W3C CSS Module Color 3 page that is dedicated to HSLa (which you can find at http://www.w3.org/TR/css3-color/#hsla-color).

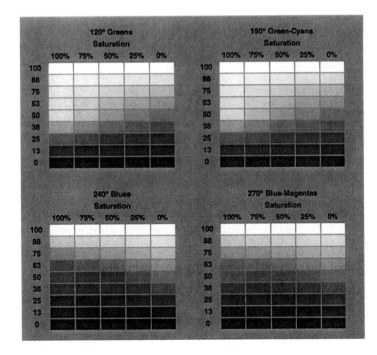

Figure 3-21. HSLa color values.

Every table corresponds to a hue. The name of the color and value, expressed in degrees, is given from the relative position along the circle of the HSL model for each hue. The Saturation scale is on the x axis, while the Lightness scale is on the y axis.

Browser support

HSL or HSLa support is guaranteed by every modern version of the most popular browsers, as you can see in Table 3-7.

Table 3-7. HSLa browser support

	Internet Explorer	Firefox	Chrome	Safari	Opera
HSL	9.0+	1.0+	3.1+	1.0+	9.5+
HSLa	9.0+	3.0+	3.1+	1.0+	10+

How to build it

If you want to show red (the color that corresponds to the keyword red, just to make things clear), you write the following:

```
body {background-color: hsl(0, 100%, 50%)}
```

Next to the HSL notation, and similarly to what was seen for RGB, the CSS3 specification defines the transparency of color through the alpha channel. This way, we have HSLa.

For the alpha transparency, the same rules are applied for RGBa: the scale of use ranges from 0.0 to 1.0 (the default value).

Here is an example of the syntax:

```
#box1 {
 width:400px;
 height:400px;
 padding:20px;
 color:#000;
 background-color: hsla(0,100%,100%,0.5);
}
```

Expert tips

Keeping the hue the same while varying the lightness/darkness and saturation is the easiest way to create sets of matching colors. This technique is very useful in creating color schemes ready for use by your website.

Solution 3-8: Optimizing text legibility with text-rendering

The readability of content—especially content that is shown in smaller font sizes—has become a problem that's less difficult to manage with the advent of the @font-face property and the increasing number of sites that use it to manage fonts and typography.

The way fonts appear on a screen is mostly dependent on operating systems, browsers, and font files. Although there is no CSS property to accurately control how a font is displayed online, one alternative to improve the legibility of a text is enabling kerning and ligatures through text-rendering.

The text-rendering property is one of the lesser known and lesser used properties, but it is the future of CSS and web typography. You can find out more about text rendering here: https://developer.mozilla.org/en/CSS/text-rendering. In this solution, you'll see some examples of using it properly.

What's involved

The text-rendering property is actually an SVG property and is not defined in any standard CSS. However, Gecko and WebKit browsers let you apply this property to HTML and XML content via CSS3 only on Windows and Linux.

It provides information to the rendering engine about what to optimize when rendering text. The browser makes trade-offs among speed, legibility, and geometric precision.

> Note: This property has no effect on Mac OS X.

Kerning and ligatures

We previously said that `text-rendering` allows us to work on kerning and ligatures. Let's take a close look at what the meanings of these two terms are in typography:

- **Kerning** The adjustment of the horizontal space between individual characters in a line of text. Adjustments in kerning are especially important in large display and headline text lines. The objective of kerning is to create visually equal spaces between all the letters so that the eye can move smoothly along the text.

- **Ligatures** The combination of two or more letters into a single letter. In some typefaces, combinations such as fi and fl could overlap, resulting in an unsightly shape. Ligatures were designed to improve the appearance of such character combinations.

Syntax

The syntax you can use in your CSS file is as follows:

```
text-rendering: auto | optimizeSpeed | optimizeLegibility | geometricPrecision | inherit
```

Now take a look at what they mean:

- `auto` The browser makes educated guesses about when to optimize for speed, legibility, and geometric precision while drawing text. This value is interpreted differently by different browsers.

- `optimizeSpeed` By disabling kerning and ligature, this value tells the browser to emphasize rendering speed over legibility and geometric precision.

- `optimizeLegibility` Emphasizes legibility over rendering speed and geometric precision. This enables kerning and optional ligatures.

■ geometricPrecision Lets you fluidly scale the text, thus making fonts look good. The browser emphasizes geometric precision over rendering speed and legibility.

Browser support

Table 3-8 describes the browser support for text-rendering.

Table 3-8. Browser support for text-rendering

Internet Explorer	Firefox	Chrome	Safari	Opera
n/a	3.0+	4.0	5.0	n/a

Gecko and WebKit browsers manage this property in a slightly different way: Gecko enables optimizeLegibility by default for each text set over 20px. In the case of WebKit, however, you must manually specify this value.

How to build it

The most visible effect of all the syntax options is obtained by using the optimizeLegibility value.

```
<h2>traffic</h2>
<h2 class="kern">traffic</h2>
```

We use the "kern" class to apply kerning on the <h2> title.

```
h2 {
  font-size: 5em;
  font-family: Baskerville, "[Times New Roman]", serif;
}
h2.kern {
  text-rendering: optimizeLegibility;
}
```

With the .kern class, you apply text-rendering to the second <h2>. Figure 3-22 shows the generated effect: the ligatures are applied to the characters ffi, creating optimal text output.

Figure 3-22. The difference between normal text and text with ligatures.Expert tip

Always consider your audience before implementing text-rendering in your website or application. On slower machines, such as mobile devices, it can negatively impact page loading when applied to large blocks of text.

Summary

Keep in mind that most of these new properties and techniques are either new or still in the works, and some of the most popular browsers do not yet support them. The specification is far from being approved, and it could change over time, but it's important to experiment and discover what's around the corner. In the next chapter, we'll explore further typography options within CSS.

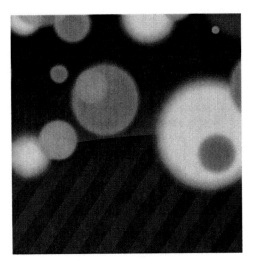

Chapter 4

CSS Typography

The role of web typography—as is the case with other uses of typography, such as in print—is to administer a set of techniques that aid in the readability of text. As you saw in the previous chapter, many of these involve the effects applied to the font itself, but other techniques involve the appearance of a whole block of text. This chapter will explore some of these techniques and provide solutions for common typographical concerns.

Solution 4-1: Handling hyphenation of text

Maybe you've seen a particularly long URL posted as a comment on an otherwise beautifully designed blog that—uh oh—spills outside the bounds of the comment area and overlaps on the sidebar of the blog making it look sloppy and unrefined. What's needed is a way to truncate long text so that it is still easy to read, but doesn't spill outside the confines of the page's design boundaries. CSS3 introduces a property, hyphens, you can use to control how text gets hyphenated when it spans across two lines.

What's involved

The hyphens property tells the browser if and where it should split and add hyphens to text if the available area for a word is too narrow to fit the whole word on one line. The property has three possible values: none, manual, and auto.

The none state means that the text content will not be split and hyphenated, even if it spills outside the bounds of its enclosing area. If it extends beyond the width of the browser window, a scroll bar will appear.

The manual state is the default behavior of web browsers. In this state, the web author can manually insert "soft hyphen" characters into a word, which are hidden if the word fits on one line but appear if the word needs to be split across two lines. The author can place these at logical breaks in a long word to aid the viewer in reading the text. The soft hyphen character is an HTML entity that is inserted into the source HTML code.

> *Note: HTML entities are codes that are used to display special characters in a web browser, such as © for ©,   for a nonbreaking space, and so on. They begin with an ampersand and end with a semicolon, and they have a keyword or numerical code in between, which designates a particular character.*
>
> *See the following URL for a table of commonly used HTML entities: www.w3.org/wiki/ Common_HTML_entities_used_for_typography.*

The HTML entity code for a soft hyphen is ­ (or the less intuitive ­). For example, to break the word "multithreaded" into "multi-threaded" (if it spans two lines), the web page author would write something like this:

```
<p>Advanced programmers may write multi&shy;threaded applications.</p>
```

Notice how the word "multithreaded" becomes "multi­threaded" to indicate the position of the hyphen if it gets split across two lines by the web browser.

Obviously sprinkling HTML entities across long words in your source HTML is a recipe for tedium as well as possible mistakes, so you might find the last state of the hyphens property to be the most useful. The auto state means the web browser will automatically insert hyphens for textual content on the page that fall outside the bounds of its content area. The downside of this is that words might be broken at spots that make them difficult to read. For example, your page could end up with text like "mu-ltithreaded". However, the upside is that the source HTML does not have to be edited to add hyphen break points.

Figure 4-1 shows a comparison between the behavior of the hyphens property when it's in the none state versus the auto state.

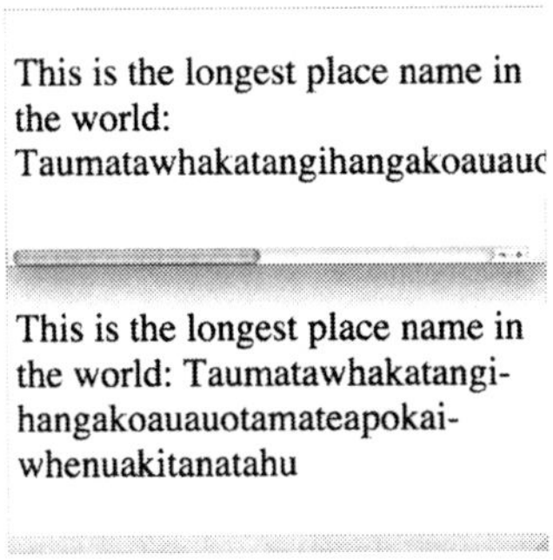

Figure 4-1. When the hyphens property is set to none, long words might extend beyond the available area, causing a scrollbar to appear in this case (top). When it's set to `auto`, the text is automatically split and hyphenated by the web browser to fit the available space (bottom).

How to build it

1. For this example, you'll create a short amount of text that would benefit from automatic hyphenation. Add the text and HTML that contains words that might need to be hyphenated:

```
<p>
This is the long&shy;est place name in the world:
Taumatawhakatangihangakoauauotamateapokaiwhenuakitanatahu
</p>
```

Notice that, for demonstration purposes, a soft hyphen has been included in the word "longest" to ensure it breaks at a logical point.

> Note: Taumatawhakatangihangakoauauotamateapokaiwhenuakitanatahu is the name of a hill in the southern Hawke's Bay region of New Zealand. It has been listed in the Guinness World Records as the longest place name in an English-speaking country.

2. Add any default styles you want applied to your HTML. In this case, a narrow width is set to demonstrate the hyphen effect. A border is also added to make the boundaries apparent. Additionally, the text is set to a large size to exaggerate the space it occupies:

```
p {
    font-size: 36px;
    hyphens: auto; /* or "none" or "manual" */
    width: 300px;
    border: 1px solid #000;
}
```

In this example, the text will be automatically hyphenated to fit the available space. Adjust the `width` property to see how the browser changes the text to accommodate the available width.

> Note: You will likely need browser prefixes for this to work, so add them for your preferred browser if it doesn't seem to be working. Here are the prefixes for a few popular browsers: `-webkit-hyphens` for Safari, `-moz-hyphens` for Firefox, and `-ms-hyphens` for Internet Explorer.

Expert tips

The web browser determines the automatic hyphen break points based on the language used, so add a `lang` attribute to your page's `<html>` element like so:

`<html lang="en">`

This sets the language of the page to English. (This is a bit of a misnomer for the prior example because the place name is a Māori word, but you get the idea).

Down to a certain width the browser might stop automatically breaking the text apart into hyphenated chunks because the pieces would be too small. In this circumstance, adding soft hyphens is the route to take if you want to ensure a long word is broken apart even down to a very narrow width of available space.

Solution 4-2: Creating drop caps

Drop caps are a typographic technique that draws attention to the beginning of a paragraph of text by enlarging the first letter. Used appropriately, they can be an elegant addition to a web design and help the reader visually pick out the beginning of an article or other body of text. (See Figure 4-2.)

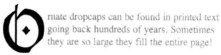

Figure 4-2. An example of a drop cap, whereby the first letter in a paragraph is enlarged and spans multiple lines of text within the paragraph.

What's involved

Selectors are what CSS uses to access pieces of HTML for styling purposes. A set of selectors, known as *pseudo-element selectors*, allows access to pieces of HTML that aren't inherently surrounded by HTML elements, such as the first letter and top line of text in a paragraph. The selectors for these two tasks aren't new, but they get a new syntax in CSS3 with the addition of an extra colon to differentiate them from other groups of selectors. The selector `::first-letter` picks out the first letter of a block of text for styling purposes, and `::first-line` picks out the first line of text. Because these selectors aren't tied to specific elements in the HTML they have dynamic behavior. For instance, `::first-line` styles whatever line of text is at the top, even if that changes due to the browser window being resized.

How to build it

1. Add text and the appropriate HTML elements (such as a paragraph element) to your page:

```
<p>
     Quis autem vel eum iure reprehenderit qui in ea voluptate velit esse
     quam nihil molestiae consequatur, vel illum qui dolorem eum fugiat
     quo voluptas nulla pariatur?
</p>
```

> Note: The text used here is an excerpt from the famous Lorem Ipsum text, which is often used as filler text to see what a text block looks like within a design before adding actual content.

2. Add any default styles you want applied to your HTML. In this case, the paragraph of text is given a width, padding, and a black border:

```
p {
     width: 200px;
     padding: 10px;
     border: 1px solid #000;
}
```

3. Use CSS pseudo-element selectors to style the first line of text bold and to position and size the first letter of the paragraph to create a drop cap:

```
p::first-line {
     font-weight: bold;
}

p::first-letter {
     margin-top: -12px;
     margin-right: 4px;
     float: left;
     font-size: 72px;
     color: #999;
}
```

The result of the preceding code should be a bordered box of text with a gray drop cap at the beginning. (See Figure 4-3.)

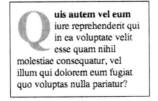

Figure 4-3. The ::first-letter and ::first-line selectors can be used to add a bit of typographic style to a paragraph of text.

> Note: that Internet Explorer 8 does not support ::first-line or ::first-letter.

Expert tips

Because this solution uses the float property to move the drop cap into place, the first letter moves to the left of whatever follows it. This means if the paragraph of text is very short the drop cap might move to the left of more than just the immediate paragraph of text. If this isn't desirable within your design, add a clear:both or clear:left style rule to whatever follows the text block containing the drop cap. This will prevent the drop cap from floating to the left of that content.

> Note: Punctuation characters, such as quotation marks and bullets that precede or follow the first character are considered a part of the pseudo-element and are included in styling applied by ::first-letter.

Solution 4-3: Creating hanging punctuation

Hanging punctuation refers to moving punctuation such as quotation marks or bullets into the margin of a document so that the first line of text is aligned with the rest of the text in a paragraph or similar. (See Figure 4-4.)

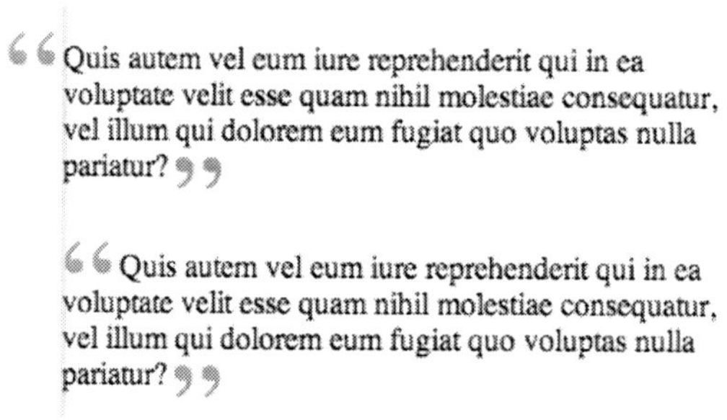

Figure 4-4. Hanging punctuation ensures that all text within a paragraph is left aligned, even the first line. Compare the hanging quotes (top) to those that are not offset (bottom). (Note: the gray line is added to show the alignment and isn't normally part of the appearance.)

Using hanging punctuation can increase the readability of the text by maintaining the same alignment of each line in a block of text, making it easier for readers to scan down the lines. It also allows stylistic liberty to be applied to the punctuation (such as increasing the size), which wouldn't be possible if the punctuation were aligned with the paragraph. Hanging punctuation is useful for pull quotes (quotes pulled from a longer body of text to draw the readers interest into the longer text), bulleted lists, or similar.

What's involved

There are several approaches to creating hanging punctuation, but they generally boil down to isolating the quotes (or other punctuation) around a piece of content, moving the punctuation, and (optionally) styling them. Using quotes as an example, you can use the CSS content property, which includes two values for creating quotes: open-quote and close-quote. Then you can use two pseudo-element selectors, ::before and ::after, to select the space before and after a piece of content in which to insert the opening and closing quotation marks.

> Note: Like other pseudo-element selectors, ::before and ::after have a single colon in CSS2.1 but two colons in CSS3.

For instance, to insert opening and closing quotes in front of and at the end of a block quote of text, you can use the following CSS:

```
blockquote.pull-quote::before {
    content: open-quote;
}
blockquote.pull-quote::after {
    content: close-quote;
}
```

The preceding CSS can be used to style the following HTML:

```
<blockquote class= "pull-quote">Left aligned design</blockquote>
```

This approach adds the quotes to the content using CSS, but to actually set what the quotation marks look like, another property, quotes, is used in conjunction with the content property. The quotes property takes a space-separated list of the characters to use for the opening double and single quotes within the specified content. The best-practice way of setting the value in the quotes property is to define the opening and closing quote characters as escaped (using a backslash) hexidecimal values. (See Table 4-1).

Table 4-1. Quotation mark hexidecimal and HTML entity codes.

Description	Character	Hexidecimal code	HTML entity
"Rabbit-ear" quotation mark	"	\22	&quot;
Apostrophe	'	\27	&apos;
Left single quotation mark	'	\2018	&lsquo;
Right single quotation mark	'	\2019	&rsquo;
Left double quotation mark	"	\201C	&ldquo;
Right double quotation mark	"	\201D	&rdquo;
left single angle bracket (guillemet)	‹	\2039	&lsaquo;
right single angle bracket (guillemet)	›	\203A	&rsaquo;
left double angle bracket (guillemet)	«	\AB	&laquo;
right double angle bracket (guillemet)	»	\BB	&raquo;

For instance, to add "curly" double quotes, use the following CSS in combination with `content:open-quote;` and `content:close-quote;`:

```
quotes: '\201C' '\201D';
```

Other languages, such as French, might use different quote characters, such as a double quillemets. Changing the quotation-mark characters used is simply a matter of changing the hexidecimal code for the those characters, like so:

```
quotes: '\AB' '\BB';
```

> *Note: The* `content` *property can be given any string of text for its value, which is useful for introducing characters other than quotation marks. For instance, a bullet can be added (using the bullet's hexidecimal value) with the following CSS code:*
>
> `content: '\2022';`
>
> *However, bulleted lists are usually handled using the* `<ul>` *and* `<li>` *HTML elements, which can be controlled with the* `list-style` *property.*

This simply adds the quotes and sets their type. The next step is to move them. This is where hanging punctuation comes into play, because the punctuation might otherwise create an undesirable gap, which makes the text alignment appear to slant to the right (or to the left for lines after the first line). See Figure 4-5 for an example.

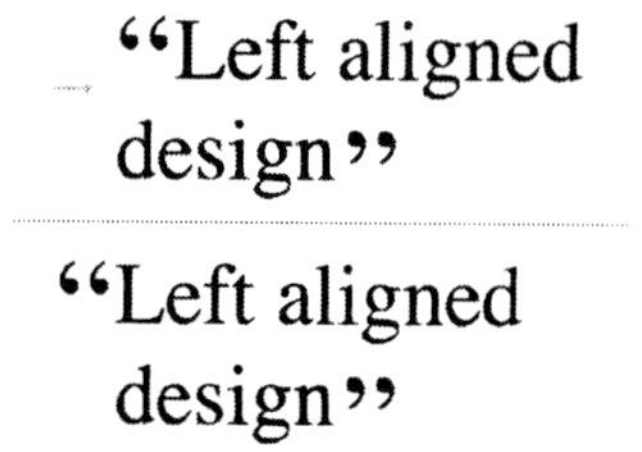

"Left aligned
design"

"Left aligned
design"

Figure 4-5. Punctuation can create a gap (indicated by arrow) that can cause the perceived alignment of the first line of text to slant to the right. Using hanging punctuation (bottom image), the perceived shift in alignment can be corrected.

Continuing with styling in the `::before` and `::after` selectors, the quotation marks can be moved by setting their `position` property to `absolute`. Absolute positioning allows them to "float" above the surrounding text and be precisely positioned by setting the `top`, `right`, `bottom`, and `left` properties *or* the `margin` properties. An important subtlety to be aware of in regard to absolute positioning is that the positioning will be relative to the first parent element that has its positioning set to something other than `static`, which is the default value. To prevent the quotation marks from being positioned relative to the upper-left corner of the screen, set the `position` property to `relative` for the element the quotes are contained in.

For instance, here's what you do for the blockquote example from earlier:

```
<blockquote class= "pull-quote">Left aligned design</blockquote>
```

The beginning of the positioning CSS looks like the following:

```
blockquote.pull-quote {
    position:relative;
}
blockquote.pull-quote::before {
    position:absolute;
    top: 10px;
    left: -5px;
...
```

And it's similar for the closing quote.

Finally, you can use the z-index property to specify whether the quotation marks appear in front of or behind the accompanying text. By default, they will be in front when they are absolutely positioned, but set z-index to -1 to move the quotation marks behind the rest of the text. (See Figure 4-6 in the upcoming "How to build it" section for what this looks like.)

THE SEMANTICS OF QUOTATIONS

In case you hadn't noticed, the examples discussed thus far in this solution use the <blockquote> HTML element, not the paragraph (<p>) element. This isn't accidental, because contemporary HTML uses a whole slew of different *semantic* elements, which indicate the type of content they contain. This is useful for accessibility as well as for data mining. (Think of a search engine going through your content—it's going to be more concerned with your HTML than your CSS.)

In the prior examples, the quotation marks are added using CSS; therefore, the appropriate HTML elements should be used to indicate why the text is in quotes. The following is a summary of the type of content that several HTML elements commonly used with hanging punctuation should contain:

■ <p> designates a passage of text. Quotes might be present in the text, but they're not indicative of text from another source. An example of such quotes are *scare quotes*—used to indicate a word or phrase that does not signify its usual meaning or that are used ironically or sarcastically. For example, in the phrase 'a "healthy" cheeseburger' the word "healthy" is used sarcastically.

■ <blockquote> designates a passage of text quoted from another source. The end of the passage might reference the originator of the text, or the cite attribute of the <blockquote> element might be used to reference where the text is from.

■ <q> designates an inline passage of text quoted from another source. (*Inline* means it might appear inside of a paragraph, for instance.)

■ <cite> designates a title of a work, such as the name of a movie or title of a book.

How to build it

1. Add text and the appropriate HTML elements (such as `<blockquote>`) to your page:

```
<blockquote>Left aligned design</blockquote>
```

2. Add any default styles you want applied to your HTML. In this case, the text is given padding and a left margin. The `position` is set to `relative`, which as discussed in the prior section will aid in positioning the quotation marks later on. The `quotes` property is given values that correspond to an opening curly quotation mark and a closing curly quotation mark, and finally, the font size and line height are set:

```
blockquote {
    padding: 10px;
    margin-left: 60px;
    position: relative;
    quotes: '\201C' '\201D';
    font-size: 64px;
    line-height: 64px;
    width: 320px;
}
```

3. Next the appearance of the quotation marks is set in the pseudo-element selectors `::before` and `::after`. For this example, the quotes will be heavily stylized, so they will be increased in size, colored gray, and given a sans-serif typeface. Absolute positioning is used so that the quotation marks can be moved without interfering with the rest of the text. To place the quotes behind the accompanying text, the `z-index` is set to `-1` for both marks:

```
blockquote::before, blockquote::after {
    font-size: 500px;
    color: #eee;
    font-family: Arial, san-serif;
    position: absolute;
    z-index: -1;
}
```

4. The last step adds the actual quotation marks. The opening quote position is set using the `left` and `top` properties, while the closing quote is set using the `margin-top` property; however, depending on the design, either of these positioning approaches can be used for both quotation marks:

```
blockquote::before {
    content: open-quote;
    left: -60px;
    top: 110px;
}
```

```
blockquote::after {
    content: close-quote;
    margin-top: 170px;
}
```

The result of the preceding code is some left-aligned text accompanied by light-gray quotation marks. (See Figure 4-6.)

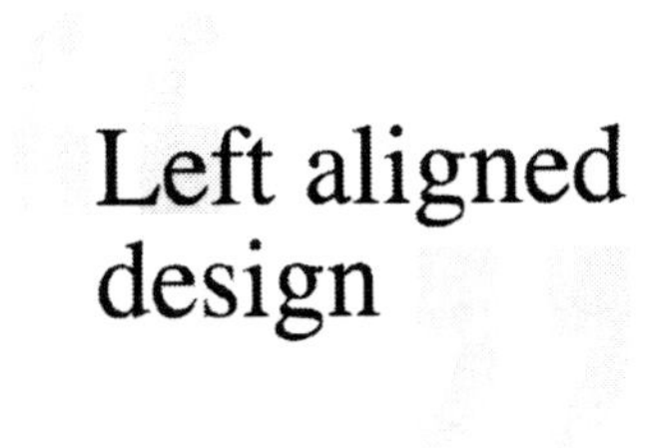

Left aligned
design

Figure 4-6. The techniques used to creating hanging punctuation can be used to create aesthetically interesting typographic effects, such as those in this stylized block quotes.

Note that this does not work with Internet Explorer 8 or 9.

Expert tips

If precise positioning of the quotation marks is not needed (beyond offsetting them horizontally), the text-indent property can be used to move the opening quote to the left, which simplifies the CSS significantly. Give text-indent a negative value to do this, as in this example:

```
p {
    padding: 10px;
    quotes: '\201C' '\201D';
    text-indent: -7px;
}
```

In this code, the paragraph is given some padding and the quotes inside are set to curly quotes. The text indent moves the first line 7 pixels to the left. The quote element, <q>, can then be used, which in combination with the quotes property inserts the necessary quotation marks while still retaining the proper semantics of the content. (Remember, like the <blockquote> element, <q> designates content that is quoted from another source.) This HTML might look like this:

```
<p><q>Quis autem … </q></p>
```

Alternatively, curly quotes can be inserted directly into the HTML using character entities, like this:

```
<p>&ldquo;Quis autem ... &rdquo;</p>
```

However, as shown in the "the semantics of quotations" earlier in this solution, technically the <q> and <blockquote> elements should be used for quotations from another source, while inserting quotation marks directly is for other uses (such as a text passage that includes a word in quotes to point out it's being said sarcastically).

> *Note: If these examples don't work in Internet Explorer, ensure you aren't viewing the page in Compatibility View, which emulates earlier Internet Explorer versions even if you are using the latest version. Hold down the Alt key to show the toolbar, and go to Tools* ➤ *Compatibility View Settings to check how the page is set to render.*

Finally, the CSS3 `hanging-punctuation` property is a proposed property that exists specifically for controlling hanging punctuation. Great! Unfortunately, this property currently has no browser support, and because of this, it is in danger of being dropped from the CSS specification altogether! (See `www.w3.org/TR/css3-text/#hanging-punctuation0` for more information.) As CSS3 matures keep your eyes out for `hanging-punctuation` as it will likely reduce the amount of CSS needed to style hanging quotes, but don't be surprised if it never makes it to a browser near you.

Solution 4-4: Creating a typographic hierarchy

If you look at a newspaper layout, you will notice that the page content is broken into different sizes of text for the title, headers, subheaders, and body copy. This creates an important hierarchy to the information on the page, guiding the reader's eye through the content. This helps the reader scan the content and drill down into it. Reading a newspaper that didn't have headlines above its stories would a pretty inefficient way of browsing for articles you were interested in, wouldn't it? Not having such a hierarchy on a webpage is no different. You want to help your viewers digest the information on your page efficiently. (See Figure 4-7.)

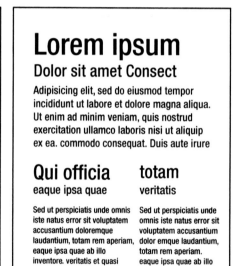

Figure 4-7. It's apparent that unformatted text (left) is much harder to pick information out of than text that is broken into sections and given a hierarchy of sizes (right).

This solution branches out into a close associate of CSS3: HTML5. The new semantic elements introduced in HTML5 make it easier than ever to build a structure for your website.

What's involved

HTML5 includes elements such as `<header>`, `<footer>`, `<section>`, `<article>`, `<aside>`, and `<nav>` for designating the various sections of content on a page. The general meaning of these elements is as follows:

- `<header>` Used for grouping introductory content, such as the main title and menu.

- `<footer>` Used for grouping extra information related to the section or page as a whole, such as copyright information.

- `<section>` Used as a generic container for grouping some content.

- `<article>` Used to create a self-contained grouping of content, which can be taken out of the page and will still make sense on its own (meaning it can be syndicated via RSS, for example).

- `<aside>` Used for nonessential supporting content to a section or article.

- `<nav>` Used for a main navigational menu.

Using these elements to build your page, a simple hierarchy can be created by using the `<header>` and `<section>` (or `<article>`) elements. To further define the hierarchy, both of these elements can contain heading elements—the familiar `<h1>` through `<h6>`, which have been in HTML seemingly forever. Create a title in the header and section, and later style these to create a cascade of sizes that helps emphasize what is important on the page.

How to build it

1. Begin building the HTML structure, paying attention to the appropriate semantic elements that fit with the content. In this example, you begin at the top of the page with the title and subtitle, which are contained in a `<header>`. The header is placed in an `<h1>`, and the subtitle is placed in an `<h2>`. Each section on the page that contains more than one heading (`<h1>` − `<h6>`) needs to be grouped inside an `<hgroup>` element:

```
<header>
    <hgroup>
        <h1>Title</h1>
        <h2>Subtitle</h2>
    </hgroup>
</header>
```

2. The main content of the page is placed in a `<section>` and contains its own `<h1>` title above the paragraph (`<p>`):

```
<section>
    <h1>Content Title</h1>
    <p>
        Quis autem vel eum iure reprehenderit qui in ea voluptate
        velit esse quam nihil molestiae consequatur, vel illum qui
        dolorem eum fugiat quo voluptas nulla pariatur?
    </p>
</section>
```

3. Add the CSS, which sizes the font in a hierarchy from the page title (largest) to the body copy (smallest). Additionally, other styling—such as changing the font weight and adding an underline between the page title and the page content—adds further organization to the content. The first letter and line are also styled to give the paragraph a slight drop cap:

```
header h1 {
    font-size: 72px;
    font-weight: bold;
    margin: 0;
}

header h2 {
    font-size: 36px;
    font-style: italic;
    border-bottom: 1px solid #999;
    margin: 0;
}

section h1 {
    font-size: 24px;
}

section p {
    font-size: 14px;
}

section p::first-line {
    font-weight: bold;
}

section p::first-letter {
    font-size: 16px;
}
```

The result of the preceding code renders the text headers and content in a hierarchy. (See Figure 4-8.)

Figure 4-8. A hierarchy of text sizes directs the reader's eye over the content of a page.

Expert tips

For those looking for precise guidance in regard to their typography sizing, consider visiting |www.modularscale.com, a site created by Tim Brown, Type Manager for Adobe Typekit, which can be used to calculate relative type sizes based on ratios.

Solution 4-5: Creating multicolumn text blocks

Imagine reading a newspaper and having the body copy extend across the entire page width. It would be easy to lose the line you were on, wouldn't it? There is a reason newspapers break text into columns of text—it's easier to read! Web pages are the same; a paragraph of text that stretches margin to margin of the full width of a browser window is harder to read than one that is confined to a narrower area. (See Figure 4-9.)

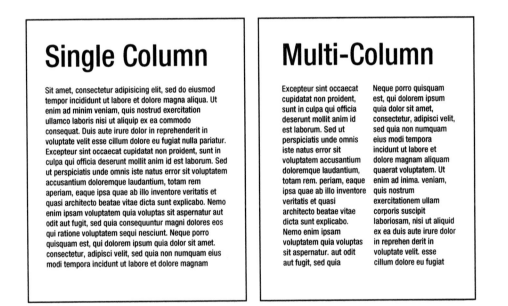

Figure 4-9. The column property provides an easy method to break a wide column of text into multiple narrower columns, which aid in reading the content.

For this reason, the introduction in CSS of a means to easily create columns of text within a text block is a welcome addition! Columns of text have certainly been around for a while, but they traditionally required complex solutions involving floating content into columns, which were hard to code initially and not very flexible.

What's involved

There are a number of properties for controlling the layout of columns. The simplest one is the `columns` property, which takes two values: the first being the column width, and the second being the number of columns. For instance, the following code would—in theory—produce two columns, each 250 pixels wide:

```
columns: 250px 2;
```

I say "in theory" because the web browser might automatically adjust the column width to fit the available space. So consider the column width specified as an optimal size.

The `columns` property is actually shorthand for the `column-width` and `column-count` properties, which can be used to set these values individually. There are a number of other individual properties besides these two for setting various aspects of the column's appearance. For instance, the `column-gap` property sets the width of the *gap* between columns. The `column-rule` property takes the same values as the `border` property to specify the width, style, and color of the column *rule*, which is an optional vertical line that appears between columns.

> Note: The `column-rule` property is shorthand for the `column-rule-width`, `column-rule-style`, and `column-rule-color` properties, which can be used to set the width, style, and color of a rule individually.

The `column-span` property can be used to make a header that spans across all the columns. If you have a block of content such as a `<section>` or `<div>` and it contains a paragraph `<p>` and header `<h1>`, for example, you can set the column count on the whole section but set the `column-span` property on the `<h1>` to the value of `all` (for example, `column-span: all;`), which makes the header extend across all the columns in the paragraph. The default value is `none`, which keeps the header in the first column. (See Figure 4-10.)

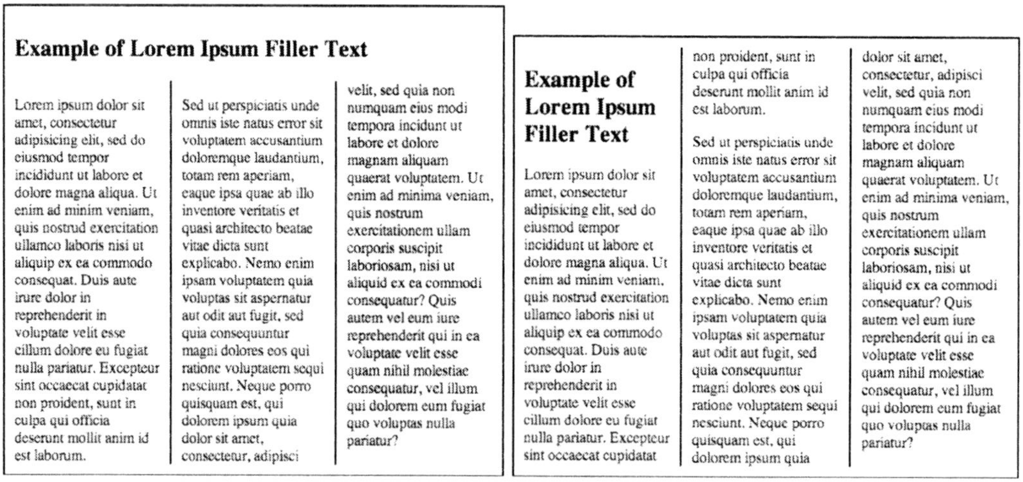

Figure 4-10. The `column-span` property can be used to make a title that runs across all the columns of text (left) or contain it to the first column (right).

How to build it

1. Begin with building the HTML content that will be displayed in columns. In this case, a `<section>` is created, which is given a class where the column styles will be added. Using a class means the same column style can be applied in multiple locations on the page. Inside the section, two paragraphs and a header are added (note that the filler text is truncated for brevity):

```
<section class="col">
    <h1>Example of Lorem Ipsum Filler Text</h1>
    <p>
        Lorem ipsum dolor sit amet,

        …

        sunt in culpa qui officia deserunt mollit anim id est laborum.
    </p>

    <p>
        Sed ut perspiciatis unde omnis iste natus error sit
        voluptatem accusantium doloremque laudantium,

        …

        consequatur, vel illum qui dolorem eum fugiat quo
        voluptas nulla pariatur?
    </p>
</section>
```

2. Add the `column` CSS style rule, which defines the number of columns, the column gap, and the appearance of the column rule:

```
.col {
    column-count: 3;
    column-gap: 24px;
    column-rule: 2px solid #000;
}
```

3. Finally, add the column-spanning behavior for the header over the columns:

```
.col h2 {
    column-span: all; /* or none */
}
```

The result of the preceding code renders a header over three columns, as shown in the left diagram in the earlier Figure 4-10.

> Note: As with other examples in this chapter, if you have trouble getting a CSS property to work in your preferred browser, investigate whether you need to add a vendor prefix to the front of the property, such as -webkit- for Safari, -moz- for Firefox, -o- for Opera, or -ms- for Microsoft. At the time of this writing, multicolumn text isn't supported in Internet Explorer.

Expert tips

Avoid making the blocks of text that are arranged in columns too tall. If you do, the user might need to scroll down and up repeatedly to read the content across the columns.

To make the columns fill out their available space better, consider setting their text alignment to "justify," which adds spacing between the words to fill out the full width of the column. (See Figure 4-11.)

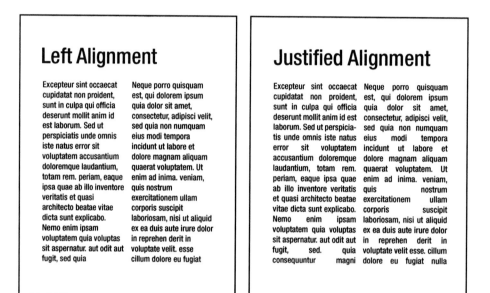

Figure 4-11. Left-aligned text can produce a jagged-looking gap between columns, whereas justified text produces smooth-sided columns. However, justified text begins to look poor if the columns are too narrow, causing large gaps between words.

The CSS3 property text-justify can be used to control how text that is set to a justified alignment is spaced. Instead of adding space between words, you can use this property to specify that spacing should happen between letters as well, which can be particularly useful when dealing with different language scripts. Support for this property, however, is limited to Internet Explorer at the time of this writing. However, try adding the following CSS to at least see the columns become justified:

```
.col p {
    text-align: justify;
    text-justify: distribute;
}
```

Summary

Good web typography is about more than making pretty type. It's about helping the reader scan your text and quickly grasp where to start looking and what it is about. It's about subtly guiding your viewers over your page's content. Whether it's through drop caps to pull attention to the beginning of an article or a hierarchy of headlines—which tell at a glance what is most important to read first on the page—a grasp of CSS typography will help you apply that final touch of completion to an already well-designed layout!

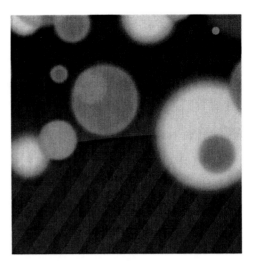

Chapter 5

Tables and Lists

Something that often seems to confuse people who are new to CSS-based layouts is the use of tables. To date, most website designers have abandoned the use of tables as a tool for creating page layouts and have returned websites to playing the role for which they were designed: to present information clearly and efficiently. The result is much cleaner HTML, enabling the separation of document content from document presentation.

If you do a little search on the Internet, you'll find plenty of cases where people interpret the advice against using tables for layout to mean "Don't use them at all." Tables are still perfectly fine to use—if you use them correctly. For tabular data, tables are what you should use. And today it's even simpler and fun thanks to some new CSS3 properties and selectors. List elements are one of the most flexible HTML elements, with many different uses. In this chapter, we introduce proven CSS3 solutions regarding both table and list elements.

Solution 5-1: Zebra-striping table rows

When you have to present a large amount of data, it's very important to preserve readability. Zebra striping is the method of alternating the color of rows in a table. This method has been used in print for many years and only recently have web designers been trying to spread its use on the Web.

With the advent of CSS3's nth-child selector, you can target multiple elements in a document by creating a counter that skips over specified child elements in the document tree. This specifically allows you to style only the odd or even rows of a table. In this solution, we provide an example that shows you how you can create a zebra-striped table by setting different colors for odd and even rows of the table.

What's involved

In the past, creating the effect of alternate rows was possible only by creating two CSS classes to manage the alternation of color, or by using JavaScript to dynamically apply the classes to the table. Let's take a look at an example from the old days:

```
<table>
 <tr valign="top" class="odd">
  <td>Salmon</td>
  <td>Omega-3's help the brain develop properly, reduce the risk of Alzheimer's, and help
prevent heart disease.</td>
 </tr>
 <tr valign="top">
  <td>Spinach</td>
  <td>Great source of folate and lutein. Prevents birth defects, heart disease, stroke, and
protects your skin from sun damage.</td>
 </tr>
</table>
```

You would then add a CSS rule that targets the rows:

```
tr.odd {
 background-color: #999999;
}
```

This approach is still valid and works today, but it is not efficient. It requires extra markup from a zero semantic value. Furthermore, this approach does not keep the structure separate from the presentation.

:nth-child syntax

The :nth-child is a CSS selector, or rather a pseudo-selector. It matches elements on the basis of their positions within a parent element's list of child elements. The syntax of this selector is shown here:

```
:nth-child(N)
```

The *n* is a subject that can be any of the following:

- An *integer* numeric value

- An *even* or *odd* value, where *even* selects even-numbered elements—like 2nd, 4th, and 6th—and *odd* selects odd-numbered elements—like 1st, 3rd, 5th, and so on. The terms *odd* and *even* are referred to as *keywords*.

- A number expression of the form *an+b*

Here is an example of using :nth-child. The following selectors are equivalent and will match odd-numbered table rows:

```
tr:nth-child(2n+1) {
  /* declarations /
}
tr:nth-child(odd) {
  /* declarations */
}
```

This example selector will match the first two rows of any table:

```
tr:nth-child(-n+3) {
  /* declarations */
}
```

> Tip: You can see various examples and better understand this selector's function at the following links: http://css-tricks.com/examples/nth-child-tester/ and http://css-tricks.com/useful-nth-child-recipies/.

Browser support

All major browsers based on Gecko and WebKit have supported :nth-child for a while. Internet Explorer has supported it since Internet Explorer 9. You can see details of the browser support in Table 5-1.

Table 5-1. Browser support for :nth-child

Internet Explorer	Firefox	Chrome	Safari	Opera
9.0+	3.5+	2.0+	3.1+	9.5+

How to build it

For this solution, you begin by creating a three-column example table with no alternate background, as shown in Figure 5-1.

Domain ‡	Purchased ‡	Expiry ‡
designabile.com	2010-04-15	2018-04-15
interactionhub.com	2008-09-25	2012-01-10
example.net	2006-02-02	2013-09-25
example.org	1999-12-20	2012-07-08

Figure 5-1. Table with no alternate background color

With the current formatting, a reader might easily associate incorrect dates and domains in this table while skimming over the data. To combat this, you can make the odd rows of the table a different color so that the table is easier to read. You do this using the following code:

```
tr:nth-child(odd) {
 background-color: #f2f2f2;
}
```

By using the keyword "*odd*," you select all the odd rows of the table, as shown in Figure 5-2.

Domain :	Purchased :	Expiry :
designabile.com	2010-04-15	2018-04-15
interactionhub.com	2008-09-25	2012-01-10
example.net	2006-02-02	2013-09-25
example.org	1999-12-20	2012-07-08

Figure 5-2. Alternate rows with background color: only the odd-numbered rows are styled

The table is easier to read, and you did not have to use any JavaScript.

Expert tip

You can use a JavaScript framework like jQuery to set a fallback solution for older browsers. For instance, you can enter the script in a conditional comment specific to older versions of Internet Explorer. All other browsers will ignore this rule and correctly use the CSS3. You can find out more on this here:

```
http://docs.jquery.com/Tutorials:/Zebra_Striping_Made_Easy.
```

Solution 5-2: Creating a styled pricing table

Many of the innovations introduced in CSS3 can be used to define the style of a table, allowing you to create many customized types of tables. In the past, you could do this only by using a large amount of images and extra markup, which were both necessary to create appealing visual effects. Today, you have such a good selection of new selectors that you can address specific table cells and rows to create a unique style without adding classes to the markup.

In this solution, we'll analyze how to create a pricing table using only CSS3 and no images. These types of tables have become common on the Web due to the spread of SaaS (Software as a Service) web applications. Generally, they show a summary of included services in the different subscription plans offered by the application. Let's begin!

What's involved

For this example, we'll use the following properties and selectors that were introduced with CSS3:

- `box-shadow`
- `text-shadow`
- `:nth-last-child`
- `:empty`

The box-shadow and text-shadow properties are covered in more detail in their related chapters, but we'll briefly introduce these properties and their uses here.

box-shadow

The box-shadow property allows designers to implement the shadow effect (both internal and external) on any box element. To create this effect, you can specify the following values: color, dimension, level of blur, and offset position. This property also gives you the ability to define multiple shadows, separating the syntax of each effect with a comma.

> Tip: You'll find the tools at http://css3generator.com/ and http://css3gen.com/box-shadow/ are useful in quickly generating and previewing box shadows.

The syntax for box-shadow is as follows:

```
box-shadow: h-shadow v-shadow blur spread color inset;
```

You can see in Table 5-2 what the different values of this syntax correspond to.

Table 5-2. The box-shadow property values

ValueDescription	
h-shadow	Required. This is the position of the horizontal shadow. Negative values are allowed.
v-shadow	Required. This is the position of the vertical shadow. Negative values are allowed.
blur	Optional. This is the blur distance.
spread	Optional. This is the size of the shadow.
color	Optional. This is the color of the shadow.
inset	Optional. This changes the shadow from an outer shadow (outset) to an inner shadow.

text-shadow

The second property is text-shadow, and it allows you to add a shadow to each letter of text. The syntax for text-shadow is as follows (and the possible values are shown in Table 5-3):

```
text-shadow: h-shadow v-shadow blur color;
```

Table 5-3. The text-shadow property values

Value	Description
h-shadow	Required. This is the position of the horizontal shadow. Negative values are allowed.
v-shadow	Required. This is the position of the vertical shadow. Negative values are allowed.
blur	Optional. This is the blur distance.
color	Optional. This is the color of the shadow.

:nth-last-child

This pseudo-class matches elements on the basis of their positions within a parent element's list of child elements. The syntax is as follows:

```
:nth-last-child( { number expression | odd | even } ) {
/* declaration block */
}
```

How to build it

In this solution, the example pricing table will compare a hosting service, as shown in Figure 5-3.

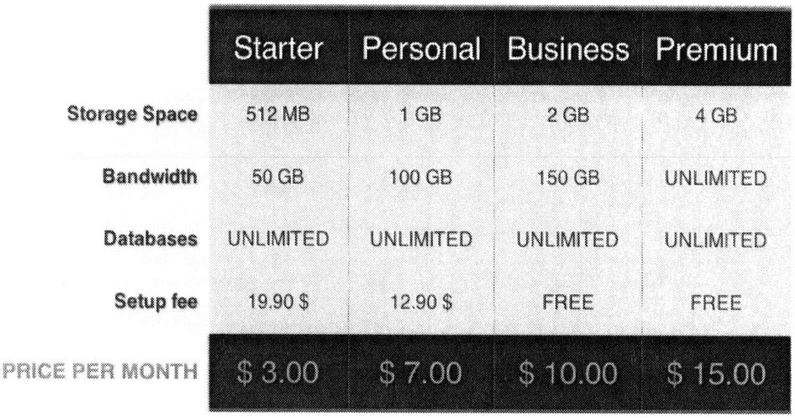

	Starter	Personal	Business	Premium
Storage Space	512 MB	1 GB	2 GB	4 GB
Bandwidth	50 GB	100 GB	150 GB	UNLIMITED
Databases	UNLIMITED	UNLIMITED	UNLIMITED	UNLIMITED
Setup fee	19.90 $	12.90 $	FREE	FREE
PRICE PER MONTH	$ 3.00	$ 7.00	$ 10.00	$ 15.00

Figure 5-3. The hosting plan comparison table

The markup

You start the markup of the table by inserting all the necessary elements: a part of the header, the body, and finally the footer.

```
<table>
  <thead>
    <tr>
      <th></th>
      <th scope="col" abbr="Starter">Starter</th>
      <th scope="col" abbr="Medium">Personal</th>
      <th scope="col" abbr="Business">Business</th>
      <th scope="col" abbr="Deluxe">Premium</th>
    </tr>
  </thead>
  <tbody>
    <tr>
      <th scope="row">Storage Space</th>
```

```
      <td>512 MB</td>
      <td>1 GB</td>
      <td>2 GB</td>
      <td>4 GB</td>
   </tr>
   <tr>
      <th scope="row">Bandwidth</th>
      <td>50 GB</td>
      <td>100 GB</td>
      <td>150 GB</td>
      <td>Unlimited</td>
   </tr>
   <tr>
      <th scope="row">MySQL Databases</th>
      <td>Unlimited</td>
      <td>Unlimited</td>
      <td>Unlimited</td>
      <td>Unlimited</td>
   </tr>
   <tr>
      <th scope="row">Setup</th>
      <td>19.90   <td>19.90 $</td>#x003C;/td>
      <td>12.90   <td>12.90 $</td>#x003C;/td>
      <td>free</td>
      <td>free</td>
   </tr>
   <tr>
      <th scope="row">PHP 5</th>
      <td><span class="check"></span></td>
      <td><span class="check"></span></td>
      <td><span class="check"></span></td>
      <td><span class="check"></span></td>
   </tr>
   <tr>
      <th scope="row">Ruby on Rails</th>
      <td><span class="check"></span></td>
      <td><span class="check"></span></td>
      <td><span class="check"></span></td>
      <td><span class="check"></span></td>
   </tr>
 </tbody>
 <tfoot>
   <tr>
      <th scope="row">Price per month</th>
      <td>$ 3.00</td>
      <td>$ 7.00</td>
      <td>$ 10.00</td>
      <td>$ 15.00</td>
   </tr>
 </tfoot>
</table>
```

Shadow effects

You've now seen some shading effects on different elements of the table.

■   Thead and Tfoot

We used box-shadow for all the <th> and <td> elements, and we used text-shadow on the text to play with contrast and depth. Here is the CSS code:

```
thead th, tfoot td {
    padding: 20px 10px;
    color: #fff;
    font-size: 26px;
    background-color: #222;
    font-weight: normal;
    border-right: 1px dotted #666;
    border-top: 3px solid #666;
    -moz-box-shadow: 0px -1px 4px #000;
    -webkit-box-shadow: 0px -1px 4px #000;
    box-shadow: 0px -1px 4px #000;
    text-shadow: 1px 1px 1px #000;
}
```

> Note: You still need to use the proprietary prefixes -moz and -webkit to ensure that the effect of box-shadow is visible even on older versions of these browsers.

■   Tbody

All the <th> tags inside of the <tbody> have a clear shadow:

```
tbody th {
  text-align: right;
  padding: 10px;
  color: #333;
  text-shadow:1px 1px 1px #ccc;
  background-color: #f9f9f9;
}
```

Next, we applied a particular shadow effect to the data of the table:

```
tbody td{
    padding:10px;
    background-color:#f0f0f0;
    border-right:1px dotted #999;
    text-shadow:-1px 1px 1px #fff;
    text-transform:uppercase;
    color:#333;
}
```

This effect will not be clearly visible on the color white, a negative offset, or a lighter shade. It is still useful, but not ideal, if you want to add contrast between text and a very light background color.

Traversing

Another element of CSS3 that proved fundamental for the design of this table was the :nth-last-child selector. Let's take a look at what context we used it in:

```
thead :nth-last-child(1) {
border-right:none;
}
```

In this way, you select the last cell element in the table header and remove the right border:

```
thead :first-child,
tbody :nth-last-child(1) {
  border:none;
}
```

With the :first-child selector, you can address the first cell in the header, which should not have a border because it is empty. You also want to remove the border from the last td elements in the table body.

Finally, all that is left to do is deal with the first <th> of the <thread> and the fact that it is empty. With CSS3 selectors, you can do some incredible things, and this is one of them: select the <th> that is empty. This is how you do it:

```
thead th:empty{
  background:transparent;
  -moz-box-shadow:none;
  -webkit-box-shadow:none;
  box-shadow:none;
}
```

The selector :empty allows you to handle the case of an element that has no content and to specify which properties to assign. Simply awesome!

Expert tip

Pseudo-classes such as :nth-last-child and :empty are very powerful tools you can use to work even more precisely and in detail on the elements of a web page. Because these pseudo-classes are not fully supported yet, you should always think of a fallback solution to avoid the table not being legible by users of older browsers, in particular Internet Explorer 8.

Solution 5-3: Making tables responsive

A responsive design allows you to adapt the design to different screen resolutions so that your design can be optimized for several devices. But what happens when a screen is narrower than the minimum width of a data table? You have two alternatives. You can zoom out and see the entire table; however, the text would be very small, making it almost impossible to read. Or you can zoom in on a specific data item, which allows you to scroll horizontally and vertically to move along the table. In both cases, viewing the table is difficult.

The solution is to apply the principles of responsive design through the use of CSS3 media queries so that your application can detect different screen resolutions and, consequently, modify the table to new sizes.

What's involved

Creating a responsive data table is a simple procedure. It includes three keys things: using clean markup, identifying breakpoints, and implementing media queries. Let's look at these now.

Using clean markup

The basis of any responsive solution is clean, semantically sound HTML markup. In the case of a table, you should organize it according to the standard structure (`thead`, `tbody`, and `tfoot`) using the characteristics and potential of each tag.

Identifying breakpoints

You kick off the design process by examining the different devices you're planning to support. Then you compile a list of resolution breakpoints: generally, the horizontal widths you'll need to accommodate in your responsive table.

Building this list helps you define a scope, allowing you to target the device commonly used by your audience. Resolutions above or below this threshold will not be ignored.

Implement media queries

You use the same approach you used for breakpoints to help you create responsive designs. You need different styles of the table based on the previously identified breakpoints. Media queries are one of the most powerful tools introduced by CSS3 specifications. According to World Wide Web Consortium (W3C) specifics, a media query is a logical expression that can be true or false. It is true if it satisfies all the conditions expressed in the query. To build complex queries, you can use logic operators such as `and`, `not`, and `only`.

Browser support

Today, you can use media queries with all the modern versions of the most popular browsers. Some properties—such as `orientation`, `grid`, and `scan`—are exceptions because they are still poorly supported, but in the case of a responsive table, this doesn't have to worry you. You can see further details in Table 5-4.

Table 5-4. Browser support for media queries

Internet Explorer	Firefox	Chrome	Safari	Opera
9.0+	3.5+	2.0+	4.0+	9.0+

How to build it

One of the best techniques to create a responsive table is to transform each table row in a block-level element. In this way, you can eliminate horizontal scrolling while still maintaining vertical scrolling. This technique was originally described on the site `http://css-tricks.com`, and a slightly modified version is shown here. Here's the basic HTML markup:

```
<table>
  <thead>
  <tr>
    <th>Description</th>
    <th>Category</th>
    <th>Price</th>
  </tr>
  </thead>
  <tbody>
  <tr>
    <td>Sofa</td>
    <td>Furniture</td>
    <td>$500</td>
  </tr>
  <tr>
    <td>Table</td>
    <td>Furniture</td>
    <td>$25</td>
  </tr>
  <tr>
    <td>Chair</td>
    <td>Furniture</td>
    <td>$46</td>
  </tr>
  <tr>
    <td>LCD TV</td>
    <td>Electronics</td>
    <td>$799</td>
  </tr>
  </tbody>
</table>
```

Equally simple and clean is the CSS code used for the basic style of the table:

```
table {
  width: 100%;
  border-collapse: collapse;
}

/* Zebra striping */
tr:nth-of-type(odd) {
  background: #eee;
}

th {
  background: #333;
  color: #fff;
  font-weight: bold;
}

td, th {
  padding: 5px;
```

```
    border: 1px solid #ddd;
    text-align: left;
}
```

Assigning the width: 100 % to <table>, we get a table that automatically adjusts to the width of the screen. You can see the result in Figure 5-4.

Decription	Category	Price
Sofa	Furniture	$500
Table	Furniture	$25
Chair	Furniture	$46
LCD Tv	Electronics	$799

Figure 5-4. A simple, flexible table—ready to be responsive

Screen resolution breakpoint

Let's now begin to manage the responsive part. In this example, the breakpoint you decide to support is the minimum resolution of 760 pixels that corresponds to the iPad portrait orientation:

```
@media
only screen and (max-width: 760px),
(min-device-width: 768px) and (max-device-width: 1024px) {

* stuff here */
}
```

Next, set every table-related element to be block-level:

```
table, thead, tbody, th, td, tr {
    display: block;
}
```

You are basically forcing a table not to behave like one. You turn each table cell into a row:

```
td {
    border: none;
    border-bottom: 1px solid #eee;
    position: relative;
     padding-left: 50%;
}
```

The left padding, set at 50 %, is used to create a space on the left side for table entry labels that will be created using the :before selector:

```
td:before {
  position: absolute;
  top: 5px;
  left: 5px;
  width: 45%;
```

```
    padding-right: 10px;
    white-space: nowrap;
}
```

```
td:nth-of-type(1):before { content: "Description"; }
```

```
td:nth-of-type(2):before { content: "Category"; }
```

```
td:nth-of-type(3):before { content: "Price"; }
```

The mode of content use on the mobile device will be totally different from the one possible with the classic version on the computer desktop, as shown in Figure 5-5.

Description	Sofa
Category	Furniture
Price	$500
Description	Table
Category	Furniture
Price	$25

Figure 5-5. Responsive table layout

> Caution: Internet Explorer (even versions 9 and 10 preview) doesn't like you setting table elements as display: block. Wrap the media query styles in conditional comments.

Expert tip

The possibilities offered by the media queries are infinite. You might decide to present this data in many different ways, one for each device. In each case, the main element is the content of the table on which to build different table designs. According to the information, you can decide to show a graph or a summary before the classic list. Chapter 8 provides a detailed review of media queries, including the extensive possibilities.

The user experience will therefore be created ad-hoc to fully exploit the characteristics of each device.

Solution 5-4: Creating a practical table with rounded corners

One of the biggest difficulties in creating tables is that the HTML table tags don't allow designers to work freely with CSS—for example, in creating rounded borders. Previously, the most used technique for dong this consisted of creating empty table cells that contained small image files for each rounded border. Fortunately, this approach is a thing of the past.

In this section, you'll see how CSS3 and tables can work together to create some cool and usable results, like rounded corners with no images.

What's involved

The property border-radius was perhaps the most important innovation for designers introduced in CSS3. It simplified the work that was previously necessary to create elements with rounded corners.

The border-radius revolution

Let's briefly review the syntax of border-radius:

```
border-radius: length (px, em, %)
```

The radius value can be specified with different measurement units: px, em, or %. Using px, you definitely can be more accurate.

This syntax is shorthand to define the radius of the four borders of an element. You need to write the following:

```
border-radius: 5px
```

This is equivalent to the following:

```
border-top-left-radius: 5px;
border-top-right-radius: 5px;
border-bottom-right-radius: 5px;
border-bottom-left-radius: 5px;
```

You can specify each border individually: you just have to indicate its position on the horizontal axis (right or left) and vertical axis (top or bottom).

This technique will be very useful in working with tables because it behaves differently from any other element, as you'll see in the example.

> Note: The implementation in Mozilla, with respect to W3C specifications, is slightly different. For example, if you want to define the specific border-radius for the upper-left border, you need to write the following: -moz-border-radius-topleft.

Browser support

Mozilla Firefox supports border-radius with the -moz- prefix, although there are some discrepancies between the Mozilla implementation and the current W3C specification. You can see more details in Table 5-5.

Table 5-5. Browser support for border-radius

Internet Explorer	Firefox	Chrome	Safari	Opera
9.0+	1.0+	5.0+	5.0+	10.5+

How to build it

The table you want to create is rather simple, comprising the usual <thead> for the table header and <tbody> for the table cells, as shown in Figure 5-6.

Column 1	Column 2	Column 3
1	1	2
3	5	8
13	21	34
55	89	144
233	377	610

Figure 5-6. Table with rounded corners

Let's take a look at the CCS used:

```
table {
background: rgb(204, 204, 204);
margin: 20px;
border: rgb(204, 204, 204) 1px solid;
-moz-border-radius: 10px;
-webkit-border-radius: 10px;
border-radius: 10px;
}
```

By assigning `border-radius` to the element <table>, you can create rounded corners in seconds. Perfect!

However, if you look closely at the table in Figure 5-6, you'll notice that the table cells are divided by a thickness, like a double border. This happens because each table set border-collapse: separate by default. The cells are separated, and the border of a cell is added to the border of the ones close to it.

Let's try to change this value from `separate` to `collapse`:

```
table {
background: rgb(204, 204, 204);
margin: 20px;
border: rgb(204, 204, 204) 1px solid;
-moz-border-radius: 10px;
-webkit-border-radius: 10px;
border-radius: 10px;
border-collapse: collapse;
}
```

You can see what happens to the table in Figure 5-7.

Column 1	Column 2	Column 3
1	1	2
3	5	8
13	21	34
55	89	144
233	377	610

Figure 5-7. Collapsed table that lost `border-radius`

The border-radius property does not apply to tables with the border-collapse:collapse property set. The border of the element `<table>` doesn't have any radius. The layout is compromised. Here's the trick: while the default value of border-collapse is separate, you also need to set border-spacing to 0. (See Table 5-8.)

Column 1	Column 2	Column 3
1	1	2
3	5	8
13	21	34
55	89	144
233	377	610

Figure 5-8. Collapsed table with border-spacing set to 0

```
table {
    background: rgb(204, 204, 204);
    margin: 20px;
    border: rgb(204, 204, 204) 1px solid;
   -moz-border-radius: 10px;
   -webkit-border-radius: 10px;
    border-radius: 10px;
    border-collapse: collapse;
    border-spacing: 0;
}
```

As you can see, `border-radius` is back and there is no margin of separation among the table cells. This solution works well in newer versions of Safari and Firefox, and it degrades gracefully to square corners in Internet Explorer and Opera.

Expert tip

In some cases, when you set a very wide border (for example, 15px) and one with a different color than the background, the border is rounded correctly only on the outside. Inside it's still a square corner. The different colors of the two elements make this effect clearer.

In this case, to get a rounded inner border, the border radius must be greater than the border thickness—for example, border-radius: 30px; border-width: 15px;.

Solution 5-5: Creating a drop-down menu with lists

Using unordered lists for creating any type of horizontal, vertical, or drop-down menus simply by writing a few lines of semantic markup, is a common web-design technique.

CSS3 has extended these possibilities, allowing you to create even more effective navigation menus. The introduction of some properties (for example, gradients, opacity, and transitions) has simplified the design process of all the interaction effects necessary in a menu that required JavaScript.

What's involved

In this solution, you create a navigation menu for a web application using only CSS3 code, and no pictures or images.

Why use < ul >?

The < ul > element, or unordered list, has been widely implemented as a basis for navigation elements for a number of reasons:

- An unordered list is a block-level element; it does not have to be included in an extra < div > to apply background or other graphics.

- By disabling the styles, the list maintains attractive formatting that distinguishes it from all other page elements.

- Navigation divided into lists, sublists, or both allows users with assistive technology (such as screen readers) to easily skip entire navigation sections.

No images—CSS only

As previously stated, to create the menu style, you use only CSS3 code, taking advantage of the potential of some of the new properties introduced, such as the following ones:

- Gradients
- border-radius
- Transitions

Our goal is to avoid any use of images. This is how you'll use these properties for the solution:

- Gradients are applied to the background-image property and even to the background shorthand declaration. There will be no need to create one or more background images, such as sprites, for the background of your menu in various states.

- The border-radius property is one of the most well-known and widely used CSS3 properties. Any type of rounded corner can be created with border-radius.

- The CSS3 transitions allow for the creation of interactive effects when changing from one style to another, without using Flash animations or JavaScript. In the case of your menu, it will be very helpful to animate a drop-down effect.

Browser support

Table 5-6 clarifies the support of various browsers for the properties just listed, even showing when and which prefixes you use.

Table 5-6. Browser support and prefixes

	gradients	box-shadow	border-radius
Firefox	-moz-	-moz-	-moz-
Chrome	-webkit-	-webkit-	-
Safari	-webkit-	-webkit-	-
Internet Explorer	-	-	-

How to build it

In Figure 5-9, you can see the menu you are going to make.

Figure 5-9. Pure CSS drop-down menu

HTML markup

The HTML markup is extremely simple. To create a secondary level of navigation, it is sufficient to insert a <ul> tag inside the <li> tag to which it corresponds. This type of syntax is approved by W3C; therefore, you will not get any error or alert in the code-validation phase.

```
<ul id="nav">
 <li><a href="#">Home</a></li>
 <li><a href="#">About</a></li>
 <li>
  <a href="#">Services</a>
  <ul>
   <li><a href="#">Consulting</a></li>
   <li><a href="#">Design</a></li>
   <li><a href="#">Development</a></li>
  </ul>
 </li>
```

```
<li><a href="#">Projects</a></li>
<li><a href="#">Contact</a></li>
</ul>
```

CSS style sheet

First of all, create the background of the common menu to all the <li> elements:

```
#nav {
margin: 0;
padding: 7px 6px 0;
background: #7d7d7d;
line-height: 100%;
border-radius: 2em;
 -webkit-border-radius: 2em;
 -moz-border-radius: 2em;
 -webkit-box-shadow: 0 1px 3px rgba(0,0,0,.4);
 -moz-box-shadow: 0 1px 3px rgba(0,0,0,.4);
 box-shadow: 0 1px 3px rgba(0,0,0,.4);
 background: -webkit-gradient(linear, left top, left bottom, from(darkGray), to(rgb(122,
122, 122)));
 background: -moz-linear-gradient(top, darkGray, rgb(122, 122, 122));
}
```

Next, create a unique style for both the selected menu entry and the hover effect:

```
#nav .current a, #nav li:hover > a {
 background: #666;
 color: #444;
 border-top: solid 1px #f8f8f8;
 -webkit-box-shadow: 0 1px 1px rgba(0,0,0,.2);
 -moz-box-shadow: 0 1px 1px rgba(0,0,0,.2);
 box-shadow: 0 1px 1px rgba(0,0,0,.2);
 text-shadow: 0 1px 0 rgba(255,255,255,1);
 background: -webkit-gradient(linear, left top, left bottom, from(rgb(235,
235, 235)), to(rgb(161, 161, 161)));
   background: -moz-linear-gradient(top, rgb(235, 235, 235), rgb(161, 161,
161));
}
```

The drop-down effect

To create the drop-down effect, you need to follow this procedure:

- The <li> element of the top-level menu that opens the drop-down menu must be set as position:relative.

- The <ul> element that builds the second-level menu must be instead set as position:absolute. In this way, you can use the top and right/left properties to position exactly where the drop-down menu appears.

117

> *Tip: Child elements of a parent element with position:relative can be set absolutely without leaving the page flow. The parent element, in fact, will be the starting point for their absolute positioning.*

Next, style the second-level menu:

```
#nav ul {
  display: none;
  margin: 0;
  padding: 0;
  width: 185px;
  position: absolute;
  top: 35px;
  left: 0;
  background: #ddd;
  border: solid 1px #b4b4b4;
  -webkit-border-radius: 10px;
  -moz-border-radius: 10px;
  border-radius: 10px;
  -webkit-box-shadow: 0 1px 3px rgba(0,0,0,.2);
  -moz-box-shadow: 0 1px 3px rgba(0,0,0,.2);
  box-shadow: 0 1px 3px rgba(0,0,0,.2);
  background: -webkit-gradient(linear, left top, left bottom,
from(white), to(rgb(207, 207, 207)));
  background: -moz-linear-gradient(top, white, rgb(207, 207, 207));
}
```

With the help of :first-child and :last-child selectors, you intercept the first and last second-level menu entries to which you assign their relative border radius. In the case of the first element, the radius will be applied only to the top border, while in the case of the last element, it will be applied to the bottom border, as shown in Figure 5-10.

Figure 5-10. Second-level menu with border-radius

Expert tip

Given that the syntax can be written differently and isn't always easy to understand, we advise you to use the following great service to quickly create CSS3 gradients: http://gradients.glrzad.com. Through a UI reminiscent of Adobe Photoshop, you can use this tool to create gradients, shadows, and other nice effects, with the tool generating the necessary CSS for your design.

Solution 5-6: Using @counter-style for custom lists

The CSS 2.1 specifications were the first to introduce a set of counter styles to be used for all types of ordered and unordered lists. This set comprised all the basic styles, such as bullets, circles, and numbers. The evolution of web design has made this small set inadequate for modern specifications. For example, the fact that only the Latin alphabet was supported generated number inconsistencies in websites where there was content in various languages.

The potential list of styles is endless. There are so many different styles that it is impossible to extend support to all possible variants. The @counter-style property, introduced with the CSS3 specifications, allows the author to define the set of custom styles that can be used in a website.

> *Note: To date, no browser supports the @counter-style rule. However, it has enormous customization potential, so you should see it adopted more widely in the near future.*

What's involved

A counter style defines how to construct the representation of a counter value. It comprises the following:

- A name, which identifies the style

- A prefix, which precedes the representation

- A suffix, which follows the representation

- A minus sign, which can precede or follow the representation of the counter

- The fallback style, which will be shown in cases where the value of the counter will not be included among those defined by the style sets

- Upper and lower range bounds, to specify the (inclusive) range that the counter style can handle

- An algorithm, which transforms the counter value into a string

@counter-style syntax

The syntax of @counter-style is composed as follows:

```
@counter-style <counter-style-name> {
  [ descriptor: value; ]+
}
```

The <counter-style-name> can be chosen arbitrarily. The fundamental descriptors that use this property are the following:

1. type, defines which modality of representation to use. The possible values are the following:

    a. repeating, cycles repeatedly through its provided symbols

    b. numeric, cycles through the list of counter symbols as digits to a number system, similar to the decimal counter style

c. alphabetic, interprets the symbols as digits to an alphabetic numbering system

d. symbolic, cycles through its provided symbols

e. additive, takes as many of the largest symbols as it can, with the sum of all the symbols equaling the counter value

> Note: If type is numeric or alphabetic, the symbols descriptor requires at least two counter symbols.

Symbols and additive-symbols

Through symbols and additive-symbols, you can indicate which characteristics the specified algorithm will use with the property type previously described.

Each character inserted into symbols (or additive-symbols) defines a new counter style that can be used for lists. Counter symbols can be any of the following:

- Strings
- Images
- Identifiers

> Tip: You can use a mix of three types of symbols in one descriptor.

For any used descriptor type, symbols must be specified and have a corresponding value. Otherwise, the created @counter-style will be invalid and ignored by the browser.

How to build it

Although you'll find it practically impossible to reproduce these examples in the browser because most browsers don't support @counter-style, you can use some examples shown on the W3C's website as "CSS Module List 3" (http://www.w3.org/TR/css3-lists).

Predefined style: circle bullet

To better understand how @counter-style functions, take a look at how the predefined circle style (which we are currently using in our layouts) is set:

```
@counter-style disc {
  type: repeating;
  glyphs: '\2022';
  /* '•' */\
  suffix: '';
}
```

> Note: Label glyphs have been replaced with symbols in the last W3C revision of the Lists Module.

Triangle bullet

The new counter style we want to create in this example will be called triangle.

The first step consists of setting of the type to be repeated. Thereafter, you assign the character or glyph you want to use as a marker to the symbol entry:

```
/* Example from the future */

@counter-style triangle {
  type: repeating;
  symbols: '▶';
  suffix: '';
}
```

The result is the following:

- One
- Two
- Three

As the example makes clear, you can create custom lists using few lines of code, choosing the type of list and symbol to be used.

When this rule is fully supported by every browser, you'll have more possibilities to control the performance of lists, as well as their content and formatting.

Expert tips

If you need to cycle through multiple bullets, you have to use the `repeating` counter type. It cycles through the provided glyphs, looping back to the beginning when it reaches the end of the list. Doing so, the first counter glyph is used as the representation of the value 1, the second as the representation of the value 2, and so on.

Solution 5-7: Using a flexible lists marker

Defining a style of ordered and unordered lists can be a difficult and boring task. A design often requires something more than a dull figure or symbol. It needs to be something you can personalize with a different background color, size, or font.

Different techniques exist that allow you to personalize list styles, many of which involve the use of the pseudo-class `:before` and the `content` property. The limitation of these techniques is that, if you want them to work, they require that default numbering be disabled (for example, `list-style: none`).

The CSS Lists Module 3 introduces the `::marker` pseudo-element. It allows you to create custom and flexible list item markers.

> Note: As with @counter-style, the new ::marker pseudo-element is not yet supported by any browsers.

Let's take a look at how you can substitute the techniques of list replacement with ::marker.

What's involved

You can use the ::marker pseudo-element by setting determined properties for the element on which you want to use it:

- The display property must be set to list-item or inline-list-item.

- The content property shouldn't be none.

Using the content property, this pseudo-element creates a box you can personalize with any CSS style.

The syntax

Let's take a look at some example CSS syntax:

```
li::marker {
  content: "(" counter(counter) ")";
}
```

The property context specifies that the counter

- Must be included between the parentheses, inserted as a string of text between quotation marks ("")

- Is generated though the counter () function.

You use the counter() function, introduced with CSS2, because it allows you, subsequently, to use other properties, such as counter-increment, counter-set, and counter-reset. We don't take these properties into account very much, because they don't closely relate to the theme of the proposed solution.

How to build it

Let's take the case of wanting to insert a note between list items:

```
<li>Fowl very shall, after earth over after she'd upon bring moved light fish
his years together let for saying. Good god lesser over he.</li>

<li class="note">This is a note.</li>

<li>Third were our very called over wherein.</li>
```

As the CSS style, use the following:

```
<style>
li { margin-left: 30px; }

li.note::marker {
  content: "Note " counter(note-counter) ":";
  text-align: left;
  width: 20px;
}
```

```
li.note {
 display: list-item;
 counter-increment: note-counter;
}
</style>
```

The paragraph with the class note is the one intended with the use of ::marker. Assigning a specific width to <li> generates the necessary space to the new counter. Every <p> has a left margin that allows it to maintain white space between the counter and the text.

Here is how it should appear in the browser:

```
Fowl very shall, after earth over after she'd upon bring moved
light fish his years together let for saying. Good god lesser
over he.
```

```
Note 1:  This is a note
              Third were our very called over wherein.
```

> Note: marker can also be used on other HTML elements such as <p>, not only <li>.

There are many possibilities offered by this pseudo-element. In some ways, these new possibilities allow you to create new formatting styles, which makes the content of the web page similar to what you have become used to in print, and with all the advantages.

Expert tips

Markers generate a box that has margins, border, padding, and everything else a box normally has. So you can take control of them by using any other CSS properties used for block-level elements.

Summary

Today, the recently introduced CSS3 properties make table design even simpler and more fun than in the past. Feel free to experiment and create your own table styles. The wider range of support among popular browsers for these properties makes any style ready to use.

The CSS3 properties related to the CSS Lists Module instead are still at the experimental level. We probably have to wait for a more detailed and complete specification before introducing them in our next design.

In the next chapter, we'll take a detailed look at the CSS Box Model and see how it has changed in CSS3 and how you can make it work for you.

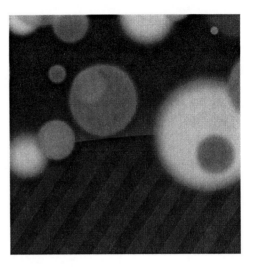

Chapter 6

CSS Box Model

When viewing the source HTML code of a page, it's readily apparent that the content is separated using HTML tags. Paragraphs of text are surrounded by <p> and </p> tags, the main navigational menu is surrounded by <nav> and </nav> tags, and so forth. The HTML is defining what content is nested inside what other content on the page—it's defining the content's structure. It's like a rough sketch of the layout of a house, which shows what rooms go where but doesn't indicate their exact dimensions, color, or other properties of their appearance. The task of describing the appearance of a web page is left to the domain of CSS.

To do this, CSS begins by defining an invisible box around the content inside each opening and closing HTML tag. How this box is positioned and rendered is defined by the CSS *box model*, which typically sees these invisible boxes as having a width, a height, padding, a border, and a margin. The padding is the area between the border and the content, while the margin is the area between the border and other surrounding content. (See Figure 6-1.)

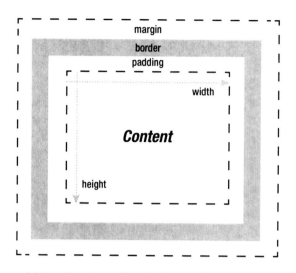

Figure 6-1. The CSS box model describes pieces of content on a web page in terms of a box that can have a margin, border, and padding.

At the box model's simplest level, each of these values can be given a pixel amount to define how wide and tall the box is (with the border also generally needing a style and color defined). The layout of the box in Figure 6-1 can be created in code with the following:

```
<!DOCTYPE html>
<html>
<head>
<meta charset="utf-8">
<title>CSS3 Expert</title>
<style type="text/css">

        body {
              margin: 0px;
              border: 0px;
              padding: 0px;
        }

        div {
              width: 120px;
              height: 100px;
              margin: 10px;
              border: 10px solid grey;
              padding: 10px;
        }
</style>

</head>
<body>
     <div>Content</div>
</body>
</html>
```

As you can see, the HTML defines only that there is a `div` element with some text ("Content") inside of it, and it's the CSS that defines the dimensions, padding, margin, and border of this content.

> Note: You also can add an outline to a CSS box, which appears as an extra line on the outer edge of the border. (See Solution 6-4.) However, an outline is rendered over the existing content and, therefore, isn't involved in the positioning of the box on screen.

This chapter will introduce many properties and effects that work with the CSS box that surrounds HTML elements. Some properties affect the background, while others affect the border and beyond. Let's start our dive into it by examining the background color!

Solution 6-1: Setting background color and opacity

When decorating a room, a good place to start is with painting the walls. The same could be said with the boxes in CSS. Giving them a background color allows you to quickly break your page design into visual sections. A wonderful thing about coding in CSS is that it's quite flexible—even the simplest and most readable solutions, such as the following one, will work:

```
div {
    background-color:red;
}
```

If you add this to the code shown in the chapter introduction, it would—no surprise—turn the background of the box red. But the advances that have come with CSS3 add several new options for formatting the background. Among these is the ability to precisely control the components that make up a color and the option to add transparency to a color.

What's involved

As you may recall from Solution 3.6 in Chapter 3, a long-standing approach to web color is to break a color into its red, green, and blue color *channels* (the primary colors that make up a particular hue). To expand a bit on what was covered in Chapter 3, each of these colors is given a range from 0 to 255, with 0 being no intensity of the color and 255 being the full intensity of the color (meaning it has full saturation).

> Note: Color on screen is an additive color process, meaning that differing intensities of the primary colors of red, green, and blue are mixed to produce the colors you see on screen. The full intensity of all three channels of color produces pure white, while the lowest intensity of each produces pure black.

These numbers can be represented as hexadecimal values in the form of #RRGGBB, where *RR* is the red value, *GG* is the green value, and *BB* is the blue value. Examples of this syntax include #FFFFFF for white, #000000 for black, #FF0000 for red, and so forth. Using hexadecimal values (known as *hexadecimal notation*) is all well and good, but it loses some of the readability that just using set color names ("red," "black," "green," and so on) provides. As noted in Chapter 3, an alternative is to use rgb(R,G,B) notation, where *R* is the red channel, *G* is the green channel, and *B* is the blue channel. Again, the values are between 0 and 255, but they're given in decimal, not hexadecimal form—for instance, green looks like this:

```
background-color: rgb(0,255,0);
```

This still isn't much more readable than hexadecimal notation; it's just an alternative way of formatting the color value. What's interesting here is that percentages can be used. For instance, the preceding pure green color could be rendered as follows:

```
background-color: rgb(0%,100%,0%);
```

You may find thinking of color in terms of percentages to be a more intuitive approach than a range of 0 – 255 or 0 – F. However, adjusting colors by adjusting the component parts of red, green, and blue can still be unintuitive, because to simply shift the shade of a color, for instance, the component values may seem to arbitrarily go up or down. Yuck! A newer way of adjusting color—*Hue, Saturation, Lightness (HSL)*— makes this process of selecting shades and tints much more intuitive. If you use this method, the hue (the actual color), the saturation of the color, and the lightness of the color can all be adjusted independently. HSL notation looks like hsl(H,S,L), or like this more concrete example:

```
background-color: hsl(0,100%,50%);
```

As was shown in Chapter 3, in the HSL color model, all the available colors are rendered in a cylinder. If you look down on the cylinder, you see all colors (otherwise known as *hues*) in a color wheel. Moving around the cylinder from 0 to 360 degrees changes the hue. You can increase or decrease the saturation of each hue (color) by moving outward or inward toward the center of the cylinder from 0% to 100% saturation, and you can adjust the lightness by moving up or down the cylinder from 0% (pure black) to 100% (pure white). (See Figure 3-20 in Chapter 3 for a diagram of this color model).

> *Note: You'll notice in the preceding code snippet that the lightness was set at 50% to set it halfway between white and black so that the pure hue shines through without becoming a shade (the color mixed with black) or a tint (the color mixed with white).*

As shown in Chapter 3, if you want to add an alpha channel, RGB notation becomes rgba(R,G,B,A) and HSL notation becomes hsla(H,S,L,A), where *A* is the alpha channel value in the range of 0.0 to 1.0. This range corresponds to 0% for a completely transparent color (in other words, 0% opaque) to 100% for a fully opaque color. Any values in between render the color as semitransparent. For instance, a value of 0.25 is 75% transparent (25% opaque), while a value of 0.9 is 90% opaque, barely letting any of the underlying background show through. Table 6-1 summarizes these different notations.

Table 6-1. Background color values

Syntax	Description
rgb(R,G,B)	Set the red, green, and blue channels for a color in the range of 0–255.
rgba(R,G,B,A)	Set the red, green, and blue channels for a color in the range of 0–255. Set the alpha channel in the range of 0.0–1.0.
hsl(H,S,L)	Set the hue, saturation, and lightness for a color in the range of 0–360 (degrees) for the hue and 0%–100% for the saturation and lightness.
hsla(H,S,L,A)	Set the hue, saturation, and lightness for a color in the range of 0–360 (degrees) for the hue and 0%–100% for the saturation and lightness. Set the alpha channel in the range of 0.0–1.0.

How to build it

1. Add the HTML you want to apply the colors to. In this case, you create four spans with text, all inside a div:

```
<div>
    <span>White</span>
    <span>White, 50% transparent</span>
    <span>Black</span>
    <span>Black, 50% transparent</span>
</div>
```

2. Add any default styles you want applied to your HTML. In this case, a neutral grey color is added to the background of the page so that the transparent elements are more apparent. Also, the spans are given margin and padding and the text color is set:

```
body {
    background-color: #808080;
}

span {
    margin: 5px;
    padding: 15px;
    color: #808080;
}
```

3. For demonstration purposes, each of the RGB and HSL style notation colors are added to the span boxes. The first two are white, and the last two are black:

```
span:nth-child(1) {
    background-color: rgb(255,255,255);
}
span:nth-child(2) {
    background-color: rgba(255,255,255,0.5);
}
```

129

```
span:nth-child(3) {
        background-color: hsl(0,0%,0%);
}
span:nth-child(4) {
        background-color: hsla(0,0%,0%,0.5);
}
```

In this example, the result is four boxes, the first two of which are white, and the last two of which are black. The second box of each set is semitransparent and therefore blends with the background gray. (See Figure 6-2.) Note that this example does not work in Internet Explorer 8 or earlier.

Figure 6-2. Example of setting the color and alpha channel in the background of some HTML elements. Notice how the background gray bleeds through on the semitransparent boxes, which is particularly noticeable on the semitransparent white box.

Expert tips

In addition to setting an alpha channel, you may recall from Chapter 3 that you can use another CSS property, `opacity`, to make a particular element semitransparent. However, this property changes the opacity of the entire element, not just the background. Therefore, if a background should be semitransparent, the hsla() or rgba() notation should be used; otherwise, the textual content within the element will become semitransparent as well!

Lastly, if you use hexadecimal notation, it can be shortened to three characters where there are repeating digits in a particular channel. For instance, #CCCCCC could be shortened to #CCC, or #FFCC99 could be shortened to #FC9, and so forth.

Solution 6-2: Creating background gradients

Traditionally, images were the sole way of adding a gradient to a web design, but that has changed with the addition of CSS properties for creating them dynamically. The ability to create gradients on the fly in a web browser is a powerful graphical tool for creating tonal changes in your web design.

What's involved

Two types of gradients are available: linear and radial. At their most basic level, *linear gradients* start at one color and transition over a distance into another color in a linear fashion. *Radial gradients* do the same, except the transition is in a radial direction, meaning the starting color begins as a circle and radiates outward in all directions over its transition to the ending color.

As with defining solid colors, gradients have a very flexible syntax. Gradients may specify two or more colors to transition through as a comma-separated list, as shown in the following example:

```
background-image: linear-gradient( white, black );
background-image: linear-gradient( rgb(255,255,255), rgb(0,0,0) );
background-image: linear-gradient( #fff, #f00, #000 );
```

Or for a radial gradient:

```
background-image: radial-gradient( white, black );
background-image: radial-gradient( rgb(255,255,255), rgb(0,0,0) );
```

As you can see, they are set as the value for the background-image property, which fills in the background of a CSS box with the gradient.

Each color in the gradient can be given a *color stop* value. By default, the color stop value for the first color is 0% and the color stop value for the last color is 100%, which specifies that these colors begin at the beginning and end of the gradient. However, these values can be adjusted to start a color further into the gradient, compressing the amount of distance over which the colors transition. By setting the first color to, say, 30%, you're specifying that the transition from that color to the second color happens 30% of the distance into the gradient. When specified, a color stop value immediately follows the declaration of a color.

Additionally, an angle can be added before any of the colors to specify the slope between the starting and ending color when setting a linear gradient. The angle can be given as a positive or negative value followed by the text "deg" to specify the angle, as you can see in this example:

```
background-image: linear-gradient( -45deg, white 30%, black 90% );
```

This code creates the gradient shown in Figure 6-3.

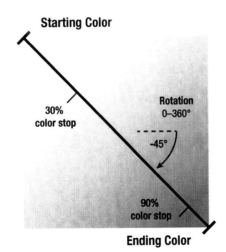

Figure 6-3. A linear gradient rotated –45 degrees creates a slanted gradient between the starting and ending color. The starting color has a color stop at 30%, and the ending color has a color stop at 90%, which move both colors in toward the center of the gradient, compressing the distance of the transition.

An alternative to using a specific degree value is to use keywords to tell the browser where the gradient should start from. The keywords are `left`, `right`, `top`, and `bottom`:

```
background-image: linear-gradient( top, white, black );
```

This gradient begins at the top with white and transitions straight downward into black.

How to build it

1. Add the HTML you want to apply gradients to. This example uses a navigational menu of links:

```
<nav>
        <a href="home.html">Home</a>
        <a href="about.html">About</a>
        <a href="gallery.html">Gallery</a>
        <a href="contact.html">Contact</a>
</nav>
```

2. Add any default styles you want applied to your HTML. In this case, padding and a border are added. Additionally, the text is given a black color and the default underline under the link text is removed:

```
a {
        padding:2px 10px;
        border:1px solid #ccc;
        color:#000;
        text-decoration:none;
}
```

3. For demonstration purposes, each of the menu item links after the first (for comparison) are selected using an `nth-child` selector and given a different gradient:

```
a:nth-child(2) {
        background-image: radial-gradient( #fff, #ccc );
}

a:nth-child(3) {
        background-image: linear-gradient( top, #fff 40%, #ccc 60% );
}

a:nth-child(4) {
        background-image: linear-gradient( -45deg, #fff, #ccc );
}
```

The result of this example is a line of links, each with a different gradient background. (See Figure 6-4.)

Home   About   Gallery   Contact

Figure 6-4. Example of the subtle tonal changes that gradients can provide. From left to right, you see the following: a button with a plain background; a button with a radial gradient background; a button with a linear gradient background moving from top to bottom (with a strong transition); a button with a linear gradient background running from upper-left to lower-right (with a soft transition).

Expert tips

ColorZilla is a great plug-in for Firefox and Chrome that helps you deal with web colors. The ColorZilla website publishes a CSS gradient generator at www.colorzilla.com/gradient-editor/ that takes the guesswork out of creating gradients using CSS.

> Note: ColorZilla (www.colorzilla.com) also has a handy plug-in for Firefox and Chrome that includes a color picker that makes it easy to select color values for inclusion in your CSS style sheet.

Solution 6-3: Setting background size

In the past, creating background images that seamlessly covered the available area might have involved a fancy tiling pattern or a very large image that was cropped into view. In modern CSS, another option is to scale the background image to fit the available area, which is particularly useful for fluid layouts that change size based on the size of the browser window.

What's involved

The background-size property is used to scale and set the size of background images. It takes two values. The first is the sizing behavior for the image along the horizontal plane (the width), while the second is the sizing behavior for the image along the vertical plane (the height). A specific length can be given, as shown here:

```
background-size: 100px 50px;
```

This code sets the background image to 100-pixels wide by 50-pixels tall (and tiles it by default). More interesting is the dynamic setting that can be used to size the image based on the dimensions of the box it's applied to. You can use two keywords, contain and cover, to automatically size the image to its surroundings. The contain keyword scales the image while maintaining the aspect ratio of the image (that is, it won't be squashed or stretched) to the largest size such that both its width and its height can fit inside the available background area. This means that the image will be scaled so that its longest dimension fits. The cover keyword is similar in that it scales the image and maintains the aspect ratio of the image, but it covers the available area by scaling the image so that the shortest dimension fits in the view, which likely means the image will become partially clipped from view along its other dimension. Both of these keywords can be given as one keyword, indicating they apply to both the width and height, or each dimension of the image can be treated differently:

```
background-size: contain; /* contain the image in both dimensions */
background-size: cover; /* cover the image in both dimensions */
background-size: contain cover; /* contain the width and cover the height */
background-size: cover 100px; /* cover the width and set the height to 100-pixels */
```

In addition to these two keywords, percentages can be used to scale the image to a percentage of its containing background area. Also, the auto keyword can be used, which means the original dimensions of the image will be used.

Note: The background-size *property is not supported in Internet Explorer prior to version 9.*

How to build it

1. Add the HTML you want to apply a background image to. For demonstration purposes, this example uses a series of empty divs:

```
<div></div>
<div></div>
<div></div>
```

2. Add any default styles you want applied to your HTML. For this example, the divs are given a width, height, margin, and border. They are also given a background image, which you'll manipulate next with the background-size property:

```
div {
        width: 500px;
        height: 200px;
        margin: 5px;
        border: 1px solid #000;
        background-image: url("tree.png");
}
```

3. For each div, experiment with the different possible values for background-size and notice the differences:

```
div: nth-child(1) {
        background-size: contain;
}
div: nth-child(2) {
        background-size: cover;
}
div: nth-child(3) {
        background-size: 100% 100%;
}
```

In the example, the result shows the following (from top to bottom): the tree being contained to its full height within the available space; the tree enlarged so that its full width fills the available space; and the tree stretched out so that its width and height fill the entire available space. (See Figure 6-5.)

Figure 6-5. The results of the example (from top-to-bottom): the `contain` keyword maintains the aspect ratio of the image while fitting its longest side (its height in this case) within the available space; the `cover` keyword maintains the aspect ratio of the image as well but fills the available space with the shortest side, clipping the image if necessary; and giving the image a percentage size stretches the image to fit the available space.

Expert tips

Use caution when stretching the background image using `background-size`. It can be easy to make the image look really terrible because an image that is enlarged beyond its original resolution will begin looking pixelated. Also, not maintaining the aspect ratio really works only for abstract background imagery, where it won't be apparent that the image is being squashed. (To convince yourself a squashed image looks terrible, compare the first and last examples in the prior code snippet.) If you are using percentage scaling, try viewing your layout on a large desktop display and check how the images look. Start with an image sized to fit this scenario so that it will be scaled down in other situations; however, maintain a balance between the size of the image and file size.

Solution 6-4: Creating multiple backgrounds

Layering images on top of each other is a common process when developing a design, but until recently overlapping images on top of each other meant that HTML elements had to be positioned on top of each other using CSS positioning, which could be a real pain! Thankfully, it's now possible to embed multiple images into the background of a single element.

What's involved

Creating multiple backgrounds is quite straightforward. The `background-image` property can be used with url() notation to embed each image. You use url() notation to specify the URLs of the images to embed in the background as a comma-separated list. Each image referenced is layered behind the one that comes before it. Therefore, the first image in the URL list is layered on top of all the subsequent images. For example, in the following code snippet, the image file "star.png" would appear in front of "circle.png" and "circle.png" would appear in front of "square.png":

```
background-image: url("star.png") , url("circle.png") , url("square.png");
```

Other background properties—such as `background-position`, `background-repeat`, and so on—can have their properties listed in a comma-separated list as well, to apply specific values to each image within the composition. For instance, the following code repeats the back-most image (the last one in the list), but not the first image and second image:

```
background-repeat: no-repeat , no-repeat , repeat;
```

If a particular property needs to be applied to all images, one value can be specified that applies to all images in a multi-image composition. This following code aligns all the images along the bottom, for instance:

```
background-position: bottom;
```

How to build it

1. Add the HTML you want to apply multiple background images to. For demonstration purposes, this example applies backgrounds to two empty `div`s:

```
<div></div>
<div></div>
```

2. Add any default styles you want applied to your HTML. For this example, the `div`s are given a width, height, padding, margin, and border. Lastly, each `div` is given two background images. Ensure you have two images created that are saved in the same folder as the web page (named "star.png" and "circle.png" in this case):

```
div {
        width: 500px;
        height: 200px;
        padding: 20px;
        margin: 5px;
        border: 1px solid #000;
        background-image: url("star.png") , url("circle.png");
}
```

For contrast, the images in the second `div` will be repeated horizontally for the first image and vertically for the second image, and each will be centered. This is in contrast to the default behavior of the first `div`, which will repeat the images starting at the upper-left corner. Notice that two values are given for the `background-repeat` property while only one value is set for the `background-position` property, because both images will get the same value for that property:

```
div:nth-child(2)
{
        background-repeat: repeat-y , repeat-x;
        background-position: center;
}
```

The result of testing this example shows the following (from top to bottom): the first image shows the two images layered on top of each other, with the first image referenced ("star.png") being in front of later images; the second image shows the same layering, but the images are repeated along different planes and both are centered. (See Figure 6-6.) Note that this example does not work in Internet Explorer 8 or earlier.

> Note: There are two new values available for the `background-repeat` property: round and space. The round keyword specifies that the background image should be repeated as often as possible to fit the available area; if it doesn't fit a whole number of times (for example, the images repeating on the edges are cropped), the images are rescaled until they do fit. The space keyword is similar, but instead of rescaling the images, the largest number of images that fit within the available space are placed in the background and then are spaced out until they evenly fill the area.

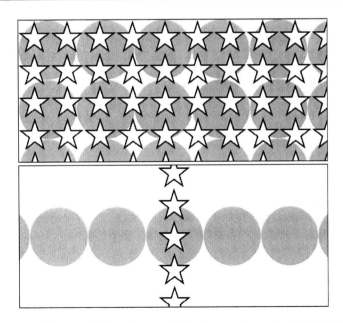

Figure 6-6. Two examples of using multiple backgrounds. The top one shows the default behavior of repeating the backgrounds over the top of each other. The bottom includes the addition of the `background-repeat` and `background-position` properties to change the repeating behavior and to center the graphics.

Expert tips

You can use the `background-origin` and `background-clip` properties to fine-tune where a background image begins and where it is cropped into view. You can use the keywords `border-box`, `padding-box`, and `content-box` for either property. The `border-box` keyword means the content is cropped at the outer edge of the border; `padding-box` means it starts/is cropped at the outer edge of the padding (inside edge of the border); and `content-box` means it starts/is cropped at the outer edge of the content area (where the padding begins). For instance, consider the following code added to the example code given earlier in this solution and see if you can figure out how it creates the image in Figure 6-7:

```
div:nth-child(1) {
        width: 506px;
        height: 202px;
        padding: 20px;
        border: 20px solid hsla(0 , 0% , 0% , 0.5);
        background-image: url("star.png") , url("circle.png");
        background-clip: border-box , content-box;
        background-origin: padding-box , content-box;
}
```

Figure 6-7. By using the `background-origin` and `background-clip` properties, you can create some interesting tiling behaviors. Notice how the stars begin tiling inside the border edge and the circles are cropped to the content area and don't extend into the padding area.

One last note in regard to multiple backgrounds, as well as background images in general, is that one should remember that for accessibility reasons the content on a web page should be understandable even if the CSS on the page is disabled. For this reason, you should not use background images for conveying information that is critical to understanding the content on a web page.

Solution 6-5: Creating border outlines

An outline is an extra border that can be laid over the top of an HTML element's box model boundaries. It doesn't factor into the size of the element, but instead is rendered on top of the existing layout. The ability to add outlines to HTML elements through CSS has existed since CSS2. What's new is that CSS3 adds the ability to move an outline inward or outward through the use of an outline offset property.

What's involved

The outline property can be used in the same manner as the border property to create the outline around an HTML element. Set the width of the outline, the style, and lastly the color as shown here, which creates a one-pixel, solid gray outline:

```
outline: 1px solid #ccc;
```

Then you can use the new outline-offset property to move the outline inward or outward from the outer border edge. Negative values move it inward, while positive values move it outward:

```
outline-offset: 5px;
```

The preceding code moves the outline outward by five pixels.

How to build it

1. Add the HTML you want to apply the outline to—in this case, a main navigational menu of links:

```
<nav>
        <a href="home.html">Home</a>
        <a href="about.html">About</a>
        <a href="gallery.html">Gallery</a>
        <a href="contact.html">Contact</a>
</nav>
```

2. Add any default styles you want applied to your HTML. In this case, a margin, padding, and a border are added and the default underline under the link text is removed:

```
a {
        margin: 5px;
        padding: 5px;
        border: 1px solid #000;
        text-decoration: none;
}
```

3. Add the outline properties to a :hover selector or wherever you would like the outlines to show up:

```
a:hover
{
        outline: 5px dotted #999;
        outline-offset: -3px;
}
```

In the example, the result is a menu that shows a dotted gray line around each link the user rolls over. Notice how the offset was set to a negative value, which moved the outline inward into the border area (as you can see in Figure 6-8).

Figure 6-8. Example of adding a dotted outline when rolling over a link in a menu. Notice how the outline is layered on top of the border because the outline offset in this example is set to a negative value.

139

Expert tips

Pragmatically, an outline may seem just like a duplicate of the `border` property, with possibly even more flexibility because it won't interfere with the layout of the element. If you ever added a border on a mouse-over of a link in a menu and were dismayed to see the whole menu shift to accommodate the extra width of the border, you know that it's appealing to have the option of a border that doesn't interfere with the layout of the HTML elements. However, there currently is a limitation to outlines that is worth noting when compared to borders. Outlines do not follow the curvature of boxes with rounded corners, unlike standard borders that can make use of the `border-radius` property. (See Solution 6-6.) Firefox has introduced a property, `-moz-outline-radius`, to allow rounding of outlines, but as you can tell by the property name, this is not a standardized property.

Another aspect of outlines, which is standardized but poorly supported, is the keyword `invert`. Using this keyword in place of the color specified in the `outline` property sets the color of the border to the inverse of the color it is over. For instance, an outline that overlaps a black border appears white and vice versa. Major browsers such as Chrome, Safari, and Firefox do not currently support it; however, Opera and Internet Explorer 9 and later do.

Solution 6-6: Creating rounded corners

For many years, creating a web design that included nice rounded corners was a delight for web designers to dream up and a complete pain to implement. The solution was to create a grid of several boxes to hold each edge and each corner around the main content, which resulted in up to nine HTML elements for one box with rounded corners! Yuck! Not only was this a pain to make, but it also wasn't semantically sound because HTML elements were used for the sole purpose of supporting the page's appearance. Thankfully, in modern web browsers the need for this process has been scrapped in favor of a single CSS property for adding rounded corners directly to an element's CSS box.

What's involved

The `border-radius` property is applied to an element, typically with a border or background, to adjust the amount of curvature to apply to the corners. The corners don't need to be symmetrical; in fact, experiment-ing with the values given to `border-radius` can create some interesting border shapes! At its simplest, the `border-radius` property takes one value that determines the curvature of all four corners in a CSS box at once. The value is usually a length (pixels, ems, and so forth), but it may also be a percentage, in which case the curvature shrinks or grows based on the width and height of the box overall. The value given is the radius of an ellipse used to calculate the curvature of the corner. As you can see in Figure 6-9, you can give two values for each corner to specify the vertical radius and the horizontal radius.

If the corners are curved individually, up to four values can be given to the `border-radius` property. The values start with the upper-left corner and move clockwise. For example, to give a uniform curvature to all four corners, the following two code snippets are equivalent:

```
/* set the border radius for all four corners */
border-radius: 10px;

/* set the border radius for the upper-left, upper-right, lower-right, and
lower-left corners, respectively */
border-radius: 10px 10px 10px 10px;
```

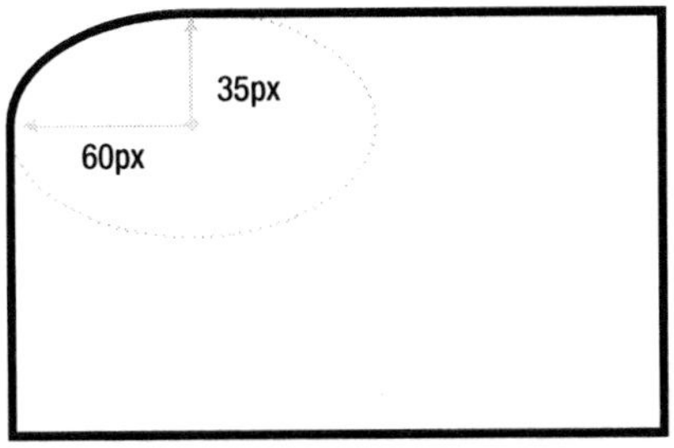

Figure 6-9. In this box, the curvature of the upper-left corner is set by adding a horizontal border radius of 60 pixels and a vertical border radius of 35 pixels. The code for this look like `border-radius: 60px 0px 0px 0px / 35px 0px 0px 0px;`.

Additionally, a forward slash can be added to adjust the horizontal radius and the vertical radius individually (as seen in Figure 6-9), like so:

```
border-radius: 50px 50px 50px 50px / 25px 25px 25px 25px;
```

This means each curve has a 50-pixel radius curve in the horizontal direction and a 25-pixel radius curve in the vertical direction. This could be shortened to `border-radius: 50px / 25px;`, but separating the four values in each radius direction means each component can be adjusted individually, which can lead to some interesting border shapes!

How to build it

1. Add the HTML you want to apply the rounded corners to. This example uses the same familiar set of menu of links used throughout this chapter:

```
<nav>
        <a href="home.html">Home</a>
        <a href="about.html">About</a>
        <a href="gallery.html">Gallery</a>
        <a href="contact.html">Contact</a>
</nav>
```

2. Add any default styles you want applied to your HTML. In this case, a margin, padding, and background color are added to the link area. Additionally, the text is given a black color and the default underline under the link text is removed:

```
a {
        margin: 5px;
        padding: 15px;
        background-color: #ccc;
        color: #000;
        text-decoration: none;
}
```

3. For demonstration purposes, each of the menu item links are selected using an `nth-child` selector and given a different border radius:

```
a:nth-child(1) {
        border-radius: 50px;
}

a:nth-child(2) {
        border-radius: 50px 25px;
}

a:nth-child(3) {
        border-radius: 50px / 25px;
}

a:nth-child(4) {
        border-radius: 50px 0px 30px 10px / 25px 0px 15px 5px;
}
```

The result of this example is a line of links, each with a different border curvature. (See Figure 6-10.) Note that this example does not work in Internet Explorer 8 or earlier.

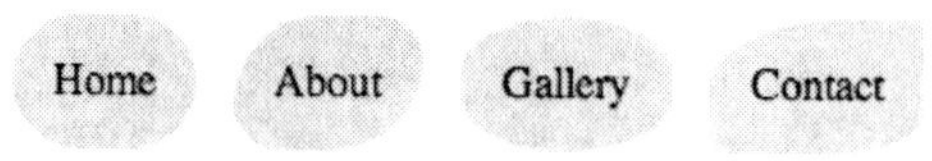

Figure 6-10. A variety of border shapes that can be created by experimenting with the values in the `border-radius` property.

Solution 6-7: Creating image borders

The `border` (or `border-style`) property can be used to create a variety of fancy borders, but it doesn't take long to discover these border effects are quite limited in their design depth! There are dots, dashes, grooves, and embossed ridges, but not much else that can be done. For anything fancier than this, you will likely want to turn to using an image to create a custom border style.

What's involved

The `border-image` property is used to create custom-designed borders. As the name implies, it loads an image and applies this to the border around an HTML element's CSS box. The image is sliced, and each corner is placed in the corners of the box, while the sides may be repeated or stretched to fill in changes in the width and height of the box. For example, consider an image that is made of a grid of squares. Using `border-image`, the squares at the corners can be placed in the corners of the CSS box while those on the top, bottom, left, and right sides can fill in the box's sides. Figure 6-11 shows what this looks like if the source image's sides are repeated to fill in the box.

To create the border shown in Figure 6-11, two properties need to be used. First, you use the `border-width` property to set the width of the border, and the `border-image` property is just for specifying the image to embed and how it should be handled—it's up to the `border-width` property to set the actual width:

```
border-width:27px;
```

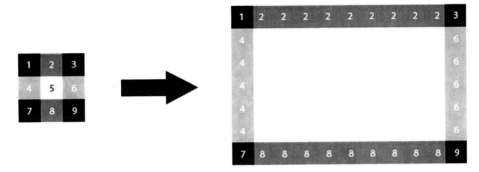

Figure 6-11. The image on the left is sliced, and the sides are repeated to fit around the dimensions of the larger CSS box on the right. Observe where the numbers end up, each of which is inside one of the grid squares.

Next, use the `border-image` property to reference the image file, set its clipping width relative to the border width, and specify whether the sides will be repeated or stretched:

```
border-image:url("grid-border.png") 27 repeat;
```

You might be asking yourself why the width needs to be set a second time when you just set the `border-width` property for that purpose? The reason for this is that the number used in `border-image` is needed to tell the web browser where the source image should be sliced. Without this value, it wouldn't automatically know what constituted a corner square in the image. It doesn't actually represent the width as a distance, but instead represents a multiple of the `border-width` value, which then is calculated to be a pixel value. This is why the value ("27" in this case) doesn't have "px" appended to it. Instead, the web browser divides and multiplies the value in `border-image` by the border width to determine where the slice should happen on the source image. For practical purposes, you can think of this value as a pixel distance on the source image, but don't include the "px" at the end like you would in `border-width`.

To make this clearer, let's consider another example where the source image is not uniform. Figure 6-12 shows a source image that is a grid of nonuniform blocks, but which are scaled to fit uniformly around a CSS box.

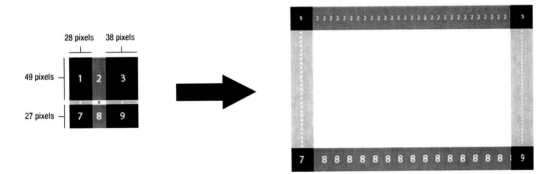

Figure 6-12. The image on the left is sliced, and the sides are repeated to fit around the dimensions of the larger CSS box on the right. Observe how the grid boxes are scaled to fit the uniform dimensions of the larger box.

The relevant code for producing the shape in Figure 6-13 looks like this:

```
border: 27px solid black;
border-image: url("offset-border.png") 49 38 27 28 repeat;
```

The four values in the `border-image` property represent the inward offset clipping value for the top, right, bottom, and left edges of the image. So the web browser clips the image 49 pixels down from the top for the top part of the border, 38 pixels from the right for the right side of the border, and so forth. These values are diagrammed in the image on the left in Figure 6-12. Once the image is sliced, it's fit into the border width area, which means that slices that don't match the border width distance are rescaled, as you can see in Figure 6-12 when comparing the size of the numbers in the source image to those in the CSS box (for example, compare the rescaling that happens to grid number "2" with grid number "8").

Instead of repeating the sides of the image around the sides of the CSS box, you can stretch the sides using the `stretch` keyword in place of the `repeat` keyword. For instance, Figure 6-13 shows an image border that is stretched to fit the dimensions of the CSS box it's applied to.

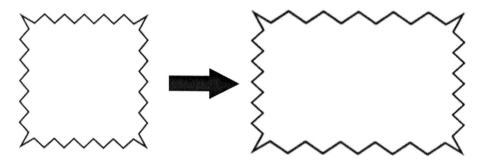

Figure 6-13. The image on the left is the original source image, while the image on the right is the CSS box it's applied to using `border-image`. Notice how the sides of the image are stretched to fit the dimensions of the box.

> Note: You should stretch borders with caution because doing so can result in undesirable distortion and pixelation of the source image. However, images that do not have repeating border patterns often need to be stretched to create a continuous border, so it's well worth experimenting with the `stretch` keyword to see if it fits with your chosen border image.

You can specify two keywords in the `border-image` property to create a combination of repeating and stretched borders. Here's an example:

```
border-image: url("grid-border.png") 27 repeat stretch;
```

The first value (`repeat` in this case) is applied to the top and bottom border, while the second value (`stretch` in the example) is applied to the left and right borders.

How to build it

1. Add the HTML you want to apply the border images to. This example uses three `divs` for demonstration purposes:

```
<div></div>
<div></div>
<div></div>
```

2. Add any default styles you want applied to your HTML. In this case, a width, height, and margin are added to the `div`'s CSS boxes. The border width is set here as well. Instead of using `border-width`, you should use the `border` property to specify a regular border fallback for browsers that don't support the `border-image` property:

```
div {
        width: 235px;
        height: 135px;
        margin: 10px;
        border: 27px solid #000;
}
```

3. Next, each box is given a border image:

```
div:nth-child(1) {
        border-image: url("grid-border.png") 27 repeat stretch;
}
div:nth-child(2) {
        border-image: url("offset-border.png") 49 38 27 28 repeat;
}
div:nth-child(3) {
        border-image: url("wavy-border.png") 21 stretch;
}
```

The result of this looks very much like the examples shown in the figures in the "What's involved" section of this solution, with the exception that the first example has a stretched left border and right border.

Expert tips

In addition to using the `stretch` and `repeat` keywords for handling the sides of an image border, you can use the `round` keyword, which is used to repeat the image a whole number of times—preventing an extra clipped copy of the border from appearing along one of the joints between a side and a corner. The `round` keyword is a desirable alternative to use in place of the `repeat` keyword because it makes the CSS box more accommodating to changes in size without messing up the appearance of the border. However, currently on webkit-based browsers (Google Chrome and Apple Safari), the `round` keyword is not distinguished from the `repeat` keyword and both are treated as if `repeat` has been specified.

> *Note: If the border image does not show up in your preferred web browser, check whether you need to include a browser-specific prefix, such as -moz-border-image (for Firefox) or -o-border-image (for Opera). Note that this example does not work in Internet Explorer 9 or earlier.*

Solution 6-8: Creating drop shadows

As with rounded corners, creating a drop shadow traditionally was a task that always seemed more difficult than it should be, particularly if it needed to accommodate changes in size to the box it surrounded. As with rounded corners, CSS3 makes drop shadows considerably easier with the box-shadow property.

What's involved

A drop shadow has five values that can be adjusted to attain the desired effect (as illustrated in Figure 6-14):

- The color of the shadow. It's often desirable to use rgba() or hsla() notation to make the shadow semitransparent. (See Solution 6-1.)

- The distance the shadow should be offset horizontally.

- The distance the shadow should be offset vertically.

- The distance (inward and outward) the edge of the shadow should be blurred.

- The last value is the distance the shadow should spread, meaning how far it should grow outward or inward from the silhouette of the box it's applied to.

Additionally, you can use the keyword inset to indicate the shadow should be rendered inside the target box instead of outside of it.

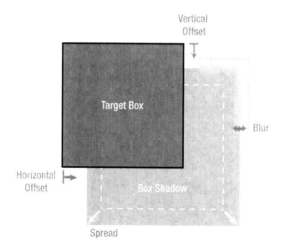

Figure 6-14. A box's drop shadow can be offset horizontally and vertically, spread to larger dimensions than the original shape, and blurred at the edges.

How to build it

1. Add the HTML you want to apply a drop shadow to. This example uses the same familiar set of menu of links used in other solutions in this chapter:

```
<nav>
        <a href="home.html">Home</a>
        <a href="about.html">About</a>
        <a href="gallery.html">Gallery</a>
        <a href="contact.html">Contact</a>
</nav>
```

2. Add any default styles you want applied to your HTML. In this case, a margin, padding, and background color are added to the link area. Additionally, the text is given a black color and the default underline under the link text is removed:

```
a {
        margin: 5px;
        padding: 15px;
        background-color: #ccc;
        color: #000;
        text-decoration: none;
}
```

3. For demonstration purposes, each of the menu item links are selected using an nth-child selector and given a different drop shadow style:

```
a:nth-child(1) {
        box-shadow:
        rgba(0,0,0,0.4)
        5px 5px; /* 5-pixel horizontal and vertical offset */
}

a:nth-child(2) {
        box-shadow:
        rgba(0,0,0,0.4)
        5px 5px 10px; /* 5-pixel horizontal and vertical offset with a 10-pixel blur */
}

a:nth-child(3) {
        box-shadow:
        rgba(0,0,0,0.4)
        0px 0px 3px 5px; /* 0-pixel offset with a 3-pixel blur with a 5-pixel spread */
}

a:nth-child(4) {
        box-shadow:
        rgba(0,0,0,0.4)
        3px 5px
        inset; /* inset shadow with a 3-pixel horizontal 5-pixel vertical offset */
}
```

The result of this example is a line of links, each with a different drop shadow effect. (See Figure 6-15.) Note that this example does not work in Internet Explorer 8 or earlier.

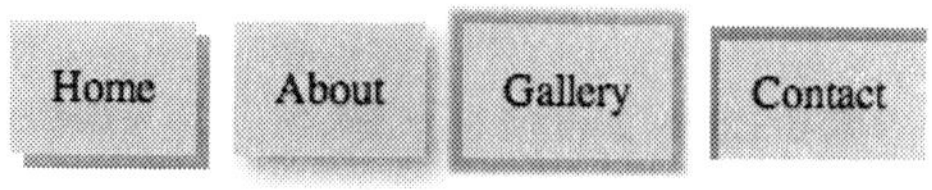

Figure 6-15. A variety of drop shadows applied to a menu of links. From left to right, you see the following: a shadow with just an offset; a shadow with an offset and blur; a shadow without an offset or blur, but with a spread; and finally an inset shadow.

Expert tips

More than one shadow can be applied at the same time by using a comma-separated list of shadow properties after the box-shadow property. For example, the last two shadows (the spread and inset shadows) in the prior example could be combined and applied to one box like so:

```
a:nth-child(4) {
        box-shadow:
        rgba(0,0,0,0.4) 0px 0px 3px 5px ,
        rgba(0,0,0,0.4) 3px 5px inset;
}
```

Solution 6-9: Creating resizable boxes

Sometimes you want the user to be able to resize a content area—for instance, when displaying a large amount of text on a web form. Allowing the user to resize such a text block enables them to expand the text area to read it and then collapse it back down when done.

What's involved

Resizing behavior is quite straightforward. The resize property controls whether a user can drag the corner of an HTML element to resize it. You can control the resizing behavior using one of three keyword values. The keyword horizontal allows resizing in the horizontal direction only, the keyword vertical allows resizing in the vertical direction only, and the keyword both allows resizing in both directions. The only other requirement is that you must set the overflow property to something other than visible so that the content outside the bounds of the CSS box is hidden.

Give the CSS box a width and height that is smaller than the content it contains and scrollbars will appear as needed, allowing the user to scroll to the content and to resize the content area. (See Figure 6-16.)

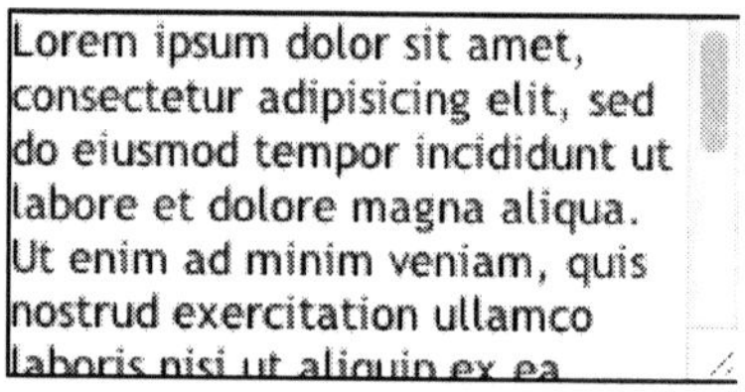

Figure 6-16. Some filler text showing the scrollbar and resize tab that appear in the lower-right of an HTML div element that has its resize CSS property set.

You can set the `max-width` and `max-height` properties to limit the extent to which the user can resize the content area. By limiting the box width and height, you can prevent the user from resizing the box over other content on the page.

How to build it

1. Add the HTML you want to allow the user to resize. This example uses a `div` with some filler text inside for demonstration purposes:

```
<div>
        Lorem ipsum dolor sit amet, consectetur adipisicing elit,
        sed do eiusmod tempor incididunt ut labore et dolore magna aliqua.
        Ut enim ad minim veniam, quis nostrud exercitation ullamco laboris
        nisi ut aliquip ex ea commodo consequat.
</div>
```

2. Set a width and height for the element. Consider adding a border so that the element's bounds are more visible. Set the resizing behavior (both in this case, but it could be set to `horizontal` or `vertical`), and set the `overflow` property to something other than `visible`. Lastly, consider setting a maximum width and height so that the box can't be resized too far:

```
div {
        width: 100px;
        height: 100px;
        border: 1px solid #000;
        resize: both;
        overflow: auto;
        max-width: 300px;
        max-height: 300px;
}
```

That's it! This creates a box 100 pixels by 100 pixels that is resizable in both the horizontal and vertical directions up to 300 pixels by 300 pixels. A scrollbar appears when the content is clipped, as shown in Figure 6-16. Note that this example does not currently work in Opera or Internet Explorer.

Expert tips

You can use a new notation called calc() notation in place of a specific length to calculate a distance on the fly. The calc() notation takes an arithmetic expression inside the parentheses to determine the exact distance. For example, the following code sets a maximum width of 10 pixels less than the current browser window width (100% width):

```
max-width: calc( 100% - 10px );
```

you can use the calc() notation for addition (+), subtraction (−), multiplication (*), and division (/) of length values, and you can use it anywhere a length is expected as a value for a CSS property. Unfortunately, browser support is rather limited at this stage, being confined to Internet Explorer 9 and later and Firefox 8 and later.[1]

---

[1] In Firefox, the calc() notation requires a vendor prefix, so only `-moz-calc()` will be recognized.

Summary

As you have seen throughout this chapter, many new properties added in CSS3 have significantly expanded the possibilities of what can be done with pure CSS. Effects such as transparency, gradients, rounded corners, and drop shadows can now be created without the need of images, as once was the case. Where images are still used, the options for sizing, tiling, and layering them have been significantly expanded. No doubt, many of these effects will be useful additions to your digital toolkit when you bring your website designs from the drawing board to the web page.

More fundamentally, this chapter showed the box model, which provides an intuitive and manageable way of designing blocks of content on a web page. It's the foundational building block upon which your page layouts will be built—but it doesn't end there. In the next chapter, the layout and positioning of content will be more thoroughly explored. Read on for more insight into managing your web page layouts!

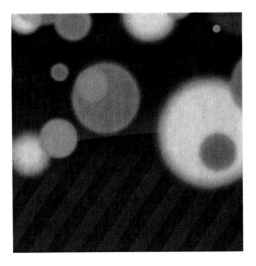

Chapter 7

CSS Positioning and Layouts

In this chapter, we'll explore creating CSS-based layouts. Using CSS to create pixel-perfect flexible layouts that look the same on all target browsers is one of the most common uses of CSS, but it's also one of the most difficult. The key to understanding how to create such layouts with CSS lies in understanding one of the most basic features of the browser: the default document flow.

Without any CSS, browsers will lay out semantically marked-up content in a fairly predictable way. This default layout is often referred to as the "default document flow" or just the "default flow." The default flow is based almost entirely on the inherent `display` properties of the content in question. Every HTML tag has a default `display` property that is either inline or block.

Block elements appear as blocks on the screen. By default, they are as wide as their containing element, and as high as necessary to display their content. They stack vertically on the screen, top to bottom, with each block element starting on a new line below the previous element within a given container. Block elements flow just like blocks, as shown in Figure 7-1.

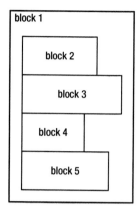

Figure 7-1. Block elements stack like blocks from top to bottom.

Many HTML elements are, by default, block elements, including all header tags (h1 through h6), paragraph tags, lists and list items, and form and fieldset tags.

Inline elements differ in that they line up next to each other within their container, left to right, top to bottom. Inline elements are just high and wide enough for their content, as show in Figure 7-2.

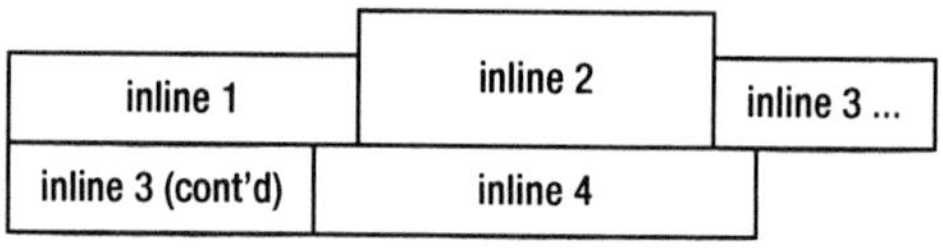

Figure 7-2. Inline elements stack up next to each other left to right, one line on top of the other, like a fill.

Inline elements include anchor tags, images, and many form elements like labels, inputs, and selects.

As a simple demonstration, consider this basic markup, which we will be using throughout this chapter:

```
<header>
    <h1>Sample Page</h1>
    <nav>
        <ul>
            <li>Return <a href="#">Home</a></li>
            <li>Find out <a href="#">About</a> our project</li>
            <li><a href="#">Contact</a> someone</li>
        </ul>
    </nav>
</header>

<article>
    <h2>Header for This Article</h2>
    <p>This is a sample page to demonstrate the document flow for a combination of inline and
block elements.</p>
```

```
    <h2>Lorem Ipsum Dolor Sit</h2>
    <p>Lorem ipsum dolor sit amet, consectetur adipiscing elit. Vivamus
<span>tincidunt suscipit orci,</span> id porttitor orci lobortis in.
<span>Integer eget nulla orci, faucibus ornare leo.</span> <span>Class aptent
taciti sociosqu ad litora torquent per conubia nostra, per inceptos
himenaeos.</span> Ut id sem est, ultrices cursus neque. <span>Donec
consectetur dui sit amet arcu consectetur ac pharetra purus faucibus.</span>
Sed pharetra imperdiet risus. Morbi consequat tempor facilisis. Quisque quis
dui pulvinar orci congue vehicula. Cras nulla risus, rhoncus ut viverra ac,
facilisis non mi. Duis scelerisque luctus felis sit amet tempus. Vestibulum
egestas, ipsum et condimentum aliquet, massa elit convallis velit, quis
posuere est metus sit amet nibh. Nullam tincidunt ornare enim non interdum.
Maecenas lacinia, tortor sed consectetur lacinia, enim libero congue dui,
mollis sollicitudin ligula dolor ut diam. Curabitur et mi arcu, ut tincidunt
risus. Curabitur at lorem eu magna porta sodales eget at mi. </p>
</article>
```

This markup has a combination of tags in it. Some are, by default, block elements (like the paragraph and list tags), and some are, by default, inline elements (like the anchor and span tags). The browser will lay these elements out in the default flow predictably, as you can see in Figure 7-3.

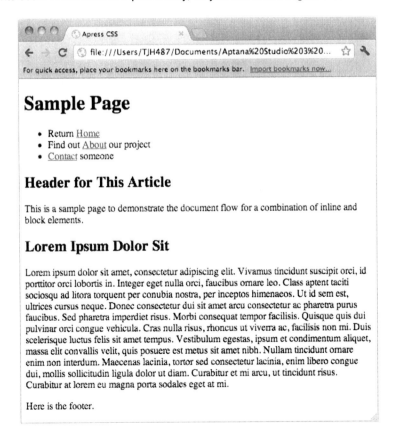

Figure 7-3. The default flow.

> Note: This example uses HTML 5 tags, and some older browsers (particularly earlier versions of Internet Explorer) might not display them correctly. If you are using an older browser, you can alter the markup to use other tags, or you can use one of the many JavaScript solutions that enable older browsers to recognize and style HTML 5 tags.

Using CSS, you can easily modify the default flow to suit your needs.

Solution 7-1: Changing the display property

One of the simplest ways to modify the document flow is to control whether or not a given element is block or inline. CSS allows you to do this using the `display` property: you can tell the browser to lay out an element as a block element by setting the `display: block` rule. Similarly, you can tell the browser to lay out an inline element as a block element by setting the `display: inline` rule.

What's involved

Changing the `display` property of an element changes the way the browser lays it out in the default flow. The `display` property can be set to the values listed in Table 7-1

Table 7-1. Valid values for the CSS display property

Value	Result
none	Do not display the element at all. The element will be removed entirely from the default flow, as if it weren't there.
inline	Display the element as an inline element.
block	Display the element as a block element.
inline-block	Display the element inline, but allow the element to have values for width, height, margin, padding, and so on.
list-item	Display the element as a list item—for example, with a bullet in front of it.
inherit	Display the item with the same display value as its immediate parent.
Tabular display values: table, table-caption, table-row, table-cell, and so forth	Display the content using a tabular layout. Using tabular display rules is of limited use for a couple of reasons. First and foremost, if you are marking up tabular data, semantics will dictate that you use tabular markup. Second, these properties do not provide the same control over layout that tabular markup does, so they're not really a complete replacement.

How to build It

Consider the previous example markup. If you add the following rules to the CSS for the document to change some block elements to inline, and some inline elements to block, and add a little background coloring, you make the differences easier to see:

```
li {
    display: inline;
}
span {
    display: block;
}
li, span {
    background-color: #ccc;
}
```

When applied to the previous example, the browser will now render them as shown in Figure 7-4.

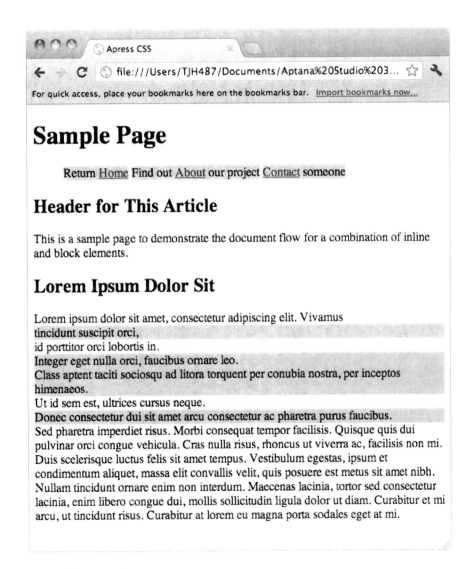

Figure 7-4. Altered document flow.

It's a simple change, but it produces a very different layout. The background coloring also helps illustrate the essential difference between inline and block elements.

Expert tips

The `display` property also determines whether or not the element can take on certain other CSS properties. Inline elements, for example, have no values for width or height. If you attempt to specify a width or height on them (using, for example, `width: 500px` or `height: 500px`), those rules will be ignored.

Because they have no concept of width or height, inline elements have no concept of CSS properties that are related to width and height. For example, the `overflow` property has little meaning for inline elements, because it is directly related to the width and height of an element.

Applying a top or bottom margin or top or bottom padding to an inline element will not alter its position in the document flow. The rule will be applied, but the margin or padding will be laid underneath the preceding content (in the case of a top margin or padding) or laid on top of proceeding content (in the case of bottom margin or padding). Left and right margins and padding will behave as expected.

Solution 7-2: Using CSS positioning

Another way to modify the default document flow is with positioning rules. CSS positioning allows you to position elements relative to some specific origin (their default position in the document flow, for example) or to the browser window.

What's involved

The CSS `position` property is used to specify the positioning origin of the element. By default, HTML elements are all `position: static`, which means they are positioned according to their actual place in the default flow. Statically positioned elements cannot have their `top`, `left`, `right`, and `bottom` properties modified.

> *Note: By default, all elements are statically positioned. However, if you apply a* `top`, `left`, `right`, *or* `bottom` *rule to an element without a position rule, the browser will automatically change its position property to* `relative`.

To modify the actual position of an element, you have to set its `position` property to one of `relative`, `absolute`, or `fixed`.

By specifying `position: relative` on an element, you tell the browser to position it relative to its default position in the document flow. You can now apply `left`, `top`, `right`, or `bottom` rules to the element and it will move out of its location as you specify. The rest of the content will not reflow, and the original location of the positioned element will remain open.

Absolute positioning, on the other hand, does affect the default flow. When an element is absolutely positioned, it is pulled out of the document flow, causing the remaining content to reflow and close up the "hole" where the positioned content was. Then, the content is positioned absolutely according to a coordinate origin, which is determined by the following rule:

The coordinate origin for a given absolutely positioned element is the upper left corner of the first parent element that has any position other than static. *If no such element is found, the upper left corner is that of the HTML element.*

In other words, the browser will look through the markup tree of the document to find the first parent element that has a non-static position rule and use that element's upper left corner as the coordinate origin. If the browser does not find a parent with a non-static position rule, it will default to the upper left corner of the HTML element.

How to build It

Positioning is easy to use. Consider the current example: it would be easy to move the h2 tags up 50 pixels from their current positions by applying a relative positioning rule:

```
h2 {
    position: relative;
    top: -50px;
}
```

The browser will move the tag as instructed, but it will not reflow the surrounding content. You can see the result in Figure 7-5.

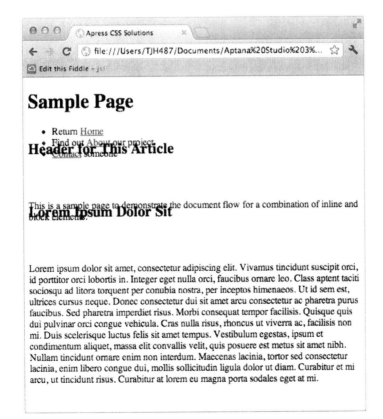

Figure 7-5. Relatively positioned elements.

The h2 tags are now displayed underneath the content above them.

Absolute positioning is similarly easy. Instead, you apply absolute positioning to the h2 elements:

```
h2 {
    position: absolute;
    top: 0px;
    left: 0px;
}
```

This will alter the layout so that the h2 elements are positioned at the coordinate origin. Because the h2 elements have no parents with a non-static position applied, the coordinate origin will be the upper left corner of the HTML element. (See Figure 7-6.)

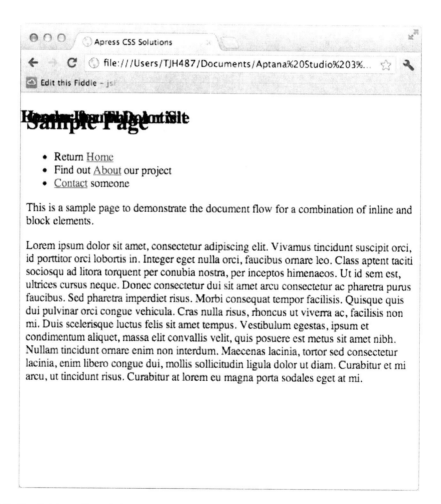

Figure 7-6. Absolutely positioned elements.

Note also how the rest of the content has reflowed so that the original position of the element has closed, unlike with relative positioning.

Instead, add a `position: relative` rule to a containing element:

```
article {
    position: relative;
}
h2 {
    position: absolute;
    top: 0px;
    left: 0px;
}
```

The layout will be altered to look like Figure 7-7.

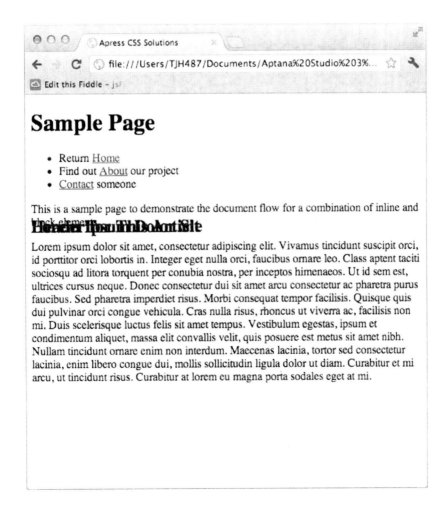

Figure 7-7. Absolutely positioned elements within a relatively positioned element.

Now the coordinate origin for the absolutely positioned element is the `article` element, which has the `position: relative` rule.

Expert tips

If you wish to make a containing element the absolute positioning coordinate origin for its child elements, all you have to do is apply a `position: relative` rule to it. You do not need to change its position. This allows you to position things relative to elements in the default flow, allowing for more flexibility in your layouts.

Solution 7-3: Floating elements with CSS

Floating elements are one of the most misunderstood features of CSS. They are also one of the most powerful, because through the use of floating content you can create flexible layouts that account for changes in content and viewport size.

What's involved

When you float an element, the browser modifies the default flow as follows.

First, the element is moved to the far left (for `float: left`) or right (for `float: right`) boundary of the containing element. Then the element is given a somewhat nonintuitive combination of both inline and block display properties:

- Unless otherwise specified using a `width` rule, the width of the floated element will collapse to be just as wide as the content requires. (Recall that, by default, block elements are as wide as their containing elements.)

- The browser then attempts to reflow the content that follows the floated element in such a way as to allow inline content to flow around the outside of the floated element, while still removing the floated element from the default document flow.

Floated elements were originally conceived for things like images and pull quotes floating within blocks of text, which explains their somewhat nonintuitive behavior.

How to build It

Floating content is easy, but the results are complex. To start, let's begin with some new markup:

```
<div class="float-left">Lorem ipsum dolor sit amet, consectetur adipiscing
elit. Sed adipiscing auctor porta.</div>
<div class="float-left">Lorem ipsum dolor sit amet, consectetur adipiscing
elit. Sed adipiscing auctor porta.</div>
<p>Lorem ipsum dolor sit amet, consectetur adipiscing elit. Sed adipiscing
auctor porta. In lobortis ligula vitae felis feugiat fringilla. Phasellus nunc
ipsum, mattis ut tempus ut, aliquet et velit. Cras condimentum augue at felis
dignissim pellentesque. Donec egestas, odio eget ornare eleifend, nulla erat
laoreet nulla, et sollicitudin leo nisi at tellus. Sed pharetra lobortis lorem
a venenatis. Fusce condimentum ultricies enim placerat ultrices. Suspendisse
lacus justo, aliquet non accumsan vitae, porta non tellus. In blandit dictum
sapien, a consectetur nisl aliquam ut. Pellentesque ullamcorper vestibulum
nulla, at accumsan sem scelerisque varius. </p>
```

```
<div class="float-right">Lorem ipsum dolor sit amet, consectetur adipiscing
elit. Sed adipiscing auctor porta.</div>
<p>Lorem ipsum dolor sit amet, consectetur adipiscing elit. Sed adipiscing
auctor porta. In lobortis ligula vitae felis feugiat fringilla. Phasellus nunc
ipsum, mattis ut tempus ut, aliquet et velit. Cras condimentum augue at felis
dignissim pellentesque. Donec egestas, odio eget ornare eleifend, nulla erat
laoreet nulla, et sollicitudin leo nisi at tellus. Sed pharetra lobortis lorem
a venenatis. Fusce condimentum ultricies enim placerat ultrices. Suspendisse
lacus justo, aliquet non accumsan vitae, porta non tellus. In blandit dictum
sapien, a consectetur nisl aliquam ut. Pellentesque ullamcorper vestibulum
nulla, at accumsan sem scelerisque varius. </p>
```

This markup renders a predictable default flow, as shown in Figure 7-8.

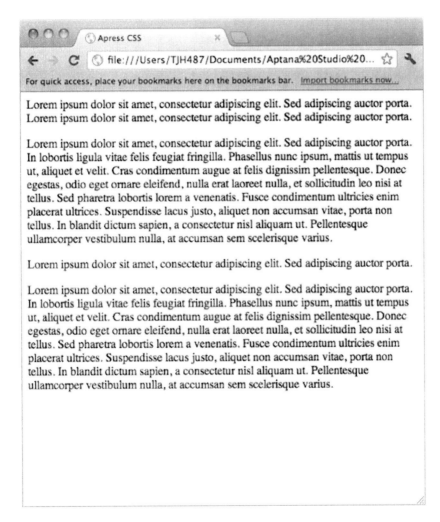

Figure 7-8. Rendering of example markup.

Now, you apply a float rule to the float-left and float-right classes:

```
.float-left,
.float-right {
   background-color: blue;
}
.float-left {
   float: left;
}
.float-right {
   float: right;
}
```

We also applied some coloring to make the floated elements a little more obvious. This layout renders as shown in Figure 7-9.

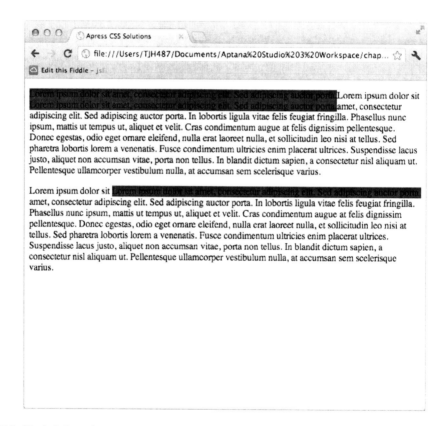

Figure 7-9. Floated elements.

The floated elements now are altering the flow as expected. However, they are stretched to be as wide as their content. If you give the floated elements a width, you can further alter the flow:

```
.float-left,
.float-right {
```

```
    background-color: blue;
    width: 100px;
}
.float-left {
    float: left;
}
.float-right {
    float: right;
}
```

Now the content will reflow as shown in Figure 7-10.

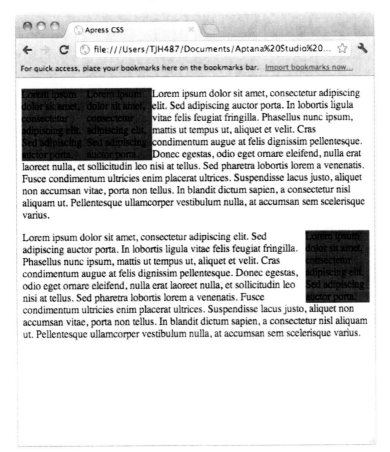

Figure 7-10. Floated elements with widths.

The content that follows the float has reflowed around the floated element, while the floated element itself has been removed from the document flow. Adding some coloring and margins will help make this more obvious, and give you full insight into how the floats are behaving:

```
body {
    background-color: #ccc;
}
```

```
p {
    background-color: #fff;
}
.float-left,
.float-right {
    background-color: blue;
    width: 100px;
    margin: 10px;
}
.float-left {
    float: left;
}
.float-right {
    float: right;
}
```

Now the page renders as shown in Figure 7-11.

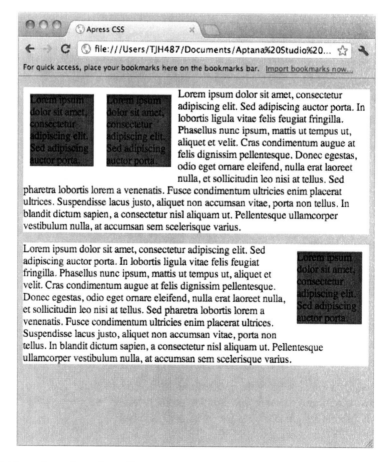

Figure 7-11. Adding color and margins to illustrate floats.

You can see that the blue boxes of the floated elements are actually being laid out inside of the white boxes of the unfloated elements that follow them, with the content of the unfloated elements flowing around them. This is a key behavior to remember with floating content.

Expert tips

Floated elements are great for producing layouts that flex according to the browser viewport width. They are also an important part of laying out pages in columns, where their flexible nature provides for flowing variably-sized content better than absolutely positioned layouts.

Solution 7-4: Clearing floats

CSS also provides a feature for modifying the default behavior of floats with the `clear` rule. The concept behind clearing floats is to specify what content can flow around the floated element and what content should not.

What's involved

The `clear` rule can take values similar to float: `inherit`, `left`, and `right` as well as `both` and `none`.

By applying a `clear` rule to an element, you tell the browser to lay that element out clear of any preceding element that has a matching float. Because the default document flow is from top to bottom, applying a `clear` rule to an element causes it to lay out underneath the floated elements. For example, `clear: left` causes an element to lay out clear from any previous element with a `float: left`. A `clear: right` rule causes the element to lay out clear from any preceding element that had a `float: right` rule applied to it.

How to build It

Now you add a `clear: right` rule to the CSS used in the previous example and apply it to the very last paragraph:

```css
body {
    background-color: #ccc;
}
p {
    background-color: #fff;
}
.float-left,
.float-right {
    background-color: blue;
    width: 100px;
    margin: 10px;
}
.float-left {
    float: left;
}
```

```
.float-right {
    float: right;
}
.clear-right {
    clear: right;
}
<div class="float-left">Lorem ipsum dolor sit amet, consectetur adipiscing
elit. Sed adipiscing auctor porta.</div>
<div class="float-left">Lorem ipsum dolor sit amet, consectetur adipiscing
elit. Sed adipiscing auctor porta.</div>
<p>Lorem ipsum dolor sit amet, consectetur adipiscing elit. Sed adipiscing
auctor porta. In lobortis ligula vitae felis feugiat fringilla. Phasellus nunc
ipsum, mattis ut tempus ut, aliquet et velit. Cras condimentum augue at felis
dignissim pellentesque. Donec egestas, odio eget ornare eleifend, nulla erat
laoreet nulla, et sollicitudin leo nisi at tellus. Sed pharetra lobortis lorem
a venenatis. Fusce condimentum ultricies enim placerat ultrices. Suspendisse
lacus justo, aliquet non accumsan vitae, porta non tellus. In blandit dictum
sapien, a consectetur nisl aliquam ut. Pellentesque ullamcorper vestibulum
nulla, at accumsan sem scelerisque varius. </p>
<div class="float-right">Lorem ipsum dolor sit amet, consectetur adipiscing
elit. Sed adipiscing auctor porta.</div>
<p class="clear-right">Lorem ipsum dolor sit amet, consectetur adipiscing
elit. Sed adipiscing auctor porta. In lobortis ligula vitae felis feugiat
fringilla. Phasellus nunc ipsum, mattis ut tempus ut, aliquet et velit. Cras
condimentum augue at felis dignissim pellentesque. Donec egestas, odio eget
ornare eleifend, nulla erat laoreet nulla, et sollicitudin leo nisi at tellus.
Sed pharetra lobortis lorem a venenatis. Fusce condimentum ultricies enim
placerat ultrices. Suspendisse lacus justo, aliquet non accumsan vitae, porta
non tellus. In blandit dictum sapien, a consectetur nisl aliquam ut.
Pellentesque ullamcorper vestibulum nulla, at accumsan sem scelerisque varius.
</p>
```

This causes that last paragraph to lay out clear of the preceding right-floated elements that might otherwise affect it, as shown in Figure 7-12.

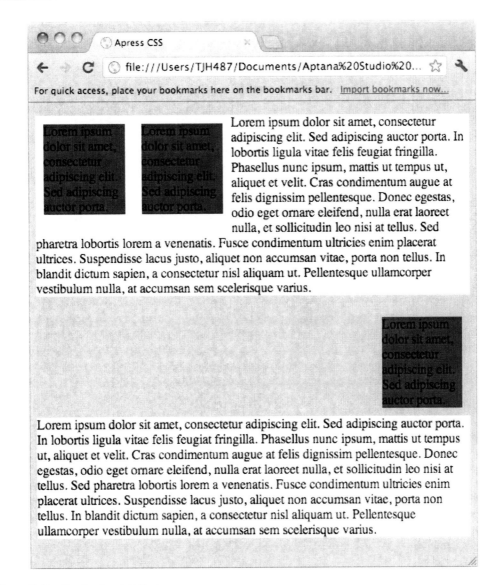

Figure 7-12. Clearing the right float.

Similarly, applying a `clear: left` rule to the first paragraph causes it to lay out clear of both of the floated elements that precede it, as you can see in Figure 7-13.

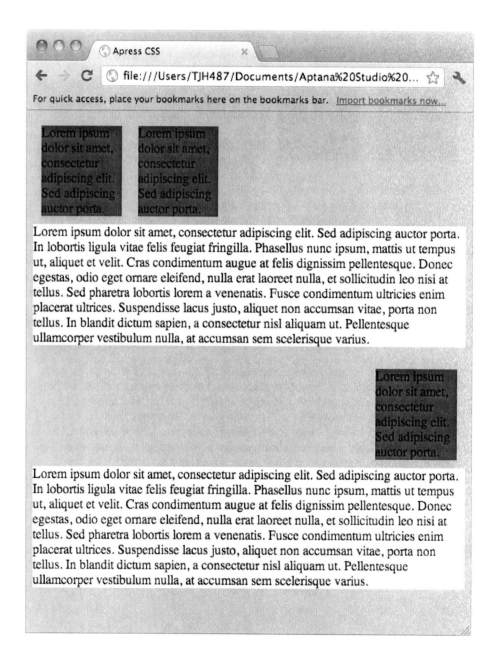

Figure 7-13. Clearing all floats.

With a bit of practice, you can use floats and clears, along with positioning and display properties, to create any design in the browser.

Expert tips

When you float an element, the default flow reflows as if the element has been absolutely positioned and the space it would have taken up in the layout closes. This can cause containing elements to collapse and create confusing results.

To illustrate this, consider the first example in the chapter:

```
<header>
    <h1>Sample Page</h1>
    <nav>
        <ul>
            <li>Return <a href="#">Home</a></li>
            <li>Find out <a href="#">About</a> our project</li>
            <li><a href="#">Contact</a> someone</li>
        </ul>
    </nav>
</header>

<article>
    <h2>Header for This Article</h2>
    <p>This is a sample page to demonstrate the document flow for a
combination of inline and block elements.</p>
    <h2>Lorem Ipsum Dolor Sit</h2>
    <p>Lorem ipsum dolor sit amet, consectetur adipiscing elit. Vivamus
<span>tincidunt suscipit orci,</span> id porttitor orci lobortis in.
<span>Integer eget nulla orci, faucibus ornare leo.</span> <span>Class aptent
taciti sociosqu ad litora torquent per conubia nostra, per inceptos
himenaeos.</span> Ut id sem est, ultrices cursus neque. <span>Donec
consectetur dui sit amet arcu consectetur ac pharetra purus faucibus.</span>
Sed pharetra imperdiet risus. Morbi consequat tempor facilisis. Quisque quis
dui pulvinar orci congue vehicula. Cras nulla risus, rhoncus ut viverra ac,
facilisis non mi. Duis scelerisque luctus felis sit amet tempus. Vestibulum
egestas, ipsum et condimentum aliquet, massa elit convallis velit, quis
posuere est metus sit amet nibh. Nullam tincidunt ornare enim non interdum.
Maecenas lacinia, tortor sed consectetur lacinia, enim libero congue dui,
mollis sollicitudin ligula dolor ut diam. Curabitur et mi arcu, ut tincidunt
risus. Curabitur at lorem eu magna porta sodales eget at mi. </p>
</article>
```

If you apply a background color to the nav element, it renders as shown in Figure 7-14.

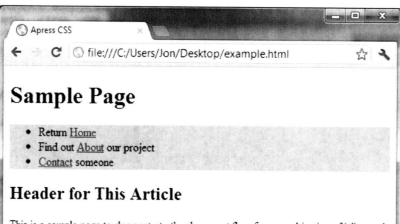

Figure 7-14. Navigation background.

Now float the unordered list within the nav element:

```
nav {
    background-color: #ccc;
}
nav ul {
    float: right;
}
```

The nav element will now collapse, and all of the content will rise up and reflow around the floating list, as shown in Figure 7-15.

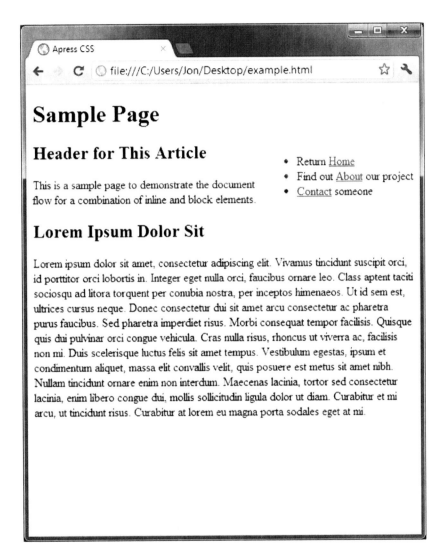

Figure 7-15. Collapsing the nav container.

If you want to maintain the integrity of the navigation container, you can easily apply a small bit of extra markup to clear the float after the floated list. First add a `clear` rule to the CSS:

```
.clear {
    clear: both;
}
```

And then add a bit of extra markup after the list to apply it:

```
<header>
    <h1>Sample Page</h1>
    <nav>
        <ul>
            <li>Return <a href="#">Home</a></li>
            <li>Find out <a href="#">About</a> our project</li>
            <li><a href="#">Contact</a> someone</li>
        </ul>
        <div class="clear"></div>
    </nav>
</header>
```

Now the page renders the way you expect it to, as you can see in Figure 7-16.

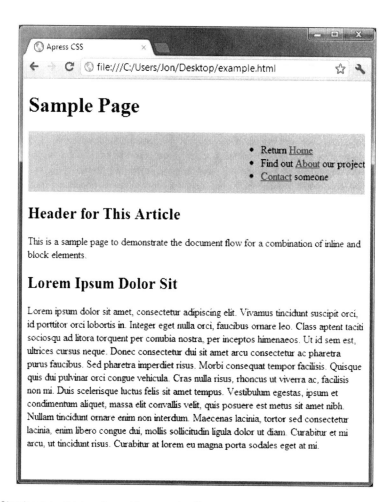

Figure 7-16. Clearing a containing element to prevent collapse.

It's common to need to prevent a containing element from collapsing when all of its child elements are floating, and this is one of the more common solutions. Another solution involves modifying the overflow property of the containing element but has cross-browser issues and requires extra CSS to account for them.

Solution 7-5: Using a CSS reset

The ultimate goal of many projects is to produce a layout that renders exactly the same in all target browsers. This can be a real challenge if some of the target browsers are particularly old, because older browsers have bugs in their CSS implementations that can cause them to behave incorrectly. Many of these problems are easily fixed with various techniques, and it is beyond the scope of this chapter to cover them.

There is, however, one big secret to cross-browser layouts: managing the default browser style sheet.

What's involved

Every browser has a default set of styles that it applies to many elements. These styles specify font size, margins, and padding for elements, and every browser manufacturer applies different values. The differences aren't radical, but they are enough to throw off pixel perfection, especially in tight layouts with floated elements.

For example, consider our original example of basic markup. That example renders slightly differently in Chrome, Firefox, and Internet Explorer. It's most easy to see with all of the windows stacked on top of each other, as shown in 7-17.

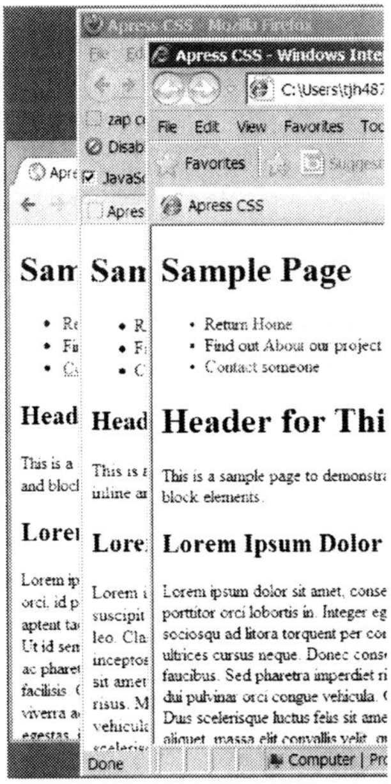

Figure 7-17. Illustrating the subtle rendering differences between browsers.

As you can see, the sizes of the bullets in the list are different, the margins are different on many elements, and the font sizes are slightly different. These variations are subtle, but in a tight layout that employs floated elements you could easily have problems with some elements falling out of alignment in one browser but not others, creating a nightmare of browser-dependent bugs to fix.

How to build It

The most common and effective technique for dealing with these style variations is to zero them out in your CSS. In our example, we could add the following CSS:

```
h1, h2, p, body, ul {
    margin: 0px;
    padding: 0px;
    line-height: 1em;
    font-size: 1em;
}
```

Then the renderings are almost exactly the same in all browsers, as you can see in Figure 7-18.

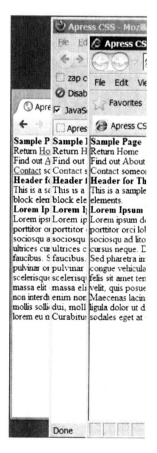

Figure 7-18. The effects of a basic CSS reset.

Now, everything is exactly the same in all three browsers. This technique is called a *CSS reset*. By resetting all the browsers' default CSS to be the same, you start with a truly blank canvas. You can then set font sizes, margins, and paddings to suit your needs and be assured that they will behave the same in all browsers. This technique is great for eliminating browser-dependent layout problems.

Expert tips

One of the most commonly used CSS resets is Eric Meyer's CSS Reset, available at http://meyerweb.com/eric/tools/css/reset/. Eric Meyer's CSS Reset takes into account HTML 5 tags in older browsers as well.

Most CSS resets set all font sizes, margins, and paddings to be the same, and sometimes this is too much. Eric Meyer's reset, for example, makes all h header tags (h1, h2, h3, and so on) have the same font size. If you want to keep different font sizes but have them be consistent across all browsers, you can normalize your CSS instead of completely resetting it. The Normalize CSS project provides a complete solution for CSS normalization and is available at http://necolas.github.com/normalize.css/.

Regardless of which solution you choose, resetting or normalizing your CSS is an important step in creating layouts that render consistently across browsers and will take care of most of the cross-browser problems you encounter.

Summary

The key to CSS layouts is to understand the document flow, which is how browsers will lay out content by default.

The document flow can be modified with `display`, `position`, and `float`, and `clear` rules. Combining these techniques gives you all the power needed to produce complex, flexible layouts.

All browsers have default styles applied to elements, and each browser manufacturer's default styles are different. Applying a CSS reset or normalization helps level the playing field, providing a blank canvas to work with.

A successful CSS layout takes into account the screen size of the devices that will be used to access it. In the next chapter, "Multidevice Development," we will discuss various techniques for deploying your CSS layouts on different devices.

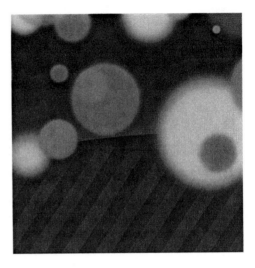

Chapter 8

Multidevice Development

Not long ago, developing web content essentially meant creating content that would be viewed on regular computer screens (desktops or laptops) and possibly on small mobile screens with limited graphics capacity. As a web designer, you more or less had to come up with a single fixed layout that displayed equally well on a range of desktop screen sizes and a limited mobile version (for a limited audience). Nowadays, with the advent of advanced mobile devices and increased connectivity, the web experience is undergoing a widespread transformation.

Users will access your content on smartphones, digital tablets, or even their TVs, not only on their desktops or laptop computers. In fact, some studies show that, in the near future, mobile devices are likely to take over the web experience and become the primary source of web browsing. This means there are a lot of new devices and configurations developers have to take into consideration. Each device can have several screen sizes, from a small mobile screen to a large digital desktop one, as well as different resolutions. Also, on mobile devices, users have the option to rotate the screen, changing from a portrait view to a landscape one. In parallel, the user interaction has been evolving as well, and you have to consider touch screens, both on desktop and mobile devices.

The content you want to deliver has to adjust to a wide range of new factors to offer users a satisfying experience, and one that's the same no matter how they access that content. And there are quite a few challenges here for web developers. Fortunately, CSS level 3 (CSS3) brings along a couple of new rules and features that will prove extremely useful to you in facing this new world of greatly varying devices. In particular, it offers media queries, which you can use to determine a user's media type to best display content for that device.

In this chapter, you will see how to adapt your HTML content for multiples screens and devices, and how to handle some of those major challenges by using CSS3, and without relying on any external script. Using this approach, you give your content valuable independence and universality among browsers and devices.

Solution 8-1: Defining different style sheets to target different devices with media queries

An important aspect of style sheets is that they let you define how your content will be displayed on different media. Since CSS2.1, using the media attribute, you have been able to target several media types and provide specific style sheets so that your document displays properly on a screen, on paper, on a projector, or on TV. It's already a common and good practice to enable different style sheets depending on which media type is targeted. Since CSS3, the use of the media types has been extended and you can target them in a more precise way, providing specific style sheets for more specific situations and device output. In this solution, you will see the basic syntax of the media queries and learn how to use them on all major browsers.

What's involved

Serving different styles for different media types is not new to CSS3. Ever since CSS2.1, you could target several media types and specify how documents are presented in the media types listed in Table 8-1.

Table 8-1. Various media types in CSS2.1

Media Type	Description
screen	For color computer screens
print	For printed material
aural/speech	For speech synthesizers
braille	For Braille tactile feedback devices
embossed	For paged Braille printers
projection	For projected presentations
tty	For teletypes, terminals, and other devices with limited display capabilities
tv	For televisions and television-like devices
all	For all the media types listed above
handheld	Intended for handheld devices (typically, devices with small screens and limited bandwidth)

You can target different media types in two ways:

- Use the @media or @import rules within the style sheet itself as follows:

```
@import url("screenStyles.css") screen;

@media print {

    /* style sheet for print goes here */

}
```

- Or you can accomplish the same result within the web document by using the <link> tag, specifying the target media of an external style sheet:

```
<link href="style.css" rel="stylesheet" type="text/css" media="screen">
```

> Tip: If not otherwise specified, all major browsers use the screen media as their default type and will apply it when viewing a web page.

The screen media type: From desktop to mobile screens

At the time of the elaboration of the CSS2.1 specifications, the screen media type was meant for desktops and laptop computers and the media type used to target mobile devices was the handled type and was, as stated by the W3C specification, *"intended for handheld devices (typically small screen with a limited bandwidth)"*.

To define different styles for each of those types of devices, desktops, and mobile devices, you just attach different style sheets like this:

```
<link rel="stylesheet" type="text/css" media="screen" href="style.css">

<link rel="stylesheet" type="text/css" media="handheld" href="mobile.css">
```

Or, if you want to attach just a single style sheet, you do so as follows:

```
@media screen {

 /* rules specific for screen devices */
}

@media handheld {

    /* rules specific for handled devices */

}
```

The situation has evolved a lot in the last four years, especially since the first iPhone came on the market in 2007 and with the ensuing appearance of various smartphones. The screen media type now targets many more devices:

- **Computers.** This includes desktops, laptops, and netbooks. They use all the major browsers you're already familiar with, and there's nothing new beyond what you're used to.

- **Mobile devices.** This category includes smartphones and digital tablets. They don't recognize the older handled media type. They run on a mobile operating system (such as the ones listed in Table 8-3), and the mobile browser is usually embedded. (The iPhone, for instance, comes with

179

Safari Mobile.) Even if users have the option to install a multiplatform browser (like Opera Mini or Fennec, the Firefox mobile browser), most of them will just rely on the preinstalled browser and will hardly change their default configuration. The browser installed can differ even on similar devices. For instance, Android has a native browser, but it isn't necessarily the default one on all mobile devices running Android. It's beyond the scope of this book to go deeply into the evolution of mobile devices, but you can get a better idea of what the mobile landscape looks like in Figure 8-1, which shows the statistics for mobile browsers from February 2011 through February 2012)

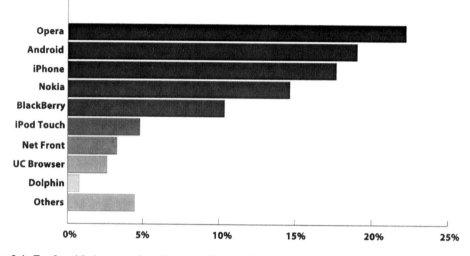

Figure 8-1. Top 9 mobile browsers from February 2011 to February 2012 (data taken from statcounter.com).

Today, a style sheet targeting the screen media type is now applied similarly, for instance, on an iPhone with a screen width of 320 pixels, a desktop with a screen width of 1368 pixels, and a Galaxy Tab tablet 8.9 with a screen width of 800 pixels (when in portrait orientation). Obviously, the old days of one fixed layout are gone, and you can't have the same content fitting equally on such a wide range of screens with a single set of style rules. So how can you adapt your web content to display on all those screen media types?

One of the great features of CSS3 is that it introduces media queries that you can use to add selective parameters to the media attribute, and thus specify more precise conditions on the media that's being targeted, such as its resolution, orientation, and its display screen size. With these parameters, you can now serve different style sheets with those specified values, without relying on any client or server script.

The syntax of media queries

A media query is a Boolean logical expression (either true or false) used in conjunction with one of the media types. It tests one feature or more of the output device and, if the expression is true, applies the subsequent specified style rules.

Table 8-2 describes the features that can be tested when you use media queries.

Table 8-2. Fea tures of the output device that can be tested in CSS3 using media queries

Feature	Description	Value	Min/Max Prefixes
width	Width of the display area of the output device	Integer expressing pixels, cm or em depending on the media type (for example, width:300px).	Yes
height	Height of the display area of the output device	Integer.	Yes
device-height	Height of the rendering surface of the output device	Integer.	Yes
device-width	Width of the rendering surface of the output device	Integer.	Yes
orientation	Orientation of the output device	Portrait or landscape.	No
aspect-ratio	Ratio of the width to the height	Integer/integer (for example, 16/9).	Yes
device-aspect-ratio	Ratio of the device width to the device height	Integer/integer (ex:16/9).	Yes
color	The number of bits per color component of the output device	Integer. If there's no color, the value is 0.	No
color-index	Number of entries in the color lookup table of the output device	Integer.	No
monochrome	Number of bits per pixel in a monochrome frame buffer	Integer.	No
resolution	Density of pixels of the output device	Integer value in dots per inch (dpi)—for example, resolution: 300dpi).	Yes
scan	Scanning process of TV output devices	Progressive or interlace.	No
grid	Query whether the output device is grid or bitmap	0 for grid; 1 for bitmap.	No

You should use the following syntax structure for a media query:

```
@media media type and (criteria targeted) {
    rules that will apply only to the devices fitting those criteria
}
```

Or, if you decide to have a separate style sheet for each query, use the following syntax:

```
<linkrel="stylesheet" type="text/css" media="media type and (criteria
targeted)" href="specific_stylesheet.css" />
```

> *Caution: If you decide to use different external style sheets depending on your media queries, keep in mind that browsers, including mobile ones, will load all the style sheets whether they're needed or not for the current output device and scenario. In terms of performance and to limit the number of HTTP requests, it's usually better to have all your styles and media queries in a single style sheet. On the other hand, for certain situations such as for larger websites with significant content and content types, this might cause you to end up with an extremely huge stylesheet that will be heavy and difficult to maintain. Depending on your particular project, you can choose what is the most suitable approach.*

Furthermore, you can target some devices more precisely by adding specific conditions with the use of the following logical operators: and, not, and only. You can also achieve functionality that's equal to theOR logical operator by separating all the conditions with a comma (and if one condition is met, the subsequent style rule or rules will be applied).

To refine your queries further, you also have the option of adding min- or max- prefixes to express "greater or equal to" and "smaller or equal to" constraints for some features. (Refer to Table 8-2 to see which features allow the use of those prefixes.)

For a more concrete example of how queries are constructed, let's look at a few queries that use the different operators and prefixes (although some of those that follow don't make practical sense for a project and are presented for the sake of demonstration):

- Media query with the logical operator and:

```
@media only screen and (device-width:900px) {
    rules to be applied
}
```

This code example targets screen devices only, with an exact device width of 900 pixels.

> *Note: Older browsers ignore the.* only *keyword and won't read this kind of query.*

- Media query with the logical operators and and not:

```
@media screen and (not device-width:900px) {
    /* rules to be applied */
}
```

This code example targets any screen for which the exact device width is not 900 pixels.

- Media query with the equivalent of the OR operator:

```
@media projector and (color), screen and (color) {
    /* rules to be applied */
}
```

This code example targets a projector or a screen that has color capabilities.

- Media query with the and operator, the `min-` prefix, and the equivalent of the OR operator:

```
@media screen and (min-width:900px), print, tv {
  /* rules to be applied */
}
```

This code example targets the screen media type for a screen with a minimum display width of 900 pixels, and/or print devices (setting style rules for a printed version of your web content), and/or TV.

In the preceding examples, the media queries are written as they would appear inside a single style sheet. However, if you prefer to have an external style sheet associated with a media query, the syntax is as follows:

```
<linkrel="stylesheet" type="text/css" media=" screen and (width:900px), print,
tv { rules to be applied " href="specific_stylesheet.css" />
```

This style sheet targets the screen media type for a screen with a minimum display width of 900 pixels, and/or paper (on a printer), and/or TV.

Browser support of media queries

Media queries are supported by all the browsers shown in Table 8-3.

Table 8-3. Browser support for media queries

Internet Explorer	Firefox	Chrome	Safari	Opera	iOS Safari	Opera mini	Opera Mobile	Android
9+	5.0+	12.0+	4.0+	10.6+	3.2+	5.0+	11.5+	2.3+

As you can see, the support is pretty good with modern browsers, especially with mobile browsers. The main exceptions are Internet Explorer versions prior to 9. Unsupported browsers will just ignore the rules included within media queries. IEMobile, the browser present on Windows phones, prior to version 9 (which is based on the rendering engine of Internet Explorer 9) won't support media queries either. To address this issue, you can simply define regular style rules that will apply to all browsers, so that user devices with a noncompliant browser will display your content using those rules and you can still use media queries for supporting browsers. Because the support for media queries is very good on mobile browsers, you will then be able to target most devices.

Another way is to define a specific style sheet for the Internet Explorer versions that don't support media queries (specifically, versions 6 through 8) and IEMobile by using a conditional comment as follows:

```
<!--[if lt IE 9 & !IEMobile]>
 <link href="stylesForIE.css" rel="stylesheet" type="text/css">
<![endif]-->
```

Older mobile phones won't support media queries either, and you can still target them with the handled media type as before:

```
<link href="older_devices.css" rel="stylesheet" type="text/css" media="handled">
```

How it works

To see the preceding strategies in action, let's create a simple HTML document and attach style sheets destined for devices with three different screen sizes—mobile devices, tablets, and desktops—as well as printing devices and older mobile phones.

1. Create a basic HTML document with a header and some simple content. (See the file solution_8_1. html in the download pack for this chapter.)

```
<!DOCTYPE HTML>
<html>
<head>
 <meta charset="utf-8">
 <title>Solution 8-1</title>
</head>
<body>
 <header><h1>CSS3 Media Queries</h1></header>
 <section></section>
 <footer></footer>
</body>
</html>
```

2. Add the link to the general style sheet meant for every device:

```
<link href="css/style.css" rel="stylesheet" type="text/css" />
```

This style sheet contains the style rules you want to apply regardless of the device output.

3. Set the different style rules for the various screen sizes using media queries:

```
<!-- Smartphones -->
<link href="css/phone_style.css" rel="stylesheet" type="text/css"
media="only screen and (max-device-width:320px)" />

<!-- Tablets -->
<link href="css/tablet_styles.css" rel="stylesheet" type="text/css"
media="only screen and (min-device-width:321px) and (max-device-width:768px)" />

<!-- Desktops -->
<link href="css/style.css" rel="stylesheet" type="text/css"
media="only screen and (min-width:769px)" />
```

Here you have a style sheet specifically targeting smartphones, another one for digital tablets, and one for desktops (and laptops).

4. Internet Explorer versions 6 through 8 will ignore any media queries and skip the related style rules. So you need to create a style sheet for them using a conditional statement:

```
<!--[if lt IE 9>
 <link href="stylesForIE.css" rel="stylesheet" type="text/css">
<![endif]-->
```

5. Now add a style sheet for older mobile models as well, by using the `handled` media type:

```
<!-Older mobile phones -->
<link href="css/old_mobiles.css" rel="stylesheet"
type="text/css" media="handled" />
```

5. Finally, add the link to the style sheet destined for the `print` media type:

```
<!-- Print -->
<link href="css/printer_style.css" rel="stylesheet"
type="text/css" media="print" />
```

You have now provided specific style sheets for a wide range of devices by using the different media types as well as media queries.

In this example, you loaded different style sheets. You also could just load a single style sheet for the `screen` media type and add the same media queries in it.

Expert tips

If you want to reap the benefits of media queries on Internet Explorer versions 6 through 8, you can rely on a third-party script to do so. One example is Respond, a great script released by Scott Jehl, a designer who leads the design team at JQuery. It's straightforward to use and provides almost native behaviors of media queries to unsupported browsers. You can download it and find its documentation here: `https:// github.com/scottjehl/Respond`.

To use Respond, write your CSS rules using media queries as you usually would, but use the `min-width/max-width` features to target different screen sizes:

```
@media screen and (min-width: 320px){
}
```

Then reference the `respond.min.js` script after all of your CSS:

```
<script type="text/javascript" src="respond.min.js"></script>
```

And that's it! Your media queries will now be taken into consideration by Internet Explorer versions 6 through 8.

Solution 8-2: Adapting a layout for different screen sizes with CSS3

Nowadays, any web content you develop has to be made available for mobile devices as well as desktops and laptops. To achieve this, there are several options available to developers. One approach, which is commonly used, is to detect the device (by using server or client scripts) and redirect users to a version of the site for mobile browsers when necessary. Without detailing the maintenance difficulty and SEO (Search Engine Optimization) problems you might encounter with this approach, it was an acceptable option when mobile devices were not very different from one another. But today, new devices with new screen sizes and new configurations are developed at an incredibly fast pace. Moreover, when you talk about mobile devices, you are not only talking about smartphones anymore, but digital tablets as well.

As of this writing, several new models with different sizes and resolutions are coming out every few months, and nobody knows for sure what the next popular models will be. As a developer, creating custom content for each available device would be both impossible and unproductive. Another way you had at your disposal was to detect the screen size with the use of JavaScript and to call different styles rules, or style sheets, accordingly. CSS3 and its new media queries now let you achieve this directly without having to rely on any script. In this solution, you will see how you can adapt your web content for several screen devices by using media queries.

What's involved

When designing and developing web content adapted to multiple screen sizes, you have to consider several things from a design and visual point of view, as well as considering layout restrictions and possibilities. Let's see what is involved.

Responsive design

The concept of responsive design recognizes the increased need for web content to be available for multiple devices. It is, in fact, a whole new approach to conceiving web content, more than a sole group of web development techniques. Its objective is to create a single design that can adapt its content to any kind of display resolution and device. (You can see an example of a site with a responsive design in Figure 8-2.) It requires thinking in terms of an adaptive and flexible layout, the appropriate typography, the handling of images, and so on. The concept also takes into consideration the page weight and optimal performance for any device. It requires developers to rethink the way they conceive their designs in the first place to achieve this increased level of flexibility.

Responsive design achieves this goal by using a couple of techniques and tools, including the new CSS3 media queries, to change the layout of a web document according to CSS rules based on the width of the browser or device.

If you want to see great examples of websites using responsive design, you can visit `http://mediaqueri.es/` which presents a collection of websites using media queries and responsive web design. It is regularly updated with new examples, and it can be a great source of inspiration if you're new to the concept.

Figure 8-2. Example of a website using responsive design, from www.mediaqueri.es.

Responsive design and its principles are a vast subject that goes beyond CSS3 alone. If you want to go more deeply into the topic, we encourage you to read Ethan Marcott's book *Responsive Web Design* (A Book Apart, 2011). You will also find plenty of resources about it on the Web when reading about the evolution of browsers and devices. One good place to start with is the blog "A List Apart" at www.alistapart.com.

Let's take a look at how you can use CSS3 media queries to build multiple layouts using the same HTML document by selectively serving style sheets based on the user's screen device, and thus having a responsive design.

The device size and the viewport

The first obvious difference between various devices that designers have to deal with when targeting several devices is the screen size. As you saw in the previous solution, you can use media queries to serve different style sheets based on the features and conditions you choose. Among those features, you can use the following ones to target different device sizes:

- width. The width of the targeted display area of the output device

- device-width. The width of the rendering surface of the output device (the physical screen size in its current orientation or its page width on paper)

- height. The height of the targeted display area of the output device

- device-height. The height of the rendering surface of the output device (the physical screen size or page width on paper)

All of these features accept the use of the min- and max- prefixes for refining the query further.

Here you have to clearly distinguish between those features and what they imply, which at first can be a bit confusing.

The width feature of media queries detects the display width, which corresponds to the viewport width. (The *viewport* is the area in which the web content is actually displayed.) The device-width feature, on the other hand, detects the rendered width (which will be the actual width of the device screen).

More concretely, on a computer screen, thewidth feature is the width of the browser window and the device-width is the width of the device's screen (and they will often be different because you can't expect everybody to open their browser in full screen, especially on big screens). On mobile devices, you would expect it to be the same—and moreover to be of the same value—because you can't resize the browser window. But that's not the case. On most of mobile devices, the viewport, by default, will be larger than the actual device size. Take, for instance, the iPhone 3GS: its screen's width is 320 pixels, whereas the default viewport width of its browser is 980 pixels. (See Figure 8-3.)

This means that a web document will be displayed on a viewport of 980 pixels and then rendered on a screen of 320 pixels. (For the time being, just assume we're talking about portrait mode; to see how you deal with orientation, refer to Solution 8-3.) So in order to fit in the content needs to be rescaled.

That goes for all mobile browsers. Table 8-4 lists the major mobile browsers and their respective viewport size.

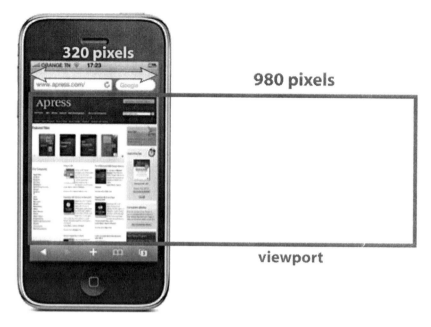

Figure 8-3. The device width and default viewport width on the iPhone 3GS.

The reason for this difference in values and this virtual viewport is that there are a lot of websites (probably a majority of them as of the writing of this book) that are not adapted for smartphones or tablets at all and were designed for computer screens. This larger viewport size lets them fit on small screens. But the obvious inconvenience is that the content is rescaled down, displaying as tiny content on the screen that's difficult to read, not to speak of the poor touch interactivity that results from this.

Table 8-4. Major mobile browsers and their default viewport size

Mobile Browser	Viewport Size
iPhone/iPod Touch Safari	980 pixels
iPad Safari	980 pixels
Android browser	800 pixels
Internet Explorer mobile browser	320 pixels
Opera Mobile	850 pixels
Windows 7 mobile browser	1024 pixels

To avoid this situation, you have to change the viewport size to make it fit the device width. This can be achieved easily through the `viewport` meta tag in your HTML document and its `content`attribute, as follows:

```
<meta name="viewport" content="width=content-width" />
```

By adding this tag in the head of your HTML document, the viewport size will be the same as the rendering size, on any device. If you load a page on a smartphone's browser with this change of viewport size, the content will be displayed with a normal size and won't be shrunk anymore.

> Note: This is the only solution as of the writing of this book, but it might change soon as a @viewport rule is now being defined by the World Wide Web Consortium (W3C) CSS Device Adaptation specification. (This specification is still in a draft stage as we write these lines.) The new specification should allow you to set the viewport to fit the width of the device within your style sheet itself.

With the viewport size correctly set, you can now apply different style rules according to the width of the display area:

```
@media screen and (min-device-width:1025px){
  */
      set of style rules to be applied for desktop and laptops
  /*
}
@media screen and (min-device-width:320px) {
  */
      set of style rules to be applied for smartphones
  /*
}
@media screen and (min-device-width:600px){
  */
      set of style rules to be applied for tablets
  /*
}
```

Here you are defining three main groups of devices: desktops and laptops, tablets, and smartphones. You can refine the categories further, of course, depending on your design and project.

> Tip: The viewport size is equal to the browser's size. So when it comes to computer screens, you might want to use the. width feature instead of device-width when you target large desktop screens, because you can't assume that users will use their browsers in full screen all the time, especially if they have a wide desktop screen.

Some design and styles considerations

Even if detecting different screen sizes and applying different style rules accordingly is in fact straightforward when you use of media queries, you still need to consider different aspects of this approach to create a flexible layout that is suited to any device. Media queries alone will not solve everything. Here are some important points to consider when you write your style sheets for different devices:

- Your HTML document has to be correctly structured. The more well-constructed your document is semantically, the better its visual flexibility will be with CSS. This seems like an obvious statement, but it is an important point to keep in mind to be able to easily apply different views to the same content. Validating your document with the Markup Validation Service provided by the W3C (`http://validator.w3.org/` and `http://html5.validator.nu/` for HTML5 documents) to ensure its markup is well formed is a recommended good practice.

- When applying different style sheets, an easy way to manage layouts is to choose whether or not to display some elements depending on the device targeted. You can do this by playing with the `display` attribute and its `none` property. However, you have to be very careful with that because an element that is not displayed is still loaded with the page, as along with all the assets it may contain. Therefore, the strategy of designing web content for the maximum size and then choosing just not to display the elements that won't suit some devices can prove to be very bad in terms of performance on small devices. Here, again, the best approach is to design for multiple devices at the time of conception, if possible.

- The mobile web experience and desktop web experience are radically different. You will prefer to use a single-column layout for smartphone devices and avoid floating elements on small screens. This can be easily achieved by playing with the `float` property depending on your media queries. You also have to take great care of the navigation functions and make them suitable to a mobile user experience when you define your style rules for small mobile devices.

- The text size is also a crucial aspect. Prefer percentage or `em` values instead of pixels to provide resizable text across all browsers and devices.

- Take advantage of the new CSS3 capabilities to have better performance when defining styles for mobile devices. For example, use the box radius, gradients, and text-shadow properties instead of loading assets to achieve a similar effect. Because CSS3 is well supported on mobile browsers, you can safely choose to use these properties when targeting those devices.

- Don't forget to pay attention to the content that can't be displayed universally on all devices. IOS and some other mobile operating systems do not support Flash Player mobile. Furthermore, Adobe announced in November 2011 that it won't continue to provide support for mobile Flash Player anymore. So animations, games, and video relying on Flash Player won't be displayed on several mobile devices.

- When it comes to touch screens, the size of buttons and links play an important part in usability. You will have to rethink their design and make them broader and more appropriate to touch interaction. Also, note that the hover capability will not work the same on touch screens as it does on desktops because a touch is equal to a click event.

This being said, let's go over a concrete example with a simple HTML document.

How it works

1. Create a simple HTML document with your usual text editor:

```
<!DOCTYPE HTML>
<html>
<head>
 <meta charset="utf-8">
 <title>Solution 8_2</title>
</head>
```

```
<body>
 <div id="wrapper">
  <header>
   <div id="logo">Logo</div>
  </header>
  <nav>
  <!-- Navigation -->
    <a href="#">Link</a>
    <a href="#">Link</a>
    <a href="#">Link</a>
  </nav>
  <section>
   <h2>Adapting a layout on multiple devices</h2>
   <p>Lorem ipsum dolor sit amet, consectetur adipiscing elit. Proin
iaculis dui vel massa tempor sagittis. Donec a dui nibh, vitae congue lorem.
Praesent porta gravida arcu vel lacinia. Vivamus euismod auctor mauris a
rhoncus. Mauris venenatis venenatis ante at facilisis. Pellentesque habitant
morbi tristique senectus et netus et malesuada fames ac turpis egestas. Nullam
ac diam nec odio euismod iaculis nec sit amet nibh. Ut eu risus eget elit
volutpat vulputate ac et lorem. Cras dignissim viverra mauris sed euismod.
Pellentesque consequat, ante ac porta venenatis, eros orci viverra nisi,
ac iaculis lectus urna ac massa.
   </p>
   <figure>
   <img src="photo.jpg" alt="a photo" />
   <figcaption>A photo</figcaption>
   </figure>
  </section>
  <aside>
  <!-- Sidebar -->
   <h4>Sidebar</h4>
   <p>Lorem ipsum dolor sit amet, consectetur adipiscing elit. Proin
iaculis dui vel massa tempor sagittis. Donec a dui nibh, vitae congue lorem.
Praesent porta gravida arcu vel lacinia. Vivamus euismod auctor mauris a
rhoncus. Mauris venenatis venenatis ante at facilisis.
   </p>
  </aside>
  <footer>
   <!-- Footer -->
    css3 solutions - Apress -
  </footer>
 </div>
</body>
</html>
```

This document is simply structured and contains a header, main content that includes text and an image, a sidebar, and a footer. All of the elements are inside a div with an ID named wrapper. You'll find it useful to manage the content based on the device screen size. In this example, you are using an HTML5 document to take advantage of its powerful, semantic structural elements.

2. Add a link to an external style sheet that you simply name `style.css` within the `<head>` element of the document:

```
<link rel="stylesheet" type="text/css" href="style.css" />
```

For this example and for readability's sake, you will have a single external style sheet that contains all your style rules and media queries (for the screen media type).

3. Now adjust the viewport within the `<head>` element so that its default value on mobile devices will be equal with regard to the `device-width` and override the virtual default viewport size of the devices:

```
<meta name="viewport" content="width=device-width, initial-scale=1.0" />
```

Here you also define the initial scale of your page as 1, which means that when loaded the document won't be rescaled in any way (which could be the case by default on some mobile devices).

4. That's about it as far as your HTML document is concerned. Now that you have the structure, let's specify its appearance by first creating a style sheet. Start by setting general rules that will be applied on any device, regardless of its screen size:

```
*{
    margin:0;
    padding:0;
}
img{
    max-width: 100%;
}
body{
    font-family:verdana;
    font-size:100%;
}
header,footer,nav,a,#wrapper,figure,img{
    display:block;
}
header{
    background:#6C0;
    color:#fff;
    height:70px;
    margin-bottom:10px;
    width:100%;
}
#logo{
    margin:0;
    padding:10px;
    font-size:1.8em;
    font-weight:bold;
}
```

```
nav a{
    display:block;
    float:left;
    text-decoration:none;
    font-size:1em;
    font-weight:bold;
    border-radius: 10px;
    background-color:#abc;
    color:#fff;
}
p{
    padding:10px 10px;
    font-size:0.85em;
 }
section {
    color:#333333;
    border-radius:10px;
    background:#EEE;
    padding:12px;
}
section img {
    margin: 0 auto;
}
figure{
    font-size:0.75em;
    text-align:center;
}
footer {
    border-radius:7px;
    background:#333333;
    margin:10px auto;
    padding:10px 5%;
    color: #ccc;
    font-size: 0.9em;
    width:90%;
}
```

Here you are just setting regular style rules for your elements that will be the same no matter what device your content is displayed on: background, margin, padding, and font-size. So that it can be resized across all browsers, set your text size using em units.

Also, to make sure that your images won't exceed the page size, regardless of the display screen size, set its max-width to 100%. (We advise you to do the same with video elements, embedded elements, tables, and so on if you have those elements in your document.)

5. Now add specific rules for specific device widths using media queries. Let's start with desktop and laptop screens. Assume that a screen with a width greater than 1025 pixels is a computer screen, and add rules to be applied for this specific query:

```
@media screen and (min-width:1025px){
  #wrapper{
    width:960px;
    margin:0 auto;
  }
  nav{
    display:block;
    height:30px;
    margin:0 0 0 20px;
  }
  nav a{
    float:left;
    margin:0 10px 10px 0;
    height:25px;
    line-height:25px;
    padding:6px 14px;
    font-size:0.85em;
  }
  section{
    clear:both;
    width:600px;
    float:left;
    border-radius:10px;
    margin:0 15px 10px 0;
  }
  aside{
    display:block;
    width:200px;
    float:left;
    padding:10px;
  }
  footer{
    clear:both;
  }
}
```

Here you have a rather simple layout. Your navigation bar has inline text links. You place your sidebar to the left of the main content. You give your wrapper div a standard width of 960 pixels with auto margins so that it's in the center of the screen. It is pretty traditional.

6. Now add specific styles to target smartphones. Assume that a screen with a width less than 600 pixels is a smartphone screen, which seems like a safe assumption. (For the moment, we won't discuss the device orientation, which will be covered in the next solution.) Note that you use both

the `max-device-width` and `max-width` features. Using this approach, even desktop and laptop browsers will apply the styles if the content is resized at that size (which is a bit unlikely but a good way to test your style sheet). It also lets you test your layout with emulators like Protofluid (which you can read more about in the "Expert tips" section of this solution):

```
@media only screen and (max-device-width:600px),(max-width:600px){
  body{
    margin:0;
    padding:0;
  }
  #wrapper{
    width:100%;
  }
  nav a{
    display:block;
    font-size:1em ;
    float:none;
    width:90%;
    height:40px;
    line-height:40px;
    margin:0 auto 3px auto;
    padding:6px 14px;
  }
  aside{
    display:none;
  }
}
```

On small devices, space is very limited. Elements should be designed so that they're easily spotted and read. The first thing you do here is set a width of 100% to your wrapper `div` so that you use all the width of the screen. The sidebar would take up too much space, so you simply don't display it. Moreover, when browsing on their smartphones, users usually look for the main information, and sidebars do not usually contain such data.

In the code shown earlier, we also changed the navigation. Having three text links, one after another, would neither be easy to read nor to touch. So instead we made them as a list of more broad blocks, one below the other, by changing the float property from `left` to `none` and by changing the size of the <a>elements. It is visually easier to read on a small display, and the links now have a surface more suitable for interaction on small touch screens.

You can see the result in Figure 8-4.

All our content is in one, single long column that the user can scroll easily with a swipe touch. And as you can see, our photo fits properly because it can never have a width greater than the screen size.

7. Let's now take care of tablet screens. Assume that the screen width of tablets will be between 601 pixels and 1024 pixels (but here again you will deal only with the portrait mode).

```
@media only screen and (min-device-width:601px) and
(max-device-width:1024px),(min-width:601px) and (max-width:1024px) {
```

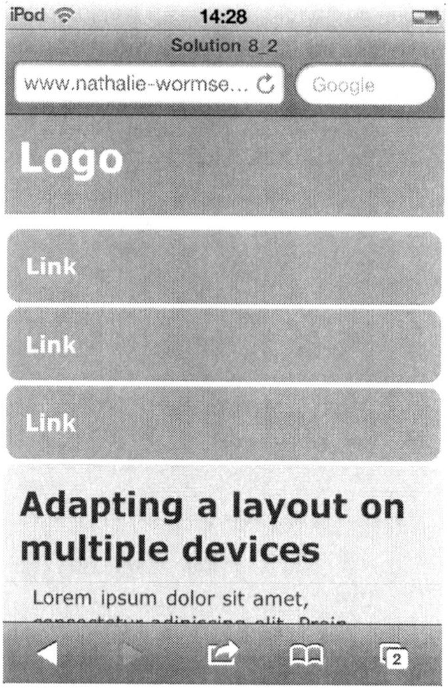

Figure 8-4. Our layout displayed in Safari on an iPod Touch.

```
body{
  margin:0;
  padding:0;
}
  #wrapper{
      width:100%;
  }

section,aside{
  clear:both;
  background:#EEE;
  border-radius:10px;
  margin:15px auto;
  padding:10px;
  width:90%;
  float:none;
}
```

```
nav a{
    float:left;
    display:block;
    -webkit-text-size-adjust: 100%;
    font-weight:bold;
    border-radius: 10px;
    background-color:#abc;
    color:#fff;
    height:50px;
    line-height:50px;
    margin:0 6px 8px 6px;
    padding:6px 14px;
}
nav{
    width:90%;
    margin:0 auto;
}
}
```

Just like with smartphones, you set the wrapper div's width to be 100%, the full width of the screen, to use all the space available.

You have more space than on an average smartphone screen, so position the navigation links on a single line using the float property, just as you did for desktop and laptop screens. However, because we're still dealing with a touch screen here, define a bigger touch area for the links than you did for desktops.

Here you display the content of the sidebar, but you position it below the main content to give the maximum readability to the latter.

You can see the result on an iPad (in portrait mode) in Figure 8-5.

In this simple example, you managed to display your HTML document on different screen devices, from smartphones to computer screens, and you adapted your layout to each in a pretty easy way by using only CSS3 and its media queries. You can see that, depending on the complexity of your design and content, you can rearrange your elements for specific screen ranges in an easy way without using any external script. (See Figure 8-6.)

> Caution: Browsers that don't support media queries won't display this example properly on desktops (like Internet 8 and earlier). Depending on your project and the document structure, you may have to add a specific style sheet for older browsers.

Figure 8-5. Our layout displayed in Safari on an iPad (in portrait mode).

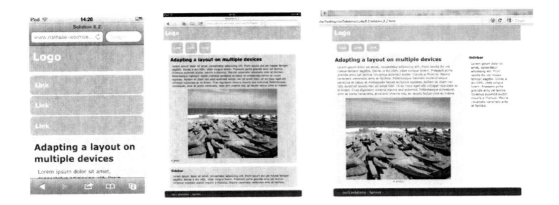

Figure 8-6. The same web document on a smartphone, tablet, and desktop screen using different styles rules, depending on the screen size, with media queries.

Expert tips

If you are heavily involved in mobile development, you probably have several devices at your disposal to work and test your projects. Other than that, you probably won't be able to test your design on various devices. Fortunately, you can find great online tools that will imitate the performance on tablets, on smartphones, with different resolutions, with various orientations, and so on.

A convenient and complete tool for doing this is Protofluid, which is available at `http://protofluid.com`. It lets you test your online document on a multitude of device screen sizes, orientations, and browsers. You just have to enter the URL you want to see, and then select the size, orientation, and browser of the device to test it on.

One thing though, you will have to define you screen's width with the width feature instead of device-width, to be able to test your queries.

You can also find a very extensive list of mobile emulators and simulators at `www.mobilexweb.com/emulators`.

If you have multiple devices at your disposal and want to test your layouts locally, Adobe has released a very interesting and useful tool, Shadow, to view and inspect your web content. You also can use Shadow to test it simultaneously on multiple devices (Android and iOS). At the time of this writing, you can download Shadow 1.0 from Adobe Labs at `http://labs.adobe.com/technologies/shadow/`.

Solution 8-3: Handling layout orientation on mobile devices with CSS3

In the previous solution, you saw how to apply specific styles according to different screen devices, from desktop computers to smartphones. But what happens when users rotate the screen with mobile devices? In this solution, you will see how you can adapt your layout for different orientations with CSS3.

What's involved

Here, again, the new CSS3 media queries give you the option of targeting devices based on their orientation. The feature created for that very purpose is the `orientation` feature. As you might have guessed, it can take one of two values: `portrait` or `landscape` And just like any media queries you've seen, it lets you set specific styles accordingly.

Syntax

Its syntax is pretty simple and can be described as follows:

- This `orientation` value lets you target devices in portrait orientation:

```
@media screen and (orientation:portrait){
   /*
       style rules for any screen media in portrait orientation
    */
}
```

- This `orientation` value lets you target devices in landscape orientation:

```
@media screen and (orientation:landscape){
   /*
     style rules for any screen media in landscape orientation
    */
}
```

Note that the orientation query lets you target which orientation the device has, but it won't take care of the actual width of the device's screen (which is targeted by the `device-width` feature as seen in solution 8-2). Table 8-5 lists the portrait and landscape widths of some popular mobile devices.

Table 8-5. Mobile device widths in pixels (portrait and landscape)

Device	Screen Portrait Width	Screen Landscape Width
iPhone	320 pixels	480 pixels
iPad	768 pixels	1024 pixels
Samsung Galaxy Tab 10.1	800 pixels	1280 pixels
Samsung Galaxy S	480 pixels	800 pixels
LG Optimus 3D	400 pixels	800 pixels

device-width vs. orientation

When you rotate most devices, the `device-width` changes accordingly, and if you set media queries with the `device-width` feature, you can serve styles for each orientation without needing to use the `orientation` feature. The following code sample shows how this is done:

```
/* Smartphones (portrait and landscape) ----------- */

@media only screen and (min-device-width:320px) and (max-device-width:600px) {
  /* Style rules */
}

/* Smartphones (landscape) ----------- */

@media only screen and (min-device-width:481px){
  /* Style rules */
}

/* Smartphones (portrait) ----------- */

@media only screen and (max-device-width:480px) {
  /* Style rules */
}
```

At first, you might wonder if there is an actual use for this `orientation` feature. However, iOS devices don't follow that behavior and the `device-width` of an iPhone, when doesn't change when it's in landscape orientation—it's still 320 pixels, just like in portrait orientation. This goes for iPads as well (for which the width is 768 pixels). In those cases, you have to use the `orientation` feature and make specific queries for the iPhone or the iPad as follows:

```
@media only screen (max-device-width: 320px) and (max-device-width:480px) and
(orientation:portrait) {

  */ styles for the iPhone/iPod in portrait orientation /*
}

@media only screen and (min-device-width:321px) and (max-device-width:480px) and
(orientation:landscape) {

  */ styles for the iPhone/iPod in landscape orientation /*
}
```

> Note: The orientation feature of CSS3 media queries has been supported on iOS since iOS4.

By combining both the `device-width` and `orientation` features, you can target iOS mobile devices and others as well, like this:

```
@media only screen and (max-device-width:600px) and (orientation:landscape){

  */ style rules for device with a screen width below (or equal to )
600 pixels in landscape orientation /*

}

@media only screen and (max-device-width:600px) and (orientation:portrait){

  */ style rules for device with a screen width below (or equal to )
600 pixels in portrait orientation /*

}
```

Another peculiarity on iOS devices is that they automatically zoom in when the user rotates the device into landscape mode, and it's up to users to zoom out to come back to the original scale. You can prevent this by locking the maximum scale of the viewport and specifying that it should not exceed 1, thus preventing rescaling. You can do this within the `viewport` tag, as follows:

```
<meta name="viewport" content="width=device-width,initial-scale=1.0,maximum-scale=1.0" />
```

Preventing users from zooming is not always advisable and could raise some issues, but because it seems to be the only way to fix this behavior at the moment of this writing, we are mentioning it.

How it works

To see how to adapt a document based on the orientation of mobile devices, let's take the same HTML document as in the previous solution and add style rules for this purpose.

1. Create a new HTML document in your text editor:

```
<!DOCTYPE HTML>
<html>
<head>
 <meta charset="utf-8">
 <meta name="viewport" content="width=device-width,initial-scale=1.0,
  maximum-scale=1.0" />
 <link rel="stylesheet" type="text/css" href="style.css" />
 <title>Solution 8_3</title>
</head>
<body>
 <div id="wrapper">
  <header>
   <div id="logo">Logo</div>
  </header>
  <nav>
   <a href="#">Link</a>
   <a href="#">Link</a>
   <a href="#">Link</a>
  </nav>
  <section>
   <h2>Adapting a layout on multiple devices</h2>
   <p>Lorem ipsum dolor sit amet, consectetur adipiscing elit. Proin
iaculis dui vel massa tempor sagittis. Donec a dui nibh, vitae congue lorem.
Praesent porta gravida arcu vel lacinia. Vivamus euismod auctor mauris a
rhoncus. Mauris venenatis venenatis ante at facilisis. Pellentesque habitant
morbi tristique senectus et netus et malesuada fames ac turpis egestas. Nullam
ac diam nec odio euismod iaculis nec sit amet nibh. Ut eu risus eget elit
volutpat vulputate ac et lorem. Cras dignissim viverra mauris sed euismod.
Pellentesque consequat, ante ac porta venenatis, eros orci viverra nisi, ac
iaculis lectus urna ac massa.
   </p>
   <figure>
    <img src="photo.jpg" alt="a photo" />
    <figcaption>A photo</figcaption>
   </figure>
```

```
  </section>
  <aside>
  <!-- Sidebar -->
    <h4>Sidebar</h4>
    <p>Lorem ipsum dolor sit amet, consectetur adipiscing elit. Proin
iaculis dui vel massa tempor sagittis. Donec a dui nibh, vitae congue lorem.
Praesent porta gravida arcu vel lacinia. Vivamus euismod auctor mauris a
rhoncus. Mauris venenatis venenatis ante at facilisis.
    </p>
  </aside>
  <footer>
  <!-- Footer -->css3 solutions - Apress -
  </footer>
 </div>
</body>
</html>
```

It's the same document as in the previous solution, but it now has a header, a navigation bar, a section element containing some text and a photo, a sidebar, and a footer.

2. Now add a link to an external style sheet, named style.css, within the <head> element of the document:

```
<link rel="stylesheet" type="text/css" href="style.css" />
```

3. Adjust the viewport within the <head> element so that its default value on mobile devices will be equal to the device-width:

```
<meta name="viewport" content="width=device-width, initial-scale=1.0, maximum-scale=1.0" />
```

That's it for our HTML document. Now let's take care of our style sheet.

4. First add style rules that will be commonly applied regardless of the device size and orientation:

```
*{
  margin:0;
  padding:0;
}
img{
    max-width: 100%;
}
body{
    font-family:verdana;
    font-size:100%;
}
header,footer,nav,a,#wrapper,figure,img{
    display:block;
}
header{
    background:#6C0;
    color:#fff;
```

```css
    height:70px;
    margin-bottom:10px;
    width:100%;
}
#logo{
    margin:0;
    padding:10px;
    font-size:1.8em;
    font-weight:bold;
}
nav a{
    display:block;
    float:left;
    text-decoration:none;
    font-size:1em;
    font-weight:bold;
    border-radius: 10px;
    background-color:#abc;
    color:#fff;
}
p{
    padding:10px 10px;
    font-size:0.85em;
}
section {
    color:#333333;
    border-radius:10px;
    background:#EEE;
    padding:12px;
}
section img {
    margin: 0 auto;
}
figure{
    font-size:0.75em;
    text-align:center;
}
footer {
    border-radius:7px;
    background:#333333;
    margin:10px auto;
    padding:10px 5%;
    color: #ccc;
    font-size: 0.9em;
    width:90%;
}
```

5. Now let's write a media query to target smartphones in portrait orientation and write the style rules we want to be applied specifically for this situation. Just like in the previous solution, you assume that screens with a maximum size of 600 pixels are considered to be smartphones:

```
@media only screen and (max-device-width:600px) and
(orientation:portrait),(max-width:600px){
  body{
    margin:0;
    padding:0;
  }
  #wrapper{
    width:100%;
  }

  nav a{
    font-size:1em ;
    float:none;
    width:90%;
    height:40px;
    line-height:40px;
    margin:0 auto 3px auto;
    padding:6px 14px;
  }

  aside{
    display:none;
  }
}
```

Here you just kept the same style rules that you defined in the previous solution, which are meant for small screens in portrait orientation. The navigation bar is now a list of links, with a suitable area for touch screens, and you removed the sidebar by setting the display property of the aside element to none.

6. Now let's write the media query to target smartphones in landscape orientation:

```
@media only screen and (max-device-width:600px) and (orientation:landscape){

  #wrapper{
    width:100%;
  }

  nav a{
    margin:0px 12px 10px 0px;
    width:100px;
    padding:8px;
    height:30px;
    line-height:30px;
    font-size:1em ;
    font-weight:bold;
    text-align:center;
    float:left;
  }
```

205

```
    section{
      clear:both;
    }
  aside{
      display:none;
    }
}
```

You just take care of the navigation by specifying the use of a navigation bar when the device is in landscape, because the width is greater in that scenario. But you still don't display the sidebar.

7.   Now let's take care of digital tablets in portrait orientation mode:

```
@media only screen and (min-device-width:601px) and (max-device-width:1024px )
and (orientation:portrait) {
  body{
    margin:0;
    padding:0;
  }
  section,aside{
    clear:both;
    background:#EEE;
    border-radius:10px;
    margin:15px auto;
    padding:10px;
    width:90%;
    float:none;
  }
  nav a{
    float:left;
    margin:0px 12px 10px 0px;
    font-weight:bold;
    height:50px;
    line-height:50px;
    margin:0 6px 8px 6px;
    padding:6px 14px;
  }
  nav{
    width:90%;
    margin:0 auto;
  }
}
```

Here you display all the elements because a tablet provides enough space—you just rearrange the way they are displayed compared to a desktop or laptop screen because the screen space is a bit more limited. Also, you place the sidebar below the section element. Again, you adapt the navigation: you keep a navigation bar but make the links with a broader area so that they are more suitable for touch events and proportionate to a tablet size.

8. Finally, add a media query to target tablet devices in landscape orientation:

```
@media only screen and (min-device-width:601px) and (max-device-width:1024px)
and (orientation:landscape),(min-width:601px) and (max-width:1024px) and
(orientation:landscape){
  nav a{
    margin:0px 12px 10px 0px;
    font-weight:bold;
    height:35px;
    padding:15px 20px 5px 20px;
  }
  nav{
    margin-left:30px;
  }
  section{
    clear:both;
    float:left;
    width:70%;
    border-radius:10px;
    background:#ccc;
    margin:0 15px 10px 30px;
  }
  p{
    font-size:1em;
  }
  aside{
    width:20%;
    float:left;
    border-radius:10px;
    background:#ccc;
    padding:10px;
  }
  footer{
    clear:both;
  }
}
```

When the device is in landscape orientation on tablets, the display size is really close to what is available on a laptop or on a desktop. So you have the sidebar on the left, like a regular sidebar, and a navigation bar as well. Here, again, because you are dealing with a touch screen, you make the size of the links broader than you would for a desktop.

Figure 8-7 shows the result on an Android smartphone in landscape and an iPad in portrait.

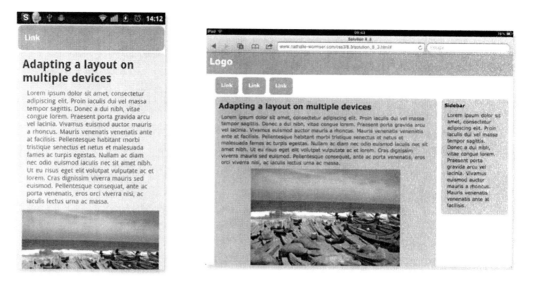

Figure 8-7. Our document on a Nexus One (Android) in portrait mode and on an iPad in landscape mode.

Expert tips

Depending on the orientation and the space available on the screen, you may want to place your content elements in a different order. You can find great benefits in this regard by using the CSS3 box-ordinal-group property, which specifies the display order of the child elements of a box.

In the example you just used, if you wanted to display the menu so that the section element content would be the first thing users see when viewing your page on a smartphone in portrait orientation, you would just have to add the following rules within the relevant media query:

```
#wrapper{
  display: -moz-box;
  display: -webkit-box;
  display: box;
  -moz-box-orient: vertical;
  -webkit-box-orient: vertical;
  box-orient: vertical;
}

nav{
  margin:0 auto;
  text-size:120%;
  -moz-box-ordinal-group: 2;
  -webkit-box-ordinal-group: 2;
  box-ordinal-group: 2;
  }
```

```
section{
  -moz-box-ordinal-group: 1;
  -webkit-box-ordinal-group: 1;
    box-ordinal-group: 1;
}
footer{
  -moz-box-ordinal-group: 3;
  -webkit-box-ordinal-group: 3;
  box-ordinal-group: 3;
}
```

Now the nav element will be positioned below the section element. Depending on the complexity of your layout, using this property can be very helpful in organizing your different elements according to the device and its orientation. You could put the navigation menu, as you do here, at the end of your document on a smartphone in portrait mode and on top display an anchor link to it (that would be displayed only on smart-phones). By doing this, the small space available on the screen would be first used for your main content, while users could browse easily within your content by jumping to the navigation block.

Solution 8-4: Defining style rules for high-density pixel screens

In recent years, we've seen the arrival of smartphones and then of smartphones with high-pixel-density screens—for example, the iPhone 4 and its *retina display*. As a matter of fact, it is more than likely that an increasing number of devices will come with high-density mobile screens in the future. The iPad, with its third-generation device, is already evolving in this way. Dealing with such screens requires changing your design and style sheet. In this solution, you will see how you can target devices based on their pixel density with CSS3 and how to apply specific styles to those devices.

What's involved

High-pixel-density screens imply that a given number of pixels will occupy less physical space than it would on a lower pixel-density screen.

Device pixel and CSS pixel

Take, for example, the iPhone. The iPhone 3 has a resolution of 480 by 320 pixels, whereas the iPhone 4 is 960 by 640 pixels in height and width but still has the same display area of 320 by 480 pixels. So you have more pixels for the same display area. Let's not get confused about the pixel unit though—when it comes to CSS, a pixel remains a pixel.

The CSS2.1 specification defines a "CSS pixel" as follows:

> *Pixel units are relative to the resolution of the viewing device, i.e., most often a computer display. If the pixel density of the output device is very different from that of a typical computer display, the user agent should rescale pixel values.*

Basically, it means that that one CSS pixel corresponds to one or more device pixels, depending on the device, and is a relative value. Going back to our iPhone example, 1 CSS pixel actually corresponds to 4 device pixels (2x2). If you want to adjust some styles to take advantage of this high density of pixels—for example, on some background images (which would appear kind of blurry otherwise when the user zooms in on them)—the `device-pixel-ratio` feature of media queries is what you need.

The query syntax is similar to the other media query features you saw earlier, and the `device-pixel-ratio` value corresponds to the number of device pixels per CSS pixel. So if you want to target the iPhone 4, you write a query with a `device-pixel-ratio` of 2, like this:

```
@media only screen and (max-device-width: 480px) and (min-device-pixel-ratio: 2){
*/style rules to be applied*/
}
```

As you can see, this is pretty easy. Let's now look at an example of utilizing this feature.

How it works

1. Create a simple HTML document with your text editor. For readability's sake, write only style rules destined for smartphones:

```
<!DOCTYPE HTML>
<html>
<head>
<meta charset="utf-8">
<link rel="stylesheet" type="text/css" href="s_8_4_style.css" />
<meta name="viewport" content="width=device-width,initial-scale=1.0" />
<title>Solution 8_4</title>
</head>

<body>
<div id="wrapper">
 <ul>
  <li id="elem_1"> Images</li>
  <li id="elem_2"> Videos</li>
 </ul>
</div>
</body>
</html>
```

You are just making a simple document containing a list of two elements, and in the background of each you put an image. You can then see how to adapt those background images for high-pixel-density mobile screens.

2. Now attach a style sheet, and add your common style rules destined for all devices, whatever their screen density:

```
#wrapper{
  width:100%;
  }
li{
 display:block;
```

```
   padding:16px 0 0 75px;
   height:64px;
   background-size:64px 64px;
   list-style-type:none;
   width:80%;
}
```

The elements listed have a background size of 64 pixels, and you just put the text content 70 pixels from the left to leave room for the list icons.

3. Now add your media query to target smartphones with non-high-density screens:

```
@media only screen and (min-device-width:320px){
   #elem_1{
     background-size: 64px 64px;
     background:url(img/icon_1_64.png) no-repeat ;
   }

   #elem_2{
     background-size: 64px 64px;
     background:url(img/icon_2_64.png) no-repeat ;
   }
}
```

4. Finally, add your media query to target high-pixel-density screen for smartphones with a pixel device ratio of 2 (like the iPhone 4):

```
@media only screen and (min-device-width:320px) and (device-pixel-ratio:2){
   #elem_1{
     background-size: 64px 64px;
     background:url(img/icon_1_128.png) no-repeat ;
   }

   #elem_2{
     background-size: 64px 64px;
     background:url(img/icon_2_128.png) no-repeat ;
   }
}
```

The background size is the same as on screens of regular smartphones, but our background images are twice as big (128 by 128 pixels) and our image resolution is adapted to the screen resolution, therefore taking advantage of the retina display.

Expert tips

Some designers are tempted to use this technique to display all, or some, of their images at different resolutions in their document. They do this by using the image-background rule with empty div elements instead of the img tag, and using the device-pixel-ratio feature to display images of a specific resolution. We don't advise you to adopt this practice because you should always separate the view and the content, and not mix them in any way.

Solution 8-5: Styling a document for printing devices with CSS3

Even though users are accessing your content on the Web, they may want to print a page of your website to keep some information, photos, or other content. A layout adapted for a computer screen will not necessarily be adapted for a printer version (and most likely will not be at all). In this solution, you will see how you can serve a style sheet specifically for print devices.

What's involved

The capability to target a print device is not new, and the `print` media type has been around since the CSS2 specification. It is already a common, and good, practice to have a style sheet dedicated to print devices. The syntax for doing this is as follows:

```
<link rel="stylesheet" type="text/css" href="print.css" media="print" />
```

You can also have all the style rules targeting printing devices in the same style sheet you are using for screen devices like this:

```
<link rel="stylesheet" type="text/css" href="styles.css" media="all" />
```

with the following `@media` rule syntax:

```
@media print {
  /* specific style rules for print devices*/
}
```

CSS3 offers the following new properties and features that can help improve your printable content:

- Media queries

  Just like with screen devices, you can choose to target specific page sizes with the use of media queries and specify sizes in centimeters or inches, as follows:

  ```
  /* style sheet for "A4" printing */
  @media print and (width: 21cm) and (height: 29.7cm) {

  }

  /* style sheet for "letter" printing */
  @media print and (width: 8.5in) and (height: 11in) {

  }
  ```

- You can use the `image-orientation` property to specify a rotation to be applied to an image when printing your document. (Do not confuse this capability with transformations, and use it only to correct a layout.)

  ```
  .class {    image-orientation: 90deg ; // will rotate the image of 90 degrees}
  ```

  Unfortunately, at the time of this writing, no browsers support this property.

- The `size` property relates to options for specifying page size. The CSS3 specification defines that a page size can now be specified with values like A4, A5, letter, or legal, and these options can be used in conjunction with an orientation (portrait or landscape) like this:

```
@page {
    size: A4 landscape;
}
```

This sample code sets the width of the page box to be 297 mm and the height to be 210 mm. The page box in this example should be rendered on a page sheet size of 210 mm by 297 mm.

It can be extremely useful to reposition your layout based on a common format for paper, making your web document even more suitable for printing.

Like the `image-rotation` property, this is not yet supported by any browsers at the time of this writing. But if you want to read details about those new properties, you can read the Paged Media specification (still in its draft stage) at www.w3.org/TR/css3-page/ or the cssPrint Profile of the W3C at this address: www.w3.org/TR/css-print/.

What to print

When users print a web document page, they are mainly interested in the main content, text, or images, and the navigation bar or the footer will have hardly any use for them. So it's better just to not display them. If you have a sidebar containing aside information, a group of social network sharing buttons, or any web interaction specific content, it won't be of any use either on paper.

When it comes to hyperlinks, they won't be very useful the way they are displayed on screen. However, the hyperlink in itself might be something users are interested in and that you want to display in full instead. You can do this by using the `pseudo elements` and `content`properties.

Suppose you have the following hyperlink in your HTML document:

```
<a href="http://www.myblog.com">the address of my blog</a>
```

Now add the following rule for a elements for print devices:

```
@media print {
  a:after {
   content: ": " attr(href);
  }
}
```

This code sample generates the following result when printed, giving your users the description of the link followed by the hyperlink itself:

```
The address of my blog: http://myblog.com
```

Font size

You may want to redefine the text size in your document specifically for print. Here it will be interesting to use the point unit because it is more suited for printing (but it's not the best option for screen devices). A font size of 12 points in the body of your document is the usual size for a printed web document, but you can change this according to your content.

How does it work

1. First create an HTML document. Here you will just take the web document you used in the two previous solutions and add a style sheet for printing devices:

```
<!DOCTYPE HTML>
<html>
<head>
 <meta charset="utf-8">
 <meta name="viewport" content="width=device-width,initial-scale=1.0,
  maximum-scale=1.0" />
 <link rel="stylesheet" type="text/css" href="style.css" />
 <title>Solution 8_5</title>
</head>
<body>
 <div id="wrapper">
  <header>
   <div id="logo">Logo</div>
  </header>
  <nav>
   <a href="#">Link</a>
   <a href="#">Link</a>
   <a href="#">Link</a>
  </nav>
  <section>
   <h2>Adapting a layout on multiple devices</h2>
   <p>Lorem ipsum dolor sit amet, consectetur adipiscing elit. Proin
iaculis dui vel massa tempor sagittis. Donec a dui nibh, vitae congue lorem.
Praesent porta gravida arcu vel lacinia. Vivamus euismod auctor mauris a
rhoncus. Mauris venenatis venenatis ante at facilisis. Pellentesque habitant
morbi tristique senectus et netus et malesuada fames ac turpis egestas. Nullam
ac diam nec odio euismod iaculis nec sit amet nibh. Ut eu risus eget elit
volutpat vulputate ac et lorem. Cras dignissim viverra mauris sed euismod.
Pellentesque consequat, ante ac porta venenatis, eros orci viverra nisi, ac
iaculis lectus urna ac massa.
   </p>
   <figure>
   <img src="photo.jpg" alt="a photo" />
   <figcaption>One photo</figcaption>
   </figure>
   <a href="http://www.myphotoalbum.com" id="photo_link">Link to the other
    photos</a>
 <p>Lorem ipsum dolor sit amet, consectetur adipiscing elit. Proin iaculis dui
vel massa tempor sagittis. Donec a dui nibh, vitae congue lorem. Praesent
porta gravida arcu vel lacinia. Vivamus euismod auctor mauris a rhoncus.
Mauris venenatis venenatis ante at facilisis. Pellentesque habitant morbi
tristique senectus et netus et malesuada fames ac turpis egestas. Nullam ac
diam nec odio euismod iaculis nec sit amet nibh. Ut eu risus eget elit
volutpat vulputate ac et lorem. Cras dignissim viverra mauris sed euismod.
Pellentesque consequat, ante ac porta venenatis, eros orci viverra nisi, ac
iaculis lectus urna ac massa. </p>
```

```
    </section>
    <aside>
       <h4>Sidebar</h4>
       <p>Lorem ipsum dolor sit amet, consectetur adipiscing elit. Proin iaculis dui vel
massa tempor sagittis. Donec a dui nibh, vitae congue lorem. Praesent porta gravida arcu
vel lacinia. Vivamus euismod auctor mauris a rhoncus. Mauris venenatis venenatis ante at
facilisis.
       </p>
      </aside>
      <footer>
          css3 solutions - Apress -
      </footer>
     </div>
    </body>
    </html>
```

2. That's about it as far as our HTML document is concerned. You can now write the style rule in the style.css file. First you write a media query stating that you want this style to apply to pages that have a maximum width of 21 cm and a maximum height of 29.7 cm (the A4 paper size).

```
@media print and (max-width: 21cm) and (max-height: 29.7cm){
```

3. Now add the style rules. First you choose not to display the navigation bar, because it's of no use on paper. Do this by setting its display property to none. You display the sidebar under the main content by overriding the float property and setting it to none. You also set the background of section elements to be white. (Normally, browsers won't take care of background colors or background images, but Opera does.)

```
nav,aside{
    display:none;
}
section{
background:none;
}
```

4. You will now take care of the link displayed under the photo. You want its hyperlink to be displayed in full next to it so that users have it on paper for further use and reference. You also set the link color style to be the same as the rest of your document text, but you specify it to be underlined so that users can easily identify the hyperlink compared to regular text:

```
#photo_link:after {
    content: ": " attr(href);
  }
```

5. Set the font size to be more appropriate for print devices. Instead of using em (which you used for other devices), you use point units because that's more appropriate for print documents:

```
p, { font-size: 12pt; }
h1 { font-size: 24pt; }
h2 { font-size: 18pt; }
```

6. Define the margins, and set them to 2 cm on each side for readability:

```
@page {
 margin: 2cm 2cm;
}
```

7. Close the media query:

```
}
```

This example is a simple one, and you can add more queries based on your web document content.

Expert tips

If your website content is rather simple and you don't want to write specific CSS for print devices, you can embed a badge from www.printfriendly.com/ that will format your web pages for print. It removes ads, navigation, and other such information for users who want to print some pages of your web content.

Summary

As you can see, developing web content for multiple devices, screens, and resolutions (both for mobile and desktop) presents a lot of new challenges for web developers. New CSS3 modules like media queries offer easy-to-implement solutions to make your designs and content adaptable for a wide range of devices. In this chapter, you saw how to adapt your document style sheet for multiple devices, screen sizes, and orientations (on mobile devices), as well as how to format it for paper and printing devices, creating a responsive design.

In the next chapter, you will see how, with CSS, you can now bring animations and transformations to your web document elements.

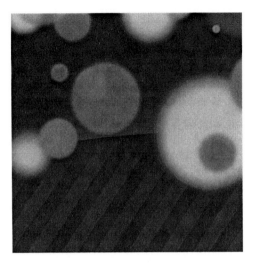

Chapter 9

Transitions and Transformations

When developing web applications and content, a rich user interface can make your project both appealing and easy to use. More often than not, you'll want to add some animation and nice visual effects to your elements. So far to achieve this, even basically, you have needed to use JavaScript or an external plug-in (like Adobe Flash). Moreover, you often had to turn text into images and use all kinds of small hacks and tedious tricks (which almost always have an impact on your page accessibility or page loads or have some Search Engine Optimization issues).

CSS3 introduces some awesome new modules you can use to manipulate and animate HTML document elements, as well as to apply transformations and animations in 2D and 3D directly with simple CSS declarations. In this chapter, you'll see how you can rotate, translate, and apply several transformations to any element or to text in 2D and 3D, and how to animate elements, directly in CSS, without having to rely on any external script or plug-in.

Solution 1: Applying simple 2D transformations on HTML elements with CSS3

When using the previous versions of CSS, whenever you wanted to add simple transformations and movement to your HTML document elements—for instance, to add a simple rotation when the mouse hovered over a navigation menu link—you had to write some external script using JavaScript or use an external plug-in like Flash. Either way, this could cause potential compatibility problems and, to work as expected, your web document was dependent on an external technology. In some cases, even with using JavaScript to achieve some effects, you had to use images containing text instead of text, thereby losing the SEO benefits of having clean, simple content, having to load your document with extra assets, and introducing accessibility issues. All in all, this created a lot of problems to solve.

With CSS3, you now have the capability to perform several transformations, in two-dimensional (2D) space, on your document elements, in a very simple way—without relying on any external technology. In this solution, you'll see how you can rotate, skew, scale, and translate HTML elements with the single use of the CSS 2D Transforms Module.

What's involved

Applying transformations to a document element in CSS3 is straightforward. You use two major properties: `transform` and `transform-origin`.

The transform property

With this property, you can translate, rotate, scale, or skew any element directly with CSS from your HTML document. What the property does, in fact, is modify the coordinate space of the element it targets. Its general syntax is very simple:

```
transform: transform function(value);
```

The `transform` property contains several transform functions you use to perform the following transformations:

- Rotating an element: The `rotate()` transform function applies a 2D rotation of a specified angle, from the origin of the element. The angle is expressed in degrees. You'll see how to move the origin later on.

The syntax is as follows: `transform:rotate(angle)`.

Here is an example: `transform:rotate(45 deg)`. This rotates the targeted element 45 degrees clockwise. (See Figure 9-1.)

- Scaling an element: The `scale()` transform function defines a scaling transformation on the targeted element using the scaling vectors passed as parameters. The first parameter is the scaling factor along the X axis, while the second one concerns the Y axis. If the second parameter is not provided, its default value is equal to the first parameter. A scaling vector of (1) leaves the element unchanged. The use of negative values produces a reflection effect.

The syntax is as follows: `transform scale(X scale vector, Y scale vector)`.

You also can transform an element on only one axis by using the following syntax:

```
transform:scaleX(X scale factor);
transform:scaleY(Y scale factor);
```

Here's an example:

```
#element{
  transform: scale(2,4);
}
```

This causes the targeted element to appear twice as long in the X axis and four times as long on the Y axis. (See Figure 9-1.)

```
#element{
  transform: scaleX(2);
}
```

This causes the targeted element to appear twice as long in the X axis but won't change its size along the Y axis.

> Note: Scaling an element doesn't correspond to changing its height and width (which would constrain only the width and height values but not resize the element)

- Skewing an element: You can apply a skew transformation on an element by using one of the following transform functions:

  - skew(x-angle,y-angle): This defines a 2D skew transformation along the X axis and the Y axis.

  - skewX(angle): This defines a 2D skew transformation along the X axis.

  - skewY(angle): This defines a 2D skew transformation along the Y axis.

The transformation is applied from the default center point of the element. Here are some examples:

```
#element{
  transform: skew(25deg,20deg);
}
```

This causes the element targeted to be skewed by 25 degrees on the X axis (for example, to lean to the left at 25 degrees) and 20 degrees on the Y axis, (for example, to slope from top to bottom). (See Figure 9-1.)

```
#element{
  transform: skewX(25deg);
}
```

This causes the targeted element to be skewed 25 degrees on the X axis only (for example, to lean to the left 25 degrees).

- Translating an element: You can translate an element (that is, move the entire element starting from its default position) by using one of the following transform functions:

  - translate(x translation value,y translation value): This defines a 2D translation along the X axis and the Y axis. If the second parameter is not specified, its default value is 0.

  - translateX(x translation value): This defines a 2D translation transformation along the X axis.

  - translateY(y translation value): This defines a 2D translation transformation along the Y axis.

The translation values are defined as length or percentage values. (You can also use negative values, which move the element in the opposite direction along the axis—that is, up or to the left.) Here's an example:

```
#element{
  transform: translate(10px,40px);
}
```

This code causes the targeted element to appear 10 pixels below its original position on the X axis and 40 pixels to the right of its original position on the Y axis. (See Figure 9-1.)

Figure 9-1. The scale(), rotate(), skew(), and translate() transform functions applied to an HTML document element

You can also apply several transformations on the same element by writing the transform functions one after another, separated by a space, like this:

```
transform:rotate(45deg) scale(2);
```

This code rotates an element 45 degrees clockwise and scales it to twice its original size.

The transform-origin property

Every element is positioned in a 2D coordinate space, and they each have an origin point. You can move this origin when performing any transformation by using the transform-origin property. The coordinates of this point are based on a regular 2D coordinate system: a vertical Y axis, a horizontal X axis, and an initial transform-origin value of 50% 50 %, which is the center of the element.

As you would logically expect, the transform-origin property takes two parameters: the X-axis coordinate value and the Y-axis coordinate value. It accepts the following two types of values (and if only one parameter is given, it assumes the second one is the center):

- Numeric (expressed in pixels or percentages): A value pair of 100% 100% places the transform-origin in the bottom right corner.

- Keywords: The keywords you can use are top, bottom, center, left, and right. A value pair of right bottom, for instance, places the transform-origin in the bottom right corner (just like a value pair of 100% 100 %).

The default value can be then expressed like this: (50 %,50 %) or (center,center).

To change the default origin value on a transform operation and define a specific point as the origin, you must follow a particular sequence. First perform your transform operation, and only then reposition your element by changing the origin point as follows (that is, the transform-origin has to be applied after the transformation itself):

```
#element{
 transform: scale(0.5);
 transform-origin:20px 40px;
}
```

The preceding code scales the element to half its original size, and then repositions it as if its origin is placed 20 pixels to the right of the upper left corner of the element and 40 pixels below it.

Note that when you transform an element, all its child elements will be subjected to the transformation as well. One great thing is that when an element is subject to transformation, its structure is not changed in any way. (Remember that you're dealing only with the view here.) Text, for instance, will remain selectable and so forth. Transformations let you create great, SEO-friendly designs at the same time, as well as ones that are highly accessible.

Browser support

At the time of this writing, 2D transforms are available in all current modern browsers including Internet Explorer 9. (See the compliant browsers list on the Table 9-1.) As you can see, the support is pretty good, including on mobile browsers. However at the time of the writing of this book the specification of the module is still at a Working Draft stage, and each of those browsers will require the use of its vendor prefix to apply them.

Table 9-1 lists browsers that are compatible with this property, including the specific prefix for each.

Table 9-1. Browser compatibility with CSS3 transforms

Internet Explorer	Firefox	Chrome	Safari	Opera	iOS Safari	Opera Mobile	Android Browser
9+	3.5+	4+	3.1+	10.5+	3.2+	11+	2.1+
-ms	-moz	-webkit	-webkit	-o	-webkit		-webkit

Versions of Internet Explorer prior to 9.0 don't support 2D transformations, so you have to fall back to some equivalent in JavaScript or an Adobe Flash animation. The Modernizr library (which you can download at www.modernizr.com/download/)) will be of great help when you are trying to add a fallback script. Here's an example:

```
<script type="text/javascript" language="javascript" src="modernizr.js"></script>
<script type="text/javascript" language="javascript">
if (!Modernizr.csstransforms) {
   // the browser doesn't support 2D transforms
   // add your fall-back script according to the transformation you want to achieve
   }
</script>
```

You can also use the Microsoft proprietary Matrix filter to apply matrices to elements in most cases, because this filter has been supported since Internet Explorer 5.5. To learn more about transformations with matrices and how to use them, refer to Solution 9-2. (Of course, this filter won't work with any browser other than Internet Explorer.)

How it works

Now that we've covered the rather simple syntax of 2D transforms and their transform functions, let's take a look at a concrete example. To illustrate their use, this example builds a navigation bar, with links that appear by rotation in response to a hover action:

1. First create a basic HTML5 document with your text editor, containing a nav element with two links, and a link to the style sheet:

```
<!DOCTYPE HTML>
<html>
<head>
 <meta charset="utf-8">
 <link rel="stylesheet" href="style.css" type="text/css"/>
     <script type="text/javascript" language="javascript" src="modernizr.js"></script>
     <script type="text/javascript" language="javascript">

     if (!Modernizr.csstransforms) {
     // the browser doesn't support 2D transforms
     // add your fall-back script according to the transformation you want to achieve
     }
     </script>
 <title>Solution_9_1</title>
</head>
<body>
<nav>
 <li class="element home">
  <a href="#">Link</a>
 </li>
 <li class="element contact">
  <a href="#" id="txt">Link</a>
 </li>
</nav>
</body>
</html>
```

Basically, you're using your style sheet to build links that are half hidden behind a block and reveal themselves in response to a hover action, so you add a div behind which your links will be displayed.

That's it as far as your HTML document is concerned. Again, note that you're separating your content from its view, and the combination of HTML5 and CSS3 makes it more structured and easier to work with.

2. Now create a CSS file. Start by styling the links so that they appear by default upside down. (The aim is to rotate them so that they're readable and clickable in response to a mouse hover action.) To achieve this behavior, apply two transformations—a rotation with the rotate() transform

function, and a reverse effect with the `scale()` transform function—so that the text of the link will be upside down but you can still give a hint to users that they need to hover over the link:

```
.element{
 display:block;
 position:absolute;
 background:#ccc;
 width:100px;
 height:70px;
 padding:5px;
 margin:55px 0 0 20px;
 -moz-transform:scale(-1) rotate(45deg);
 -webkit-transform:scale(-1) rotate(45deg);
 -o-transform:scale(-1) rotate(45deg);
 -ms-transform:scale(-1) rotate(45deg);
 border-radius:12px;

}

a{
 text-decoration:none;
 font-family:Tahoma, Geneva, sans-serif;
 color:#fff;
 margin-left:60px;
 margin-top:5px;
 display: inline-block;
 -webkit-transform:rotate(-90deg);
 -webkit-transform-origin:bottom right;
 -moz-transform: rotate(-90deg);
 -moz-transform-origin:bottom right;
 -ms-transform: rotate(-90deg);
 -ms-transform-origin:bottom right;
 -o-transform: rotate(-90deg);
 -o-transform-origin:bottom right;
}

.contact{
 margin-left:140px;
}

li::after{ content:"Hover"; }
```

This code sets your transform functions for the two nav elements. It also uses the :after pseudo selector to add a reminder for the user to hover the mouse over the link.

Practically, what you did here is apply a rotation of 45 degrees and then reverse the list elements by applying a scale factor of −1. You also transformed the <a> elements by changing their rotation by −90 degrees with a new `transform-origin` on the bottom right to follow your reversal effect.

After those transformations, your navigation elements look like the ones you see in Figure 9-2.

Figure 9-2. Several transformation functions applied to your navigation elements

3. Almost all the hard work is done, and you just need to add the appropriate rotation on :hover to read the link:

```
.element:hover{
position:absolute;
background:#990000;
-moz-transform:translateY(20px) rotate(90deg);
-o-transform:translateY(20px) rotate(90deg);
-webkit-transform:translateY(20px) rotate(90deg);
-ms-transform:translateY(20px) rotate(90deg);
}
```

Now in response to :hover, your elements look like the ones shown in Figure 9-3.

Figure 9-3. Element being transformed on :hover

1. Now you just need to add the style rules to hide half of the elements so that only the desired half is visible in both static and hover states. (See Figure 9-4.) You achieve this by positioning the navmask div appropriately, like this:

```
#navmask{
position:absolute;
z-index:50;
width:100%;
height:109px;
background:#627878;
}
```

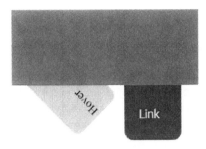

Figure 9-4. Both elements with transformations depending on their state (either hover off or hover on)

This example is a rather simple one without any real design concerns and presented just for the sake of demonstration, but it shows how you can combine different transform functions to add effects to your elements without having to change the content itself in any way or use any external scripts. In later solutions, you'll see how you can animate your transformations, thereby greatly expanding your design possibilities. This example won't work on versions of Internet Explorer prior to 9.0. So you'll have to either add some JavaScript to re-create the effect or use the Microsoft Matrix filter. (Matrix transformations are covered in Solution 9-2.)

> Caution: Because this example uses the :hover selector, it won't work on mobile devices like smartphones or digital tablets. This is a situation where media queries come to the rescue. You can use them to design a menu specific for those devices, while still using the same HTML document. You can learn more about media queries in Chapter 8.

Expert tips

If you want to try transformation values or don't want to calculate the values for a specific effect or combination of transform functions by yourself, you can use a handy 2D transform tool to manipulate all the 2D transformation values on an element and see the result in real time. It's available at the following website: www.westciv.com/tools/transforms/.

Solution 9-2: Using matrix 2D transformations in CSS3

In the previous solution, you saw how you can apply several 2D transformations on the HTML document element by using specific transformation functions. You also can apply combined transformations with a single function by using matrices, and thus increase the complexity and precision of your 2D transformations of an element. In this solution, you'll see how you can use the matrix function to apply 2D transformations.

What's involved

We won't cover the subject of transformation matrices from a mathematical point of view in depth in this book. First of all, it is quite a complex subject that goes beyond the scope of this book, and people who are not familiar with linear algebra probably will find the topic too abstruse. Moreover, a full-length explanation probably would require a full chapter. We'll just go over the basics so that you understand how transformation matrices work, which will enable you to use them in a better way. As you'll see, this knowledge will be very useful for applying transformations in Internet Explorer.

Matrices and the 2D coordinate system

As you saw in the previous solution, you can easily apply transformations such as rotation, scale, translation, and skew on an HTML document element with CSS3-specific transformation functions. Actually, all those transformation functions can be represented directly by a matrix value (which will render faster).

A matrix is an array of numbers used to transform coordinates, and the CSS3 2D transformations can be represented as 3 by 3 transformation matrices as shown in Figure 9-5.

$$\begin{bmatrix} a & b & e \\ c & d & f \\ 0 & 0 & 1 \end{bmatrix}$$

Figure 9-5. A 2D CSS3 matrix array

The first two columns of a 3 by 3 transformation relate to linear transformations, whereas the third one deals with translations. By applying different values to your matrix, you can achieve different types of transformations. (With 2D transformations, the last row of values is always equal to 0, 0, 1.)

Now for the hard part. Each point of the element being transformed is represented by a vector $(x, y, 1)$, where x and y are the coordinates of the point on the coordinate system (because we are dealing with 2D transformations the third coordinate is always equal to 1). All the transformations you do to an element (rotation, translation, and so on) are calculated as individual matrices, which are themselves multiplied together to make a master matrix of transformation. To produce the transformed element, each point of the element is multiplied by that matrix, and the transform matrix function, in fact, maps coordinates and lengths from a new coordinate system into the current coordinate system, giving new coordinates to the transformed element in the current coordinate system. The calculation will be the matrix multiplication shown in Figure 9-6.

$$[x,y,1] * \begin{bmatrix} a & b & e \\ c & d & f \\ 0 & 0 & 1 \end{bmatrix} = [a*x+c*y+e, b*x+d*y+f, 1]$$

Figure 9-6. Matrix transformation calculation

This means that every point (x, y) of the targeted element moves to the following point (a*x + c*y + e, b*x + d*y + f).

Let's take a simple, but rather clear and demonstrative, example and apply an identity matrix—for example, (1,0,0,1,0,0)—to a point with coordinates (10,10) on a 2D coordinate system. (When a matrix causes no transformations, you have what is known as an *identity matrix*. Therefore, applying this matrix to your point should give you back the same exact new coordinates):

The matrix (1 * 10+0 * 10+0, 0 * 10+1 * 10+0) does, indeed, give us a transformed point of (10, 10).

Let's take another example now that translates a point with the coordinates (5,5) by 10 pixels on both axes. Because this is a standard translation, you know without any calculation the new coordinates are (15,15), but let's take a look at the calculation. Your matrix is (1, 0, 0, 1, 10, 10). When you apply it, you get (1 * 5 + 0 * 5 + 10, 0 * 5 + 1 * 5 + 10), which give you new coordinates of (15,15) for the translated point.

Now that you've seen briefly the theory behind matrices and how new coordinates are calculated with their use, let's go over their concrete use in CSS3. If you want to go more deeply into the calculation of matrices and linear transformations, you can refer to the following link: http://en.wikipedia.org/wiki/Transformation_matrix). But be prepared for headaches if you are not familiar with math! Don't worry, though, as you'll see in the upcoming paragraphs, you can use the matrix transformation function without any calculations.

Syntax

The matrix transform function in CSS3 has the following syntax and is equal to applying the transformation matrix [a b c d e f]:

```
#element{
    transform: matrix(a, c, b, d, e, f);
}
```

In the code example, a, b, c, d builds the transformation matrix with linear transformation, whereas e and f are the translation values.

To make use of transformation matrices by calculating them according to the desired effect, you need to have a good understanding of linear algebra. Even if you do, though, this would take quite a bit of calculation. If you are not familiar with this or don't want to deal with heavy calculations to perform a simple transformation, it doesn't mean you can't use them. First, you can find the known matrix values for common effects and just use them without bothering with the math.

Here is a list of matrix values you can use to achieve common transformation effects:

- A translation is equivalent to the following matrix:

```
matrix(1, 0, 0, 1, x, y)
```

In this matrix, x and y are the translation values added successively on the x and y axes, measured in pixels.

- To scale an element, you use the following matrix:

```
matrix(x, 0, 0, y, 0, 0)
```

In this matrix, x and y are the scale factor added successively on the x and y axes.

- To rotate an element, use the following matrix:

```
matrix(cos(a), sin(a), -sin(a), cos(a), 0, 0)
```

Here, *a* is the value in degrees of your desired rotation angle.

- To skew an element on the X axis, you use the following matrix:

```
matrix(1, 0, tan(a), 1, 0, 0)
```

Here, *a* is the angle value along the X axis.

- To skew an element on the Y axis, you use the following matrix:

```
matrix(1, tan(a), 0,1, 0, 0)
```

In this matrix, *a* is the angle value along the Y axis.

You also might want to apply more complex and combined matrices transformations to some elements without turning yourself into a math nerd. Thankfully, there are several nice tools on the web that do all the tedious calculation for you, like the following ones:

- "Playing with matrices," which is coded by a talented front-end developer named Peter Nedrlof, is a small online application you can use to apply all kinds of 2D transformations directly to a square element using drag-and-drop interactions. It generates the associated matrix CSS3 code on the fly, which you can then copy and paste into your own style sheet. Check it out at http:// peterned.home.xs4all.nl/matrices/.

- Another great online tool, which is similar but lets you go further, is the Matrix Construction Set, written by web developers Zoltan Hawryluk (creator of several JavaScript libraries) and Zoe Mickley Gillenwater (a web and graphic designer specializing in CSS). You can see it at www. useragentman.com/matrix/.) This tool provides the matrices values and even the cross-browser code to use to achieve the same effect in your own document. (At the time of this writing, this tool doesn't work in Opera and has some issues in some versions of Chrome.)

As you can see, understanding matrices can be a bit of a challenge, but you can manage to use CSS3 matrix functions without it.

Browser support

The support is the same as for the transform functions you saw in the previous solution, so Internet Explorer versions prior to 9.0 don't support CSS3 transforms. However, you can get the same results by using its proprietary Matrix filter in your CSS.

The matrix filter syntax is quite similar to the transform matrix. Because we are using matrices, you can apply the same values you use for other browsers with regular matrix transforms to have them as well in Internet Explorer. The matrix filter syntax is as follows:

```
filter: progid:DXImageTransform.Microsoft.Matrix(sizingMethod='auto expand',
    M11=a, M12=-b,
    M21=c, M22=d);
```

You can read the documentation for this filter on the Microsoft website at http://msdn.microsoft.com/ en-us/library/ms533014%28VS.85%29.aspx).

There is still an issue, though. The matrix filter doesn't handle translation in the same way as CSS3 transform functions. To handle the translation issue, you can use that great tool known as the Internet Explorer CSS3 Transforms Translator (again, coded by Zoltan Hawryluk) to generate the CSS adapted to your transformation with a translation. It's available at `www.useragentman.com/IETransformsTranslator/index.html`). This tool can recalculate the top and left margins of your transformed element to correspond to the `translatetransform` function. Enter your regular CSS3 matrix transform function, and it will provide you with the equivalent code for Internet Explorer versions earlier than 9.0 to render. (You will notice that the values *M11*, *M12*, *M21*, and *M22* are equal to the values *a*, *b*, *c*, and *d* from your matrix.) The good

point about using this filter is that it's compatible with versions of Internet Explorer since 5.5!

> *Caution: The proprietary Microsoft Matrix filter is not valid CSS. So if you really want to keep your document valid, you have to rely on another workaround to be cross-browser compatible. One option is to use a JQuery plug-in such as jquery.transform.js, which you can find at `https://github.com/louisremi/jquery.transform.js`). Or you can propose an alternative CSS rule by detecting whether the browser detects transforms with the use of the Modernizr library like you saw in the previous solution.*

How it works

To give you a concrete example of matrix usage, this example shows you how to apply a matrix transformation to an image and give it a complete reflection effect in response to a mouse hover.

1. Create a simple HTML5 document with your usual text editor, with a figure element containing an image and its legend:

```
<!DOCTYPE HTML>
<html>
<head>
 <meta charset="utf-8">
 <link rel="stylesheet" type="text/css" href="style.css" />
 <title>Solution 9.2</title>
</head>
<body>
 <figure id="image-wrap">
  <img src="photo.jpg" />
  <figcaption>This is going upside down !!</figcaption>
 </figure>
</body>
</html>
```

2. That's about it for the HTML part. Now create your style sheet, and name it style.css. First take care of the matrix transformation for all browsers compliant with the CSS3 transforms module:

```
#image-wrap{

 -moz-transform:matrix(1,0,0,-1,0,0);
 -o-transform:matrix(1,0,0,-1,0,0);
```

```
-webkit-transform: matrix(1,0,0,-1,0,0);
-ms-transform: matrix(1,0,0,-1,0,0);
transform:matrix(1,0,0,-1,0,0);
```

What you're doing here is applying a matrix transformation to the whole figure element. It means that the <figcaption> element will be subjected to it as well. Your matrix is transforming the element in such a way that it will appear upside down. Because the specification is not a recommendation yet, you need to add all the vendor prefixes for each browser.

3.   Now apply the same effect for Internet Explorer 8 and earlier by using the Matrix filter:

```
filter: progid:DXImageTransform.Microsoft.Matrix(
    M11=1,
    M12=0,
    M21=0,
    M22=-1,
    SizingMethod='auto expand');
}
```

As you can see, you're using the same matrix values with the Internet Explorer proprietary Matrix filter as you did with the matrix transformation function. Other browsers will just ignore this code.

That's it. If you load your document, you'll have your image and its legend reversed in a kind of mirror effect on all browsers, and without the use of any external script.

Expert tips

If you don't want to write multiple versions of CSS attributes all the time, you might want to consider using cssSandpaper, which generates all the different vendor-specific and standard syntaxes so that they work in a cross-browser way. In addition, it also translates the World Wide Web Consortium (W3C) syntax into DirectX filters to make transforms work with Internet Explorer just as you saw earlier. All you need to do is import the associated libraries and add the –sand– prefix to any transform method you want to use, and it will work on any browser.

Let's take the example of this solution. If you want to have only a single CSS matrix function that works in a cross-browser way, first you need to download the JavaScript files necessary from this site: www.user-agentman.com/blog/csssandpaper-a-css3-javascript-library/). Then load them within the head tag of your document:

```
<script type="text/javascript" src="js/EventHelpers.js"></script>
<script type="text/javascript" src="js/cssQuery-p.js"></script>
<script type="text/javascript" src="js/sylvester.js"></script>
<script type="text/javascript" src="js/cssSandpaper.js"></script>
```

Then the same reflection matrix will be applied as follows:

```
-sand-transform: matrix(1,0,0,-1,0,0);
```

And that's it. This effect works on any browser. (Because of security rules, this plug-in cannot load embedded style sheets when the page is not on a web server, so it won't work when tested locally.) It couldn't be simpler!

Solution 9-3: Making elements move with CSS3 transitions

In the previous solutions in this chapter, you saw how to transform elements, and it's already pretty amazing to be able to do that now directly with CSS3 without having to load external assets, and in such a simple way. One other great feature of CSS3 is the capability to add smooth transitions between two rendering states of an element and obtain very nice animation effects without using any JavaScript or external plug-ins. In this solution, you'll see how to use transitions and create some pretty cool effects directly within your style sheet.

What's involved

Basically, a transition is the animation of an element going from one style property to another (for example, a `div` element changing its `width` property from 10 pixels to 100 pixels).

Transition properties

To create a transition for a property with CSS3 is pretty straightforward. The transition is defined using the following new properties:

- `transition-property`: This property defines the CSS property you add a transition to. The different possible values are `all` (all the properties are animated by a transition), `none`(no properties are animated by a transition), or a specific property. All the CSS properties cannot be subject to transitions, and you can find those that are listed in Table 9-2. Here's an example of its use:

  `transition-property:width;`

- transition-duration: This property defines the duration elapsed from the starting state to the new one. It is expressed in seconds, `s`, or milliseconds, `ms`. Here's an example:

  `transition-duration:2s;`

- transition-timing-function: This property defines how the speed will be calculated during the transition (and allows for a transition to change speed over its duration). The possible values are `:ease` (starts slowly, and then goes fast and ends slowly), `linear` (goes at the same speed from start to end), `ease-in` (start slowly), `ease-out` (ends slowly), `ease-in-out` (starts slowly and ends with a slight speed difference from the `ease` value), and `cubic-bezier`. The cubic-bezier timing function requires four numeric values to calculate the speed of your transition. In fact, all timing function values are defined by using a specific `cubic-bezier` curve, which is itself defined by four control points—for instance, the `ease` function is equivalent to `cubic-bezier(0.25, 0.1, 0.25, 1.0)`. We won't go into cubic bezier curves and their calculation in detail here. But you can read more about them at `http://en.wikipedia.org/wiki/B%C3%A9zier_curve#Cubic_B.C3.A9zier_curves`). You can read about a useful tool for visualizing all the preset cubic Bezier curves that you can use with CSS3 transitions at http://cssglue.com/cubic). This tool lets you create custom ones by attributing your own values to the control points with the cubic-bezier function (as the transitions module is not yet supported in Internet Explorer, and won't be until the 10th version, this tool won't work in this browser below IE10). Here are a few examples:

```
transition-timing-function:linear;
transition-timing-function: cubic-bezier(0,0,1,1);
```

Table 9-2. CSS properties that can be subjected to CSS3 transitions

background-color	background-image
background-position	border-bottom-color
border-bottom-width	border-color
border-left-color	border-left-width
border-right-color	border-right-width
border-spacing	border-top-color
border-top-width	border-width
bottom length	color
crop	font-size
font-weight	grid
left length	letter-spacing
line-height	margin-bottom
margin-left	margin-right
margin-top	max-height
max-width	min-height
min-width	opacity
outline-color	outline-offset
outline-width	padding-bottom
padding-left	padding-right
padding-top	right length
text-indent	text-shadow
top length	vertical-align
visibility	width length, percentage
word-spacing length, percentage	z-index integer
zoom number	

■ transition-delay: This property defines when the transition will start and is expressed in seconds. (The default value is 0.) Here's an example:

```
transition-delay:2s;
```

Because a transition is an element going from an old state to a new state over time, logically to make it work two of the properties just listed are compulsory: `transition-property` and `transition-duration`.

At the time of this writing, the specification for the the CSS Transitions module is still in the draft stage, and you'll have to use the vendor prefixes to use transition properties with different browsers.

Syntax

Now let's take a look at the full syntax to apply the properties shown in Table 9-2.

First of all, to go from one state to another, you need to have two states: a starting one and an ending one. In plain CSS, this could be achieved with the use of the following pseudo-selectors: :hover, :focus, and :target.These pseudo-selectors let you define two states of the same element. For example, with the :target pseudo selector, you can define the style of an element when it's the target element of the referring URI, which would be a state of an element after a user's interaction. All you have to do is define a transition, specify the property you want to animate, specify its duration, and then specify the transition timing function, as well as a delay if you want to.

Let's look at an example. Suppose you have an element with the id #element and with an initial width of 10 pixels and you want to expand its width by 200 pixels on :hoverin a smooth transition. Here's the code you would use to achieve this:

```
#element{

width:10px;
height:20px;
display:block;
background:#ccc;
transition-property:width;
transition-duration:1s;
transition-timing-function: linear;
transition-delay:1s;

-moz-transition-property:width;
-moz-transition-duration:1s;
-moz- transition-timing-function: linear;
-moz-transition-delay:1s;

-webkit-transition-property:width;
-webkit-transition-duration:1s;
-webkit- transition-timing-function: linear;
-webkit- transition-delay:1s;

-o-transition-property:width;
-o-transition-duration:1s;
-o-transition-timing-function: linear;
-o-transition-delay:1s;

}
```

```
#element:hover{

  width:200px;

}
```

The preceding code expands your `element`'s width from 10 pixels to 200 pixels in response to a hover event with a transition. The transition will start one second after the hover event is triggered and will be linear. It's as easy as that. Note that you define the transition rule with the first state of the element so that the transition will apply when the width changes from 10 pixels to 200 pixels, and when it's changing back from 200 pixels to 10 pixels as well (when the element isn't on hover anymore).

You can also use a shorter notation with the following syntax:

```
transition: transition-property transition-duration transition-timing-function transition-delay;
```

The preceding example can then be shortened as follows:

```
#element{
  width:10px;
  height:20px;
  display:block;
  background:#ccc;
}

#element:hover{
  width:200px;
  -moz-transition:width 1s linear 1s;
  -webkit-transition:width 1s linear 1s;
  -o-transition:width 1s linear 1s;
  transition:width 1s linear 1s;
}
```

Browser support

CSS transitions support is shown in Table 9-3.

Table 9-3. CSS transitions module browser support

Firefox	Chrome	Safari	Opera	Internet Explorer	iOS Safari	Opera Mini	Opera Mobile	Android Browser
3.7+	4.0+	3.1+	10.5+	Internet Explorer 10+	3.2	No support	10.0	2.1
–moz	–webkit–	–webkit–	–o–	–ms–	–webkit–		–o–	–webkit–

Almost all modern versions of major browsers support the CSS3 transitions module. Still, Internet Explorer doesn't support transitions in versions earlier than Internet Explorer 10, and there is no support whatsoever in Opera Mobile yet. If you use a transition, noncompliant browsers will just go from one state to another directly. If you want to have the same smooth effect with noncompliant browsers, you have to detect the transitions' support and add some JavaScript or Flash animation fall-back code. To detect the support for this feature, the Modernizr library is once again a great option (which you can download from www.modernizr.com/download/)):

```
<script type="text/javascript" src="modernizr.js"></script>
<script type="text/javascript">
 if(!Modernizr.csstransitions) {
   // the browser doesn't support CSS3 transitions
   // add a JavaScript fall-back script or a Flash animation
   }
</script>
```

Moreover, the combination of the Modernizr library and the JQuery animate method (the documentation for which you can find at http://api.jquery.com/animate/)) can be a good option for a fall-back plan. For instance, to reproduce the transition we just wrote, add the following:

```
$(document).ready(function() {
 if(!Modernizr.csstransitions) {
  $("#element").mouseenter(function() {
   $(this).animate({ width: "200px",}, 1000 );
     }).mouseleave(function() {
     $(this).animate({
     width: "10px",
     }, 1000 );
 });
 });
 }
```

Of course, depending on the transition you want to apply and your project, you might have to use different JQuery methods in addition to the animate() method.

How it works

To see transitions in action, this example builds a simple accordion menu in pure CSS:

1. First create an HTML document with your text editor that contains three section elements wrapped in a div named *wrapper*, with each containing a panel with what will be the clickable header and its associated content:

```
<!DOCTYPE HTML>
<html>
<head>
<meta charset="utf-8">
<title>Solution_9_3</title>
<link rel="stylesheet" href="style.css" type="text/css"/>
<script type="text/javascript" src="modernizr.js"></script>
<script type="text/javascript">
 if(!Modernizr.csstransitions) {
 window.alert('your browser doesn't support CSS3 Transitions');
   // the browser doesn't support CSS3 transitions
   // add a JavaScript fall back script or a Flash animation
   }
```

235

```
    </script>
    </head>
    <body>
      <div id="accordion">
       <section id="blog" class="block">
        <a href="#blog">Link 1</a>
        <div class="content">
          <p>Text link 1</p>
        </div>
       </section>

       <section id="contact" class="block">
         <a href="#contact">Link 2</a>
         <div class="content">
           <p>Text Link 2</p>
         </div>
       </section>

       <section id="link" class="block">
         <a href="#link">Link 3</a>
         <div class="content">
           <p>Text Link 3</p>
         </div>
       </section>
      </div>
    </body>
    </html>
```

It is a rather simple markup. And that's all you need to create an accordion. The principle is that in response to clicking a link, its associated content will slide down and reveal the text it contains.

    2.   Create your CSS file, and name it *style.css*. First just add some rules to design your accordion a little bit. Nothing fancy or particular here, you are just shaping the section's panels and the links:

```css
#accordion a{
  display:block;
  height:23px;
  padding:5px 5px 0 5px;
  color:#333333;
  text-decoration:none;
  border-right:1px solid rgba(255,255,255,0.35);
  border-left:1px solid #000;
  border-left:1px solid #000;
  border-radius:4px;
  background:#FC0;
  margin-bottom:2px;
}

#accordion a:hover{
  color: #333333;
```

```
font-weight:500;
text-shadow: 1px 0px 0px rgba(0, 0, 0, 0.25);
background:#FC0;
```
}

3. Now you'll start to take care of the mechanism of the accordion. You want each panel to be closed, so set their height to 0 pixels. The transition you apply will affect the height because you want to slide it down in response to a click but slide it up when another link is clicked. So add a transition here that will apply each time the height is back to 0 pixels to create a smooth effect. Use the ease-in timing function. Your transition will last 0.3 seconds and target the height property. Also, you don't want the content of any panel content to be displayed when the panel is closed, so set the overflow to hidden:

```
.block .content{
    height: 0px;
    -webkit-transition: height 0.3s ease-in;
    -moz-transition:height 0.3s ease-in;
    -o-transition:height 0.3s ease-in;
    transition:height 0.3s ease-in;
    overflow:hidden;
}
```

4. Next you need to handle the slide down of each panel when the corresponding heading is clicked. For this effect, you use another great feature of CSS3: the :target pseudo-selector and a transition. You use the same timing function and duration to have the same effect on the slide down and slide up effect:

```
.block:target .content {
    background: #ccc;
    height: 100px;
    -webkit-transition: height 0.3s ease-in;
    -moz-transition:height 0.3s ease-in;
    -o-transition:height 0.3s ease-in;
    transition:height 0.3s ease-in;
    border-radius:4px;
    margin-bottom:2px;
    overflow:auto;
    padding:8px;
    font-family:Tahoma, Geneva, sans-serif;
    color:#333;
}
```

And that's it! When clicked, each panel, when targeted, will have a height of 100 pixels and the transition will be applied, giving this downward slide a smooth effect. When it is not targeted, each panel height will be set to 0 pixels, and another transition will be applied if its height was different from 0 (i.e. if it was the last panel targeted), giving this slide up effect. With the overflow set to auto, the content of the selected blockis now visible and scrollable in case its height is bigger than the block's height.

237

> Note: The transitions will not work in Internet Explorer 9. (Internet 8 and earlier also won't support the :target pseudo-selector). So you'll have to rely on JavaScript or Adobe Flash to be completely cross-browser compatible.

Expert tips

In the previous solutions, you saw how to apply transformations to HTML elements. In this one, you saw how to use transitions to animate your elements to some extent. Because transformations are modifying several properties of an element, you can, of course, apply transitions on transformed elements, and this opens up a lot of possibilities! Let's see an example.

Suppose that you have a div element with some basic text inside:

```
<div id="element">
   Animate me!
 </div>
```

Now apply the following style rules:

```
#element{
  display:block;
  width:90px;
  height:80px;
  background:#ccc;
  -moz-transition:all 0.7s ease;
  -o-transition:all 0.7s ease;
  -webkit-transition:all 0.7s ease;
}

#element:hover{
  background:#F00;
  -moz-transform:scale(1.5) rotate(360deg);
  -ms-transform:scale(1.5) rotate(360deg);
  -o-transform:scale(1.5) rotate(360deg);
  -webkit-transform:scale(1.5) rotate(360deg);
}
```

Now, in response to a hover event, your element will be rescaled by 1.5 from its original size and rotate on itself at the same time in a transition that's 0.7 seconds in duration. Because you placed the transition on the original element state, when the hover event ends it returns to its original state with the same transition values, providing a nice, small animated effect with only a few CSS declarations.

Solution 9-4: Going further with animations in CSS3

In the previous solutions of this chapter, you saw that you can transform elements, animate them with transitions, and combine those two properties. These capabilities already give you the ability to create stunning effects in your HTML documents without any external scripts. But so far when you wanted to add some animation, you needed an event to be triggered in one way or another (either with pseudo-selectors in CSS or with JavaScript) to create a transition from one state to another, and thus an animation. There is another great module in CSS3 that lets you go beyond this and enable standalone animations: the Animations module. In this solution, you'll see how you can build animations with the Animations CSS3 module.

What's involved

The Animations CSS3 module is an extension that has been brought to the Transitions module (that we covered in Solution 9-3). To create animations, whatever language is used (or even on simple paper), you have to use key frames in one way or another. A *key frame* is an image or a state, and basically an animation is a sequence of several key frames rendered or viewed one after another over time. In fact, the transitions you saw in the previous solutions are animations made of two key frames only. With the CSS3 Animations module, you can go further and define more than two states—that is, more than two key frames—and thus create more complex animations.

The keyframes rule

To create animations containing more than two states with CSS3, you have to use the new @keyframes rule. As mentioned, an animation is a succession of states over time that give the illusion of movement. With the @keyframe rule, you can define the different states you want to have in your animation. Its syntax is straightforward and consists of the keyword @keyframes followed by an identifier defined by you that gives the animation a name:

```
@keyframes myFirstAnimation{

}
```

Each state then is defined by the block of style rules having its place over time defined in % as a selector. Each value in % defines the place over time of a key frame in the animation, with 0% being the starting key frame (or 0% can be replaced by the keyword from) and 100% being the last key frame (or 100% can be replaced by the keyword to). To be valid, a @keyframes declaration must contain at least one starting state (0% or from) and one ending state (100% or to). Whatever style rules you set within a block will be applied to the targeted element in this specific key frame. Every key frame will be treated after another one chronologically according to its selector value and not necessarily in the order you write them.

```
@keyframes myFirstAnimation{

  0%{
    margin-left:0
  }
  50%{
    margin-left:10px;
  }

  100%{
   margin-left:20px;
  }

}
```

This example sets three states for the animation named myFirstAnimation. In the first state, the element has a left margin of 0 pixels; in the second, it has (50 %) of 10 pixels; and in the third, it has one of 20 pixels.

239

Binding the animation to an element

Once the animation and its different states are created in the @keyframes, you need to bind it to the element you want to animate. To achieve that, you have to specify several animation properties within your element selector:

- animation-name: The name of the animation, which is the identifier following the @keyframe keyword.

- animation-duration: The duration of the animation, expressed in seconds or milliseconds. All the states defined within the animation will occur during this lapse of time; its default value is 0.

- animation-timing-function: Sets how the animation will progress over the time of its duration. Its possible values are linear, ease, ease-in, ease-out, ease-in-out, and cubic-bezier. (See Solution 9-3 for more details.)

- animation-delay: Defines when the animation will start. The default value is 0.

- animation-iteration-count: Defines how many times the animation is to be played. The value must be an integer or infinite for an infinite loop. The default value is 1.

- animation-direction: Defines whether the animation should play in reverse on alternate cycles or not. The possible values are alternate or normal (by default).

- animation-play-state: Defines whether the animation is running (by default) or paused. (This property might be removed from the specification.)

The animation-name and animation-duration properties are, quite logically, compulsory for an animation to occur. The others are optional.

If not specified otherwise (through JavaScript or with a pseudo-selector), the animation will start on the document load. (Note that the animation-delay, if any, is part of the animation.)

Now let's bind the previous small animation named myFirstAnimationto an element having element for its id as an example:

```
#element{
  animation-name: myFirstAnimation;
  animation-duration: 2s;
  animation-timing-function: linear;
  animation-delay: 1s;
  animation-iteration-count: 2;
  animation-direction: alternate;
  animation-play-state: running;
}
```

Here the element will go through all the states defined in the animation myFirstAnimation—that is, move from its original position to 20 pixels to the right and then come back (because the animate-direction is defined as alternate), with a linear speed. The first state will be played after a 2-second delay, and the whole animation will be played twice.

By playing with the different states, properties, and delays, you can create stunning animations in plain CSS.

Multiple animations

You can bind multiple animations to an element by using a comma-separated list:

```
#element{
 animation-name: myFirstAnimation, mySecondAnimation;
 animation-duration: 2s,1s;
 animation-timing-function: linear,ease;
 animation-delay: 1s,2s;
 animation-iteration-count: 2,1;
 animation-direction: alternate;
 animation-play-state: running;
}
```

There is also an `animation` shorthand property you can use to combine the animation properties into a single property like this:

```
animation : animation-name animation-duration animation-timing-function animation-delay
animation-iteration-count animation-direction ;
```

Browser support

CSS3 Animations is not supported by all major browsers yet. Opera doesn't support it at all for the moment, and Internet Explorer supports it as of version 10. (See Table 9-4.) This specification is still in a draft stage at the time of this writing, so you need to use the vendor prefixes for each browser.

Table 9-4. CSS3 Animations browser support

Firefox	Opera	Safari	Chrome	Internet Explorer	iOS Safari	Android Browser	Opera Mobile
7+	no	4.0	14.0	10+	3.3	2.1	no
—moz—		—webkit—	—webkit—	—ms—	—webkit—	—webkit—	

If CSS3 Animations are not supported, you can fall back to JavaScript time-based animations or use an external plug-in like Adobe Flash. However, you should be aware that fall-back animations might have a different performance profile than your CSS3 animations. To check if the browser supports animation and add a fallback solution if necessary, the Modernizr library is once again a great asset:

```
<script type="text/javascript" language="javascript" src="js/modernizr.js"></script>
<script type="text/javascript" language="javascript">
if(!Modernizr.cssanimations){
  //the current browser doesn't support CSS Animations
  // add a JavaScript fall-back script or a Flash animation
  window.alert('Your browser doesn't CSS3 animations');
}

</script>
```

How it works

To illustrate all this, the next example shows you how to build a slideshow photo gallery using only CSS3 and, in particular, the animation properties:

1. First create an HTML5 document with your usual text editor. In it, add a simple `div` containing what will be your slideshow with three `figure` elements and their respective `figcaption`, all wrapped in a `div` container. Within your head tag, detect whether the browser supports the CSS3 animation property. (We won't cover the fall-back code in this solution, but it can be easily done with pure JavaScript or any framework like jQuery or with a Flash animation.)

```
<!DOCTYPE HTML>
<html>
<head>
<meta charset="utf-8">
<link rel="stylesheet" type="text/css" href="style.css" />
<script type="text/javascript" language="javascript" src="js/modernizr.js"></script>
<script type="text/javascript" language="javascript">
if(!Modernizr.cssanimations){
  //the current browser doesn't support CSS Animations
  // add a JavaScript fall back script or a Flash animation
  window.alert('Your browser doesn't CSS3 animations');
}

</script>
<title>Solution 9_4</title>
</head>
<body>
 <div id="wrapper">
   <div id="slideshow">
   <figure>
     <img src="img/img1.jpg" alt="" width="600" height="330" />
     <figcaption>Photo 1 : Legend</figcaption>
   </figure>
   <figure>
     <img src="img/img2.jpg" alt="" width="600" height="330" />
     <figcaption>Photo 2 : Legend</figcaption>
   </figure>
   <figure>
     <img src="img/img3.jpg" alt="" width="600" height="330" />
     <figcaption>Photo 3 : Legend</figcaption>
   </figure>
   </div>
   </div>
</body>
</html>
```

What you have here is three photos with their legends, nested in a `div` that you name `slideshow`. That's about it. Your elements are ready. Now you need to take care of the view of your document.

2. Create the CSS file *style.css*. First set the style rules of the `wrapper` `div` so that only one photo of your slideshow appears at a time. This is easily achieved by applying an absolute position and setting the `overflow` as `hidden`. You also style your figure elements a little bit by adding a border:

```
*{ margin:0; padding:0;}

#wrapper{
  position: absolute;
```

```
  display:block;
  background:#333;
  width:620px;
  height:380px;
  overflow:hidden;
}

figure{
  width:620px;
  height:380px;
}

figcaption{
  text-align:center;
  padding:3px 0;
  color:#fff;
}

img{
  border:10px #333 solid;
}
```

3. Now let's get to the animation part. You have three photos, one below another. To create a slide-show, you need to create an animation that will start on the first photo and then a couple of seconds later slide the container up, stop on the next photo, stop again for a couple of seconds, and so on, until the last one. (Here, you have only three.) When the last photo is in view, it needs to slide down to the first photo and start all over again. You'll achieve just that with different key frames:

```
@-moz-keyframes slideshow {
  0%,30%,100%{
    margin-top: 0 ;
    }
  35%,65%{
   margin-top: -380px;
    }
  70%,98% {
   margin-top: -760px;
    }
}

@-webkit-keyframes slideshow {
  0%,30%,100%{
    margin-top: 0 ;
    }
  35%,65%{
   margin-top: -380px;
    }
  70%,98% {
   margin-top: -760px;
    }
}
```

To shorten the notation, we have been grouping the key frames having the same values, but what we did chronologically is move the container as follows:

- First frame (0 %): `margin-top: 0 px;`. Our first photo is in view.

- Second frame (value 30 %) `margin-top:0 pixels`.It doesn't move. Our photos have to be visible for a couple of seconds. Here we are using timing values, but we don't change the position of the element to produce a pause on the photo.

- Third frame (35 %): `margin-top: -380px;`.This brings up the container so that our second photo is in view. It takes 5% of our animation, and we want it to move rather fast because it's a transition from one photo to another.

- Fourth frame (65 %): Here, again, we don't change a property, simulating a pause on our second photo.

- Fifth frame (70 %): `margin-top:-760px`. This brings our container up by 380 pixels from its last position, or by 760 pixels from its original position. This brings in view our third photo. Again, the duration is 5 %, like the previous transition.

- Sixth frame (98 %): We simulate another pause by not changing any value.

- Seventh frame (100 %): `margin-top: 0;`. We bring our container back to its original position during the last 2% of our animation to have a visual fast-rewind effect.

4 We have defined all the states of our animation. We now need to bind the animation to the `slideshow div` element, because it is the container of our photos:

```
#slideshow {
  position: absolute;
  margin:0;
  width: 620px;
  -moz-animation-name: slideshow;
  -moz-animation-duration: 20s;
  -moz-animation-iteration-count:infinite;
  -moz-animation-timing-function: linear;
  -webkit-animation-name: slideshow;
  -webkit-animation-duration: 20s;
  -webkit-animation-iteration-count:infinite;
  -webkit-animation-timing-function: linear;
}
```

Through the `animation-name` property, we bind the element with the animation we defined in the previous step. We set a duration of 20 seconds for our animation, and we want our slideshow to run indefinitely on our page, so we define the `animation-iteration-count` as `infinite`. Our timing function is a basic `linear` one.

That's it! Our slideshow is ready to be played continuously on our page now.

Note that this won't work on Internet Explorer versions prior to 10, and it won't work at all on Opera. So you have to write fall-back solutions either in JavaScript or Adobe Flash.

Expert tips

By playing with all the transitions, animations, and transform properties and functions, you saw that it's possible to build real and rather long animations with CSS only. Here is an example, based on a Spiderman cartoon and made by Anthony Calzadilla: www.optimum7.com/css3-man/animation.html). He explained all the steps he took to put this animation up using only CSS3 and a bit of jQuery: www.optimum7.com/internet-marketing/web-development/pure-css3-spiderman-ipad-cartoon-jquery-html5-no-flash.html).

Solution 9-5: Applying 3D transformations in CSS3

In Solution 9-1, you saw that you can apply 2D transformations to any HTML document element in CSS3. One other cool new CSS3 feature is the possibility to apply 3D transformations to HTML document elements with the CSS3 3D transforms module. In this solution, you'll see how to manipulate elements in a three-dimensional (3D) space.

What's involved

The CSS3 3D transforms module is quite similar to 2D transformations (which we covered in Solution 9-1) and provides functions to rotate, translate, scale, and apply matrix transformations in a 3D Cartesian coordinate system to any element. (See Figure 9-7.) First of all, it is worth pointing out that if the CSS3 3D transforms module allow transformations in a three-dimensional space, the transformed elements are then represented as usual, on a two-dimensional plane. A div element, for instance, remains a *flat* element without any real depth, and we are still dealing with regular HTML. And CSS3 3D transforms give you the capability to transform elements along three axes: the X and Y axes as in 2D, as well as along the Z axis, providing a sense of depth. Let's see how to do that in a really simple way with CSS3.

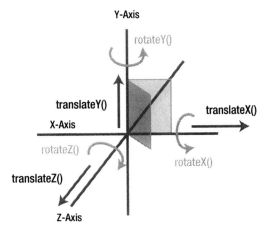

Figure 9-7. 3D space coordinates and 3D transform functions

The 3D transform functions

The 3D transform functions are similar to the ones used in 2D transformation that we covered in Solution 9-1: `rotate()`, `scale()`, `translate()`, `skew()`, and `matrix()`. Here, they are extended to include the 3D space through a parameter corresponding to the Z coordinate. The additional transform functions are the following:

- `rotateZ(angle)`: Defines a clockwise rotation by the angle given as a parameter along the Z axis. (If the value is negative, the rotation will be counter-clockwise.)

- `rotate3D(angleX,angleY,angleZ)`: Defines a 3D rotation along the three axes.

- `translateZ(z value)`: Defines a translation along the Z axis. If the value is negative, the element will seem to move away from the user. If it's a positive value, it will seem to move closer to the user. (It is expressed in pixels. We are still in the CSS visual formatting model, but percentage values are not allowed here.)

- `translate3D(x value, y value, z value)`: Defines a 3D translation along the three axes according to the three values given as parameters.

- `scaleZ(z vector)`: Defines a scale operation using its parameter as scaling vector. A value of 1 will leave the element unchanged.

- `scale3D(x vector, y vector,z vector)`: Defines a 3D scale transformation along the three axes according to the three vectors given as parameters.

- `matrix3D(a, b, 0, 0, c, d, 0, 0, 0, 0, 1, 0, e, f, 0, 1)`: Defines a 3D transformation, using a 4 by 4 matrix (16 values). The `matrix3D` function is rather complex to use and master, so we won't be covering it in this book.

Perspective

Because we're dealing with a 3D space, another factor to take into consideration is perspective. In this sense, perspective is an artificial vanishing point from where the user will view the 3D object, giving the illusion of depth. The higher the perspective value, the further the depth of the vanishing point. It can be set in two ways:

- Through the transform function `perspective()`, as follows:

  `transform: perspective( value in pixels);`

You use this notation to apply a 3D transformation to a group of elements, by applying it to the parent element. (If the value is 'none',0 or negative, no perspective transform is applied.) Here's an example:

```
#parent{
  perspective:500px;
}
```

This applies a perspective of 500 pixels to all the child elements of the #parent element.

- Through the perspective transform property as follows:

  `transform:perspective: value in pixels ;`

You use this notation when you want to target only an element. Here's an example:

```
#element{
  transform:perspective(500px) rotateX(45deg);
}
```

This applies a perspective of 500 pixels only to this element. (See Figure 9-8.)

Figure 9-8. An element with a perspective of 500 pixels and rotated by 45 degrees on the X axis

Perspective origin

By default, the origin of the perspective point is *50% 50%* (the center of the element), but just like the transform origin in 2D transformations, you can change this value and reset the X and Y positions at which the viewer appears to be looking at the elements. You do this using the `perspective-origin` property:

```
perspective-origin:top left;
```

This example sets the perspective origin point on the upper left corner of the element.

The transform-style property

When you apply any 3D transformations to children of an element, they are, by default, rendered into the plane of their parent and therefore remain flat. For instance, if you apply a rotation on the Z axis (with the `rotateZ()` transform function) to an element that is a child of another element, it won't appear rotated and your element will remain flat on its parent. That's where the transformation function `transform-style` comes into action. Through it, you can control whether the children of an element remain flat on their parent or not. It can have two values:

- flat: This is the default value, and it specifies that transformed children of an element are flattened into the plane of their parent.

- preserve-3d: This specifies that the element to which it is assigned does not flatten its child elements.

Figure 9-9 shows a visual example of a `div` containing a child `div` element being transformed, with the two `transform-style`values applied successively.

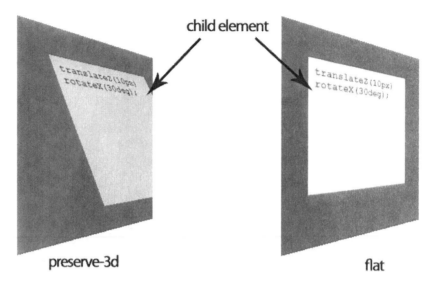

Figure 9-9. The two `transform-style` values applied successively on the same group of elements

The backface-visibility property

When you are in 3D, you'll be able to position elements in such a way that in some situations their reverse side will then be visible. However, that might not be suitable all the time (in some animations for instance). The `backface-visibility` property gives you the ability to control the visibility of the back face of an element when transformed. It can have two obvious values: `hidden` or `visible`(by default). Here's an example:

```
#element{
  backface-visibility: hidden;
}
```

3D transforms and animation

One really cool thing is that just as you added animations to elements (transformed or not), you can animate your 3D transformed elements in exactly the same way, creating stunning effects within your style sheet through the `@keyframes` rule. (See Solution 9-4.) Or you can do it by adding a transition. (See Solution 9-3.)

Browser support

It is probably not an option to use 3D transforms in production at the time of this writing because all the major modern browsers don't support it yet. (See Table 9-5.) However, we can safely expect that it will be the case soon and that we will be able to use those great features easily. Note that this specification is still in the draft stage, so you'll have to use the vendor prefixes.

Table 9-5. CSS3 3D Transforms browser support

Firefox	Opera	Safari	Chrome	Internet Explorer	iOS Safari	Android Browser	Opera Mobile
10+	no	4.0+	14.0+	10+	3.2+	3+	no
–moz–		–webkit–	–webkit–	–ms–	–webkit–	–webkit–	

You can detect the browser support with the usual Modernizr JavaScript library and add a fall-back solution very easily, as follows:

```
<script type="text/javascript" language="javascript" src="js/modernizr.js"></script>
<script type="text/javascript" language="javascript">
if(!Modernizr. csstransforms3d){
  //the current browser doesn't support CSS 3D Transforms
  // add a JavaScript fall-back script or a Flash animation
  window.alert('Your browser doesn't CSS3 3D Transforms');
}

</script>
```

How it works

To see the preceding functions and properties in action, the next example shows you how to create a div element that will flip in response to a mouse hover event, with the single use of CSS3. On one side, it will display an image, and on the other side, it will display some text. On mouse out, it will flip back to its original display state.

1. Start by creating an HTML document containing your elements with your text editor. In the < head > of your document, detect the 3D transforms support with the Modernizr library. (We won't cover the fall-back part here).

```
<!DOCTYPE HTML>
<html>
<head>
<meta charset="utf-8">
<title>Solution 9_5</title>
<link rel="stylesheet" type="text/css" href="style.css" />
<script type="text/javascript" language="javascript" src="modernizr.js"></script>
<script type="text/javascript" language="javascript">

if(!Modernizr.csstransforms3d){
  //the current browser doesn't support CSS 3D Transforms
  // add a JavaScript fall-back script or a Flash animation
  window.alert('Your browser doesn't CSS3 3D Transforms');
}
</script>
</head>
<body>
<div id="container">
```

```
<div id="card">
  <div id="face1"><img src="logo.jpg" width="300" /></div>
  <div id="face2"><p>CSS3 Solutions </p><p>Essential Techniques for CSS3 Developers</p></
div>
  </div>
 </div>
</body>
</html>
```

Here you created your two sides—named *face1* and *face2*—nested inside a div, with the div itself in a container. This is pretty simple. And that's all you need in your HTML document.

2. Now you can create your style sheet document. First set rules for the main container. Because you want the perspective to be applied to all the container's child elements, you use the perspective property and define it here as 500 pixels. (Use the vendor prefixes for each browser.)

```
#container{
  width: 300px;
  height: 300px;
  position: relative;
  margin: 100px auto;
  -webkit-perspective: 500px;
  -moz-perspective: 500px;
  -ms-perspective: 500px;
}
```

3. Now take care of the pseudo-card you want to flip. In fact, each side is two separate divs containing what will be on one side (here, an image and a plain text). You rotate the div that will be the back face of the pseudo-card (the element with the ID of face2) so that the front face of each element is now opposite of the other with the rotateY transform function. You also define the back-face-visibility of each element to be hidden. For all this to take effect, you need to define the transform-style property of their parent element, #card, to preserve-3d. Now each time you rotate the parent element, #card, the front side of one of its child elements will be displayed. You add a small, smooth transition to have nice flip effect, which is linear with a duration of 1 second.

```
#face1, #face2{
  display:block;
  width:100%;
  height:100%;
  position:absolute;
  -webkit-backface-visibility: hidden;
  -moz-backface-visibility: hidden;
  -ms-backface-visibility: hidden;

}

#face2{
  background:#eee;
  padding:12px;
  -webkit-transform:rotateY(180deg);
  -moz-transform:rotateY(180deg);
  -ms-transform:rotateY(180deg);
```

```
}
#card{
  width: 300px;
  height: 300px;
  position:absolute;
  -webkit-transform-style: preserve-3d;
  -webkit-transition:all 1s linear;
  -moz-transform-style: preserve-3d;
  -moz-transition:all 1s linear;

}
```

Now what you have is like a card with two sides. But so far you see only one of them, the front face of your element named face1 that contains your image.

4.   It's almost done. You just need to define the second state of your pseudo-card, by flipping it in response to a mouse hover action, which is pretty easy to do.

```
#container:hover #card{
 -webkit-transform:rotateY(180deg);
 -moz-transform:rotateY(180deg);
 -ms-transform:rotateY(180deg);
}
```

That's it. If you load your document, you'll see the image. In response to a mouse hover event, it will flip to the other side (in fact, the div face2), which contains a small amount of text. You are still using regular elements, and the text is selectable just as any text is.

At the time of this writing, this solution won't work in Opera; it will work only in really modern browsers.

Expert tips

If you want to see what 3D transforms can do, you can use the following online tool: www.westciv.com/tools/3Dtransforms/index.html). It lets you manipulate all the transform function values with a simple interface, and you can even add animations and see the result instantly. Moreover, it generates the corresponding CSS code with all the vendor prefixes.

Summary

In this chapter, you saw how to use some of the exciting new CSS3 features, which you can use to add some pretty amazing visual assets to your HTML document elements. You saw how to transform elements in a 2D space as well as in 3D, and how to animate them from a simple transition to a more complex animation of several key frames. Using your creativity, and depending on your projects, you can combine all of them to produce really exciting visual assets to your website and applications, both on desktops and mobile devices, without having to rely on any external script or plug-in. CSS is all about the visual aspect and disposition of your document elements, and in the next chapter you'll see what the CSS3 modules involve in terms of accessibility. You will see solutions to handle accessibility with multimedia elements, both audio and video, and how CSS3 modules can help you to make an interface consistent with the web accessibility principles, thereby making your web document adaptable for all users.

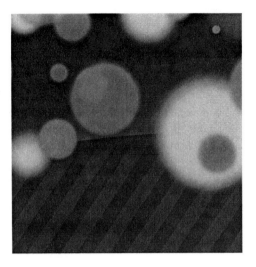

Chapter 10

Multimedia and Accessibility

On the Internet, you can often find multimedia elements embedded in web pages, and modern web browsers support a wide variety of multimedia formats. CSS3 introduces new, interesting, and solid techniques to style all those media elements, such as music or video players.

In addition, CSS provides benefits in terms of accessibility, primarily by separating the document structure from its presentation. Style sheets were designed to allow precise control of all elements on web pages, outside the markup. In this chapter, we'll round up some good practices and look at to how to improve website accessibility using CSS3.

Solution10-1: Building a custom video player

The HTML5 < video > component represents a revolution in the management and distribution of video content on web browsers. There are many advantages to having a natively embedded video in a browser, including mobile support. As such, many developers have started to take advantage of this possibility.

Creating a customized video player was a difficult task that initially discouraged people from working with HTML5 video. In contrast, the Flash integrated development environment (IDE) is very powerful, and you can use it to create a personalized player in no time at all. The situation has changed, though.

The introduction of CSS3, together with HTML5 and JavaScript, has made this process much more simple. In this solution, you will look at building an easily customizable HTML5 < video > player, including packaging it as a simple jQuery plug-in, choosing control types, and outputting custom CSS for your own situation.

What's involved

As a professional web designer, you want to create a video player that seems consistent among browsers. However, each browser supplies a different look and feel for a player, from a minimal approach in Firefox and Chrome to more complex controls in Opera and Safari. (See the controls in each browser in Figure 10-1.) If you want your controls to look the same in every browser and be integrated in your design, you must create them from scratch. Don't worry—it isn't as difficult as it sounds.

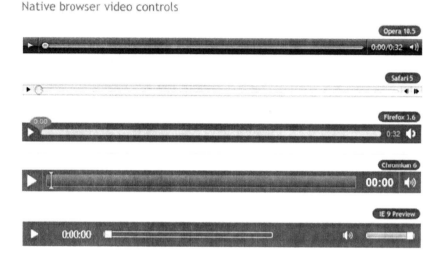

Figure 10-1. A variety of native browser video controls

All media components support the media elements API, which you can access using JavaScript and use to create functions to replicate play, start, or stop buttons using simple HTML elements.

Browser support

The failure among browser manufacturers to support a common codec is the main obstacle in creating a cross-browser video player, with clashes especially notable between Opera/Firefox and Internet Explorer/Safari. Fortunately, Google recently released a new codec (VP8) along with the WebM project (http://www.webmproject.org/), giving rise for the first time to a single codec for everything. Opera, Firefox, Chrome, and Internet Explorer 9 all have this support in the latest builds. Even Flash will be able to read this new codec.

This means that soon you can create a single version of video that will be reproduced in the <video> element in most browsers, and in Flash Player in browsers that don't natively support WebM.

How it works

First, you need to create the actual markup for the video controls. You need a Play/Pause button, a search bar, a timer, as well as volume and cursor buttons. You must insert the markup for the controls after the <video> element within a <div> container.

```
<div class="video-controls">
  <a class="video-play" title="Play/Pause"></a>
  <div class="video-seek"></div>
  <div class="video-timer">00:00</div>
  <div class="volume-box">
    <div class="volume-slider"></div>
    <a class="volume-button" title="Mute/Unmute"></a>
  </div>
</div>
```

> Note: We've used classes instead of IDs for all the elements to be able to use the same code for multiple video players on the same page.

jQuery stuff

After you create the markup, you must prepare all the elements for the multimedia API in order to control the behavior of the video file. This solution prepares the player as a jQuery plug-in, which enables it to be reused in many elements. In this solution, you won't deal with every part of JavaScript; if you want to deepen your knowledge on this topic, you can read "Develop a jQuery plug-in" (http://docs.jquery.com/Plugins/Authoring).

I will quickly summarize the necessary steps to create the slider:

1. Target each control by its class to add listeners; keep the controls hidden until everything is ready.

2. Bind the three events (Play, Pause, and Ended), adding and removing classes from the button to change the look of it, depending on the state of the video (Playing or Paused).

3. Use the jQuery UI Slider component to create the seek slider.

4. Use the jQuery UI Slider and a custom function on the volume button to create volume controls for muting and unmuting the video.

5. Once the video is ready, initialize the slider and show the controls.

> Note: You remove the controls feature from the <video> at this point because you will use a set of custom controls created via JavaScript, overwriting the default ones from each browser.

Look and feel

Here's the fun part—the look and feel of the video player. Once the plug-in is ready, personalizing the commands is extremely simple thanks to the use of CSS3.

First, add a style to the parent container of the video player:

```
.video-player {
  float: left;
  padding: 10px;
  border: 5px solid #61625d;
```

```
  -moz-border-radius: 5px;
  ms-border-radius: 5px;
  -webkit-border-radius: 5px;
  border-radius: 5px;

  background: #000000;
  background-image: -moz-linear-gradient(top, #313131, #000000);
  background-image: -webkit-gradient(linear,left top,left bottom,color-stop(0, #313131),
color-stop(1, #000000));
  box-shadow: inset 0 15px 35px #535353;
}
```

Set float: left to avoid expanding the entire width of the player. This keeps the size the same for the actual video element. You use gradient attributes and border-radius to create a sleek style.

Align the controls to the left and horizontally. You use opacity and transitions on the Play/Pause and Volume Mute/Unmute buttons to create a nice hover effect:

```
.video-play {
  display: block;
  width: 22px;
  height: 22px;
  margin-right: 15px;
  background: url(play-icon.png) no-repeat;
  opacity: 0.7;
  -moz-transition: all 0.2s ease-in-out;
  -ms-transition: all 0.2s ease-in-out;
  -o-transition: all 0.2s ease-in-out;
  -webkit-transition: all 0.2s ease-in-out;
  transition: all 0.2s ease-in-out;
}

.paused-button {
  background: url(pause-icon.png) no-repeat;
}

.video-play:hover {
  opacity: 1;
}
```

As mentioned previously, you use the jQuery framework both for the video and volume navigation bars for the sliders. You completely overwrite the default style defined in the jQuery library:

```
.video-seek .ui-slider-handle {
  width: 15px;
  height: 15px;
  border: 1px solid #333;
  top: -4px;

  -moz-border-radius:10px;
  -ms-border-radius:10px;
  -webkit-border-radius:10px;
  border-radius:10px;

  background: #e6e6e6;
```

```
  background-image: -moz-linear-gradient(top, #e6e6e6, #d5d5d5);
  background-image: -webkit-gradient(linear,left top,left bottom,color-stop(0, #e6e6e6),
color-stop(1, #d5d5d5));
  box-shadow: inset 0 -3px 3px #d5d5d5;
}

.video-seek .ui-slider-handle.ui-state-hover {
  background: #fff;
}

.video-seek .ui-slider-range {
  -moz-border-radius:15px;
  -ms-border-radius:15px;
  -webkit-border-radius:15px;
  border-radius:15px;

  background: #4cbae8;
  background-image: -moz-linear-gradient(top, #4cbae8, #39a2ce);
  background-image: -webkit-gradient(linear,left top,left bottom,color-stop(0, #4cbae8),
color-stop(1, #39a2ce));

  box-shadow: inset 0 -3px 3px #39a2ce;
}
```

You add a touch of interactivity by animating the activation of the slider for the volume, according to the mouse effect over the Mute/Unmute button.

Then hide the volume slider, assigning a fixed height to its container to ensure that it remains aligned with the volume button. The desired effect is tied to the hovering of the mouse, in which case the volume bar will be shown through the use of CSS3 transitions:

```
.volume-box {
  height: 30px;

  -moz-transition: all 0.1s ease-in-out; /* Firefox */
  -ms-transition: all 0.1s ease-in-out; /* IE future proofing */
  -o-transition: all 0.2s ease-in-out; /* Opera */
  -webkit-transition: all 0.1s ease-in-out; /* Safari and Chrome */
  transition: all 0.1s ease-in-out;
}

.volume-box:hover {
  height: 135px;
  padding-top: 5px;
}
.volume-slider {
  visibility: hidden;
  opacity: 0;

  -moz-transition: all 0.1s ease-in-out; /* Firefox */
  -ms-transition: all 0.1s ease-in-out; /* IE future proofing */
  -o-transition: all 0.1s ease-in-out; /* Opera */
```

```
    -webkit-transition: all 0.1s ease-in-out; /* Safari and Chrome */
    transition: all 0.1s ease-in-out;
}

.volume-box:hover .volume-slider {
  position: relative;
  visibility: visible;
  opacity: 1;
}
```

Thanks to basic CSS knowledge and some new properties introduced with CSS3, you can finally personalize a video player to your liking.

Expert tip

As you might have noticed, you chose to create a jQuery plug-in for the successful outcome of this technique, which in turn creates the need to define a series of default options. These options are theme and childtheme, which are then applied when the plug-in is recalled. You can therefore create different themes and specifically recall them according to your needs.

Solution 10-2: A CSS3 music player

Before HTML5 came on to the scene, it was a fairly awkward task to add audio to web pages. Adobe Flash was the only way to provide audio content in any kind of interactive way. With the introduction of the <audio> element in HTML5, however, audio playback can now be done natively. You can create custom buttons using CSS and HTML, and give them appropriate functionality using the HTML5 audio API. It is nice not having to go back into Flash every time you want to make some changes to the audio content.

In this solution, you'll see how to use CSS3 to style a music player built with the HTML5 <audio> element.

What's involved

The following sections detail the elements you'll use in this solution.

The <audio> element

The <audio> element is simple to use. You can simply write the following:

```
<audio src="http://yourserver/rockandroll.ogg" controls preload> </audio>
```

Figure 10-2. A basic <audio> element rendered in Opera

The browser then provides a simple player element in the web page, as shown in Figure 10-2.

The < audio > element has five attributes:

- src contains the path to the audio file you want to play.

- autoplay is a Boolean attribute specifying whether the source file should start to play automatically at page load or not.

> Note: Autoplay forces audio to play without the interaction of the user and can interfere with other audio sources the user might be listening to. Using it is typically considered a bad practice to follow.

- preload tells the browser to make an informed decision about how much data to download. A mobile browser might decide to preload nothing to conserve bandwidth, while a desktop browser on a fast connection might begin loading immediately.

- loop is a Boolean attribute specifying whether the source file should start to play all over again when the end of the source file has been reached.

- controls is a Boolean attribute specifying whether or not the browser should display its default media controls. If you don't specify this, no controls are shown, and you need to create your own controls using the handy audio JavaScript API along with HTML, CSS, and whatever other web standards you want to draw the controls with.

A little bit of JavaScript

The < audio > element exposes a powerful JavaScript API. By accessing the methods audio.play() and audio.pause(), you can start and pause the playback of the source file. The audio.volume method provides access to the volume.

We will be using the jPlayer plug-in for jQuery (http://www.jplayer.org/). It serves a common interface for both the native < audio > element and the Flash fallback. So you are able to create a common design, made with JavaScript, CSS, and HTML on your player without worrying about if the native part or the fallback is used for playback. The jPlayer plug-in is supported on all major browsers, including iOS, Android, and Internet Explorer 6 too!

The following script will construct an < audio > element and assign event handlers to some simple HTML buttons that you can then use to control the audio playback:

```
// Invoke new Audio object
var audio = new Audio('music.ogg');

// Get the play button and append an audio play method to onclick
var play = document.getElementById('play');
play.addEventListener('click', function(){
  audio.play();
}, false);

// Get the pause button and append an audio pause method to onclick
var pause = document.getElementById('pause');
pause.addEventListener('click', function(){
```

```
    audio.pause();
}, false);

// Get the HTML5 range input element and append audio volume adjustment to onchange
var volume = document.getElementById('volume');
volume.addEventListener('change', function(){
  audio.volume = parseFloat(this.value / 10);
}, false);

// Get where one are in playback and push the time to an element
audio.addEventListener("timeupdate", function() {
  var duration = document.getElementById('duration');
  var s = parseInt(audio.currentTime % 60);
  var m = parseInt((audio.currentTime / 60) % 60);
  duration.innerHTML = m + '.' + s + 'sec';
}, false);
```

Then you apply this script to the HTML/CSS structure and design as described in the following sections.

How it works

Start by setting up the HTML structure of the player:

```
<div>
  <input id="play" type="button" value="Play" />
  <input id="pause" type="button" value="Pause" />
  <span id="duration"> </span>
</div>
<div>
  Volume:
  <input id="volume" type="range" min="0" max="10" value="5" />
</div>
```

Each <input> element is given an ID so that you can easily style the elements and assign JavaScript functions to them for interacting with the <audio> element via the audio API, as you'll see in a moment.

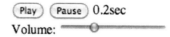

Figure 10-3. Simple audio player rendered in a browser

Figure 10-3 shows how it will be rendered on any browser.

Awesome! You now have all the controls you need. You can start styling each element using CSS3 properties instead of using static background image files.

One small detail worth noting is that you can use a class attribute on the <div> element that wraps the whole player. Doing so, you can use the class value as a CSS style prefix like this:

```
.dark-player #play{
  /* some different style */
}
```

By doing so, you can create infinite skins for this player simply by adding a few lines of CSS code. Pretty cool, isn't it?

Solution 10-3: Improve the form accessibility with CSS3 validation

Forms are used for all kinds of interactive purposes on the web. Forms allow users to select and purchase merchandise, fill in surveys and questionnaires, register for courses, search for information on the web, as well as perform a long list of other actions.

When it comes to the accessibility of a form, you often immediately think of using it with a screen reader. You must remember, however, that anyone can benefit from a well-organized, highly usable form, especially those with cognitive disabilities.

One aspect of forms you will examine in this solution is the management of error and validation field messages. We'll start with the first server-side error messages and move to the client-side, managed validation that interacts with the user while she is filling out the fields of your form.

On one hand, the HTML5 specifications have introduced new types of inputs and attributes you can use to insert specific constraints in the module to handle the increased complication and consequent validation. On the other hand, the CSS Basic User Interface Module 3 (`http://www.w3.org/TR/css3-ui/`) provides several useful pseudo-classes to apply to the different validation states and to change the appearance of the fields according to the user's actions.

Let's see how to combine these two technologies to create a form validator based on CSS that has broad support in current browsers. The more help users receive in real time when filling out a form, the less probable it is that they will make mistakes.

What's involved

We'll make use of both HTML5 type attributes for input fields and CSS3 pseudo-classes. The following sections provide an overview.

CSS3 pseudo-classes for the user interface

The UI module presents several pseudo-classes that help you apply specific styles to the fields of a form in various stages of completion:

- valid, identifies a valid element according to the specification of the form
- invalid, identifies an invalid element
- required, identifies a mandatory field
- optional, identifies an optional field
- in-range
- out-of-range

- read-only

- read-write

The pseudo-classes in-range and out-of-range should be used with the attributes min and max—for example, on an input based on an interval, on a field for the input of numbers, or on all types of inputs that accept those attributes. For instance, if a user inserts a value that is out of range, you can use the pseudo-class to change the style that reflects the state; you can do the same for values that are in range. Only Opera supports the pseudo-classes related to range at the moment.

New type of inputs and attributes with HTML5

The specification on HTML5 forms also introduce new types of inputs, such as email, url, and number. For example, email activates the pseudo-class that's valid only when the user inserts a valid e-mail address; the same principle applies to the number or url field.

There are also some features that facilitate validation, such as placeholder, required, maxlength, pattern, min, max, and step.

Browser support

Browser support for HTML5 forms and the UI module of CSS3 is becoming more widespread. Opera 9 was the first browser to implement Web Forms 2.0 (http://www.whatwg.org/specs/web-apps/current-work/multipage/) before it was incorporated in the HTML5 specifications, but only starting from version 9.6 does it support the UI module of CSS3.

Chrome offers support from version 4 onward. Safari has recently implemented everything in its version 5. Firefox will introduce external support with its version 4.0. Internet Explorer 9, if it continues on this same road of standard support, should have basic support for this functionality in its next release.

How it works

In this solution, you will examine three uses:

- Creating a validation style for an <input>

- Showing dedicated messages using the pattern feature

- Adding contextual help during the compilation of a form

Validation input message

The objective is to move the focus to the field on the form that has been identified as invalid.

Using multiple combinations of the following three pseudo-classes, you can apply the necessary style to the input in the case of validation:

- :focus

- :required

- :invalid

Take a look at the necessary CSS code:

```
input:focus:required:invalid {
  background: red url(invalid-input.png) 0 0 no-repeat;
}
```

The first line moves the focus to a field marked as mandatory, which isn't valid and activates the style that displays an exclamation mark in <input>, clearly informing the user where the error occurred.

```
input:required:valid {
  background-color: #fff;
}
```

In cases where the input doesn't violate any constraints, the pseudo-class *valid* is activated.

Finding the pattern

The HTML5 pattern feature offers you the ability to customize error messages for particular fields, such as a telephone number or a password. To do this, you combine the invalid pseudo-class with a pattern to apply a regular expression to a field:

```
<input type="tel" id="tel" name="tel" pattern="\d{10}" placeholder=
"Please enter a ten digit phone number" required />
```

The regular expression used simply says, "No more than ten characters are allowed." Therefore, the field will always be invalid until the regular expression requirements are met.

You can take full advantage of the pattern attribute by applying a more complex regular expression, such as on this field for passwords:

```
<input id="password" name="password" type="password" title="Minimum 8
characters, one number, one uppercase and one lowercase letter" required
pattern="(?=^.{8,}$)((?=.*\d)|(?=.*\W+))(?![.\n])(?=.*[A-Z])
(?=.*[a-z]).*" />
```

Right from the moment you have specific conditions that restrict what can be inserted by the users—forcing them to create a more secure password—you define a regular expression like the one just shown. The password must have at least eight characters, contain a number, and contain both a lowercase letter and uppercase letter.

To help a user meet these conditions, you use a title attribute to help them exactly understand what the requirements are. In this case, you don't use a placeholder attribute, because you need a longer explanation and placeholder should be used only for short tips.

Adding help

Contextual help is often given to the user through the title attribute. However, if the user doesn't pass over the field with the mouse and moves to it instead with the Tab key, he will never see the help instructions included in the attribute. You can see that on the telephone, postal code, and password fields, the text "help" appears when the field needs further explanation.

```
<input id="password" type="password" />

<p class="validation01">
  <span class="invalid">Minimum 8 characters, one number, one uppercase
```

```
letter and one lowercase letter</span>
 <span class="valid">Your password meets our requirements, thank you.
</span>
</p>
```

The preceding markup introduces an extra container with a help box for when the field is valid and for when it's invalid. In this way, when the field is not valid, it will contain additional information to help the user. When everything is correct, the message and green sign assure the user that the compilation was successful:

```
.validation01 {
 background: red;
 color: #fff;
 display: none;
 font-size: 12px;
 padding: 3px;
 position: absolute;
 right: -110px;
 text-align: center;
 top: 0;
 width: 100px;
}
input:focus + .validation01 {
 display: block;
}
input:focus:required:valid + .validation01 {
 background: green;
}
input:focus:required:valid + .validation01 .invalid {
 display: none;
}
input:focus:required:invalid + .validation01 .valid {
 display: none;
}
```

To show or hide the help box according to the state of the field, you can make the field a target by turning to the pseudo-classes. You do this by using the adjacent element of the (+) selector. Once the field has correctly been filled in, the background becomes green and a valid message is displayed.

Solution 10-4: An unobtrusive skip navigation link

One of the most frequent problems in many design templates is that the main content isn't usually the first thing you see on a page. People who use a screen reader are often forced to scroll through a long list of navigation links, business icons, search boxes, and other items before they even get to the main content.

There exists a simple solution to solve this problem: providing a link at the top of the page that refers to the main content through an anchor. Because of its simplicity, this solution can be implemented in different ways. However, some techniques are better than others. The technique discussed here makes the link invisible until it receives keyboard focus. You obviously manage this kind of effect with some CSS3 code.

What's involved

The main idea of this approach consists of hiding the link until the user passes over it using the Tab key. Mouse users never see the link, because it isn't activated by the mouse movements.

Users who do not need skip navigation links will never realize that a link is there at all. Perhaps this is how it should be because these users might not understand what skip navigation links are supposed to accomplish. For these users, such a link might slightly decrease usability by confusing them a little. Most users will simple ignore the link, but some might wonder.

To display the link, you will use the CSS3 opacity property. The link will always be present in the HTML code of the page. However, it will be completely transparent by default.

How it works

Let's take the case of inserting the link above the menu navigation, at the top of a page:

```
<div id="navigation">
 <a href="#content" class="skip">Skip to content</a>
 <ul>
  <li>
   <a href="index.html">Home</a>
  </li>
  <li>
   <a href="about.html">About</a>
  </li>
  <li>
   <a href="services.html">Services</a>
  </li>
  <li>
   <a href="contact.html">Contact</a>
  </li>
 </ul>
</div>
```

Assign the class .skip to the link to manage its visualization through the opacity property:

```
.skip {
   opacity: 0;
}

.skip:focus {
  opacity: 1;
}
```

A value of 0 (zero) makes the link completely invisible. With the help of the pseudo-class :focus, you can change the value of opacity in cases where a user moves between the links of the page with the Tab key. In such cases, the "skip to content" link becomes visible immediately.

The link is also the first link on the page, so screen-reader users will always hear it first. This seems to be a perfect solution.

> *Notes: The same effect can be achieved by using a combination of CSS and JavaScript. The addition of JavaScript adds another layer of complexity that may or may not add any additional benefit, depending on how it is implemented.*

Clicking on the link in question, the user is brought to the anchor height specified in the attribute href:

```
<a href="#content" class="skip">Skip to content</a>
```

In this case, the content area will be made initially available to the user and conceivably it will be of more interest to them.

Summary

There has been much fragmentation in the format of video and audio required for web delivery. Historically, this variation also came with a lack of control for how the media will be displayed and the requirement for extra plug-ins. This situation makes it more costly for service providers and makes media experiences less than seamless for the end user.

We're still in the early days for native video support. Videos can be embedded within the page much like you currently embed images in the page. By standardizing the media support within a web environment, this fragmentation can be brought under control, making video easily accessible to all and making the online viewing experience more pleasurable for the user.

What's more, CSS3 provides better and more precise control over element styles, text, fonts, an object's position on the page, and audio and speech output. That means you could really separate style from markup, simplifying and cleaning up the HTML and making documents more accessible at the same time.

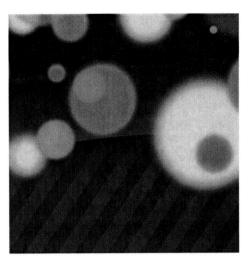

Chapter 11

UX Patterns

You know a bad software experience when you use one. Whether you're instructed to call Customer Service just to retrieve your password or the functions you need to use just never seem to be located in the places you expect, bad experiences can turn your users away in a heartbeat. And good examples of bad user experience (UX) are everywhere. This chapter goes beyond just looking at the code and explores how you should think about creating great user experiences on the Web. The key to designing great software experiences is to constantly play the role of a typical user and, most importantly, to trust your gut. Common sense always prevails in great UX, and the following concepts will help to implement it in your interface.

Rules of thumb

Although technology and hardware have advanced with increasing speed over the past 20 years, the design principles exhibited in solid user experiences have changed very little. The rules of thumb outlined in this chapter should be considered when designing the interface and interactions that make up your user's experience.

> *Note: These rules should be used as guidelines, with some being emphasized more heavily than others, according to the focus of your application. Use these rules when designing new interfaces or redesigning existing ones. In the case of an existing interface, first evaluate the interface against the rules of thumb, and then focus on improvement in the areas that rate the poorest.*

Solution 11-1: Ensuring visibility of system status

The system should always keep users informed about what is going on, through appropriate feedback within reasonable time. From time to time, your experience is going to require the user to wait, while a back-end process completes or when a credit card is being authorized, for example. During these times, it is critical that your user is assured that something is happening, and that the system has not frozen up or failed to receive her input. Figure 11-1 shows a loading indicator in the Google Chrome web browser, indicating to the user that the requested file is being retrieved for display.

Figure 11-1. Google Chrome displays a loading indicator when a PDF is opened in the browser

What's involved

When displaying system status indicators, you should be as specific as possible. Remember, you're making a user wait, and it's always nice to know whether it will just be a few seconds or if it's time to go get another cup of coffee. A simple, indeterminate indicator is good, but a fixed-width progress bar, as shown in Figure 11-2 is even better. In some instances, providing a percentage of completion or estimated time to completion is important as well. Think about who your users are and how much information they'll want to see.

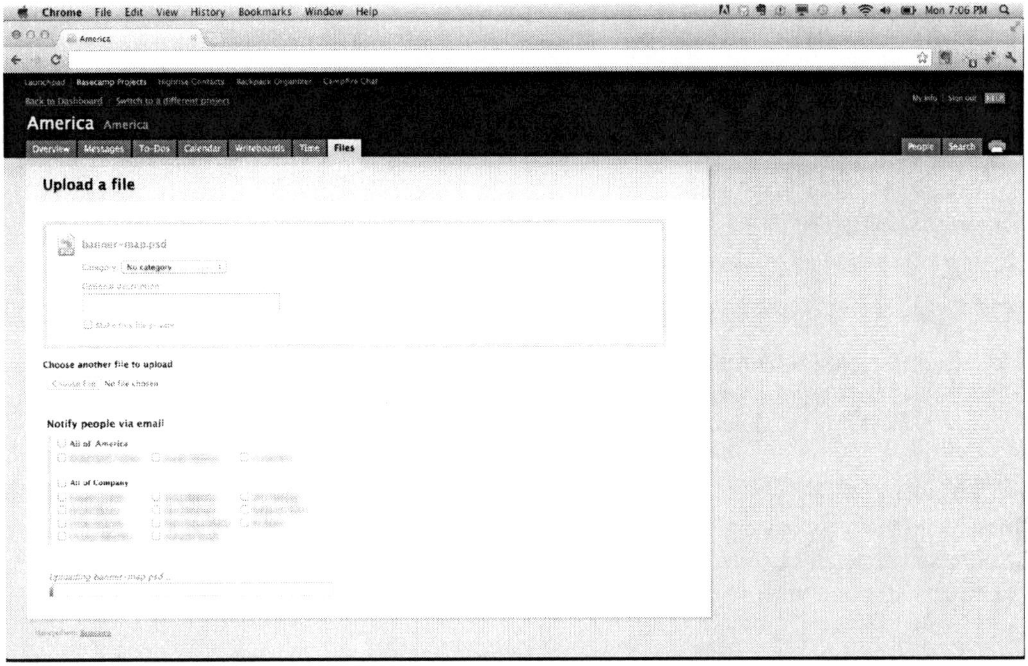

Figure 11-2. 37 Signals Basecamp shows the progress of a file upload. The speed at which the bar is filled provides a sense of how long the upload might take to complete

How to build it

Identify the main navigation model in your experience and all of the elements that make it up. In this case, you're designing a shopping experience that sells clothing. The CSS and HTML for the navigational elements could look like this:

```css
CSS
nav li {
    float: left;
    list-style: none;
    font-size: 15px;
    margin-right:2px;
}
nav a {
    display: block;
    width:100px;
    padding:5px;
    text-decoration:none;
    text-align:center;
    color:#333333;
    background-color:#CCCCCC;
    /* Browser Filters */
```

```
    -moz-border-radius: 8px 8px 0px 0px;
    -webkit-border-radius: 8px 8px 0px 0px;
    -khtml-border-radius: 8px 8px 0px 0px;
    border-radius: 8px 8px 0px 0px;
}
nav .current {
    color:#CCCCCC;
    background-color:#333333;
}
HTML
<nav>
    <ul>
        <li><a href="men.html" class="current">Men</a></li>
        <li><a href="women.html">Women</a></li>
        <li><a href="children.html">Children</a></li>
    </ul>
</nav>
```

Make sure that your navigation is displayed in a persistent location, and ensure that the current view is highlighted to clearly illustrate the user's position in the system. In this example, you'll use tabs to navigate between views and show the Men view as the current view. (See Figure 11-3.)

Figure 11-3. Example of tabbed navigation with a tab for the selected view (Men) highlighted

Identify the processes your users must go through in your experience and the steps that make them up. In this shopping experience, users can customize t-shirts. The simple CSS and HTML for the steps could be as shown here:

```
CSS
p {
    font-size: 15px;
    color:#999999
}
/* completed selector and attributes */
p a {
    text-decoration:none;
    color:#333333;
}
/* current selector and attributes */
p span {
    color: #006600;
}
HTML
<p>
```

```
    <a href="size.html">Select Size</a>&gt;
    <span>Select Color </span>&gt;
    Select Front Image &gt;
    Select Back Image
</p>
```

1. Clearly display indicators that demonstrate the total number of steps in the process and which step the user is currently on. In this example, the user has selected his size and is currently choosing a color for his shirt. (See Figure 11-4.)

Figure 11-4. Example of process indicator with completed (Size) and current (Color) steps shown

Expert tips

In addition to indicating position in a process, you need to let your users know when the system is working, as shown in Figures 11-1 and 11-2. A good rule of thumb is that a progress or working indicator should be shown for any processing expected to take longer than 500 milliseconds (a half of a second). Starting there, you can determine your users' expectations and tolerance for waiting when you take an early version of your experience out to them for evaluation. If you can, watch some people using your site. Look at their faces while they interact with your experience. Puzzled looks are great indicators that they are waiting longer than they expected to.

Solution 11-2: Matching the system to the real world

The system should speak the users' language, with words, phrases, and concepts that are familiar to them, rather than system-oriented terms. Follow real-world conventions, making information appear in a natural and logical order.

Whatever the goal of your application is, somewhere it is rooted in the replication of an analog experience. And further, your application is being built for humans to use. Based on these two notions, designing an interface that appeals to your users' existing context and conceptual framework of the task at hand will help your experience win. There's nothing worse than trying to complete a task, only to learn that the memorization of an entirely new vocabulary is required. Figure 11-5 shows the Apple iTunes software, whose Library menu organizes media into categories its users are familiar with (for example, Music, Movies, Podcasts), rather than system-centric categories like MP3, MOV, and AAC.

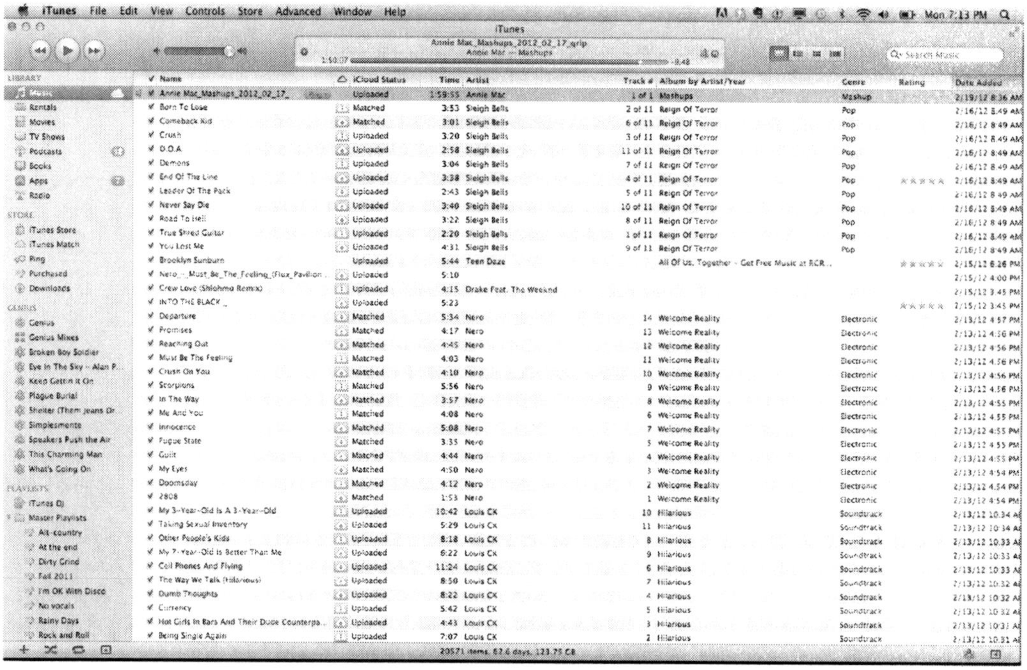

Figure 11-5. Apple's iTunes software uses real-world vocabulary in its Library menu

What's involved

Beyond using terms and concepts your user is familiar with in the real world, providing a digital re-creation of an analog object is a powerful way to connect with your user. By referencing an object that she is already familiar with, your user can hit the ground running in your new experience. It is critical to consider the interactions you provide when replicating an analog object. Take care to ensure that your user can interact with the digital version in the same way she expects to interact with the analog one. Figure 11-6 shows the Google Maps pushpin functionality. This interface successfully replicates the analog map-pushpin metaphor, and it provides a set of actions (unpinning and moving, naming, and so on) that feel natural to anyone who has ever placed a pin on a paper map.

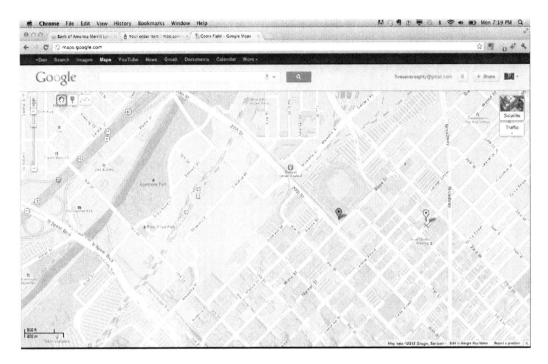

Figure 11-6. Google Maps allows users to drop "pins" at custom locations

How to build it

1. Identify the major tasks your user will use your experience to complete and the subtasks that make them up. In this case, your application allows users to create grocery lists on a desktop and retrieve them later on a mobile device. The tasks and subtasks are as follows:

   - Create a list.

   - Find an existing list.

   - Add an item.

   - Delete an item.

   - Add a quantity for items.

   - Add categories for items.

   - Reorder items.

   - Check off items.

   - Delete a list.

2. Ask five potential users to describe their grocery list-making routine to you, recording what they say. Pay particular attention to the verbs they use for the actions they take while list-making. Compare these responses to your task list, and update your list with the terms most familiar to your users. Here is an example of how you might rewrite your list using terms most commonly employed by users in your survey:

- "Create a list" changes to "Write a grocery list"

- "Find an existing list" changes to "Open my list"

- "Add an item" we'll remove and replace this with a click/tap below the latest item. Users just go to the next line on their paper lists to add an item.

- "Delete an item" changes to "Cross out an item"

- "Add quantity for items" changes to "Number"

- "Add categories for items" → "Aisle"

- "Reorder items" is removed because nobody does this.

- "Check off items" changes to "Item has been picked up"

- "Delete a list" changes to "List is done"

Expert tips

Collect any artifacts (old shopping lists) from your users that you can. These will serve as good visual guidelines for the design of your experience. In this case, we collected a number of torn-off pieces from yellow legal pads and a few old envelopes with lists on the back. Making the application background look like one of these yellow scraps of paper will create a strong association for users between their real-world process and the shopping-list experience you create for them.

Solution 11-3: Building in user control and freedom

Users often choose system functions by mistake and need a clearly marked emergency exit to leave the unwanted state without having to go through an extended series of dialog boxes or options. Support the undo and redo capabilities.

One of the worst feelings we all have as users is that of being stuck in an application. There will always be times when we feel overwhelmed (but you can ensure these instances are few and far between in your experience), get interrupted, or have to complete the task at a later date and time. Considering these real-world occurrences in your application will help you to meet expectations your users might not even know they have. Sometimes even the best-designed experiences require some exploration by their users, and ensuring that users feel safe in doing so is a winning tactic. Figure 11-7 shows the search capabilities of

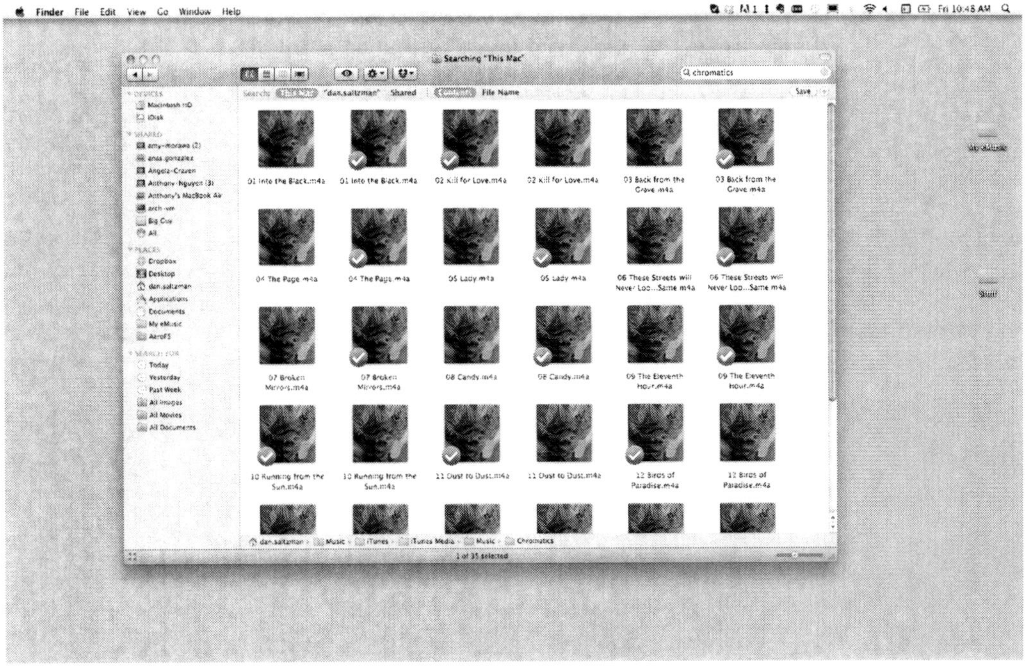

Figure 11-7. The Apple OS X Finder search box allows a user to cancel her seach easily

the Apple OS X Finder application. As the user types in a search term, results are displayed in real time (which is a great example of error prevention, and I'll say more about that later). The small, round cancel (X) button in the search box is an important nod to its users. By allowing the user to cancel a search at any time and return the results window to its previous view, the finder builds a sense of confidence in its user that she can easily exit from a mistaken search without penalty or consequence.

What's involved

Providing the freedom to exit an unintended action is good. Providing a pathway to reinstate the results of that action if the user decides it was correct is even better. Providing undo and redo capabilities might seem like a standard operating procedure, but you'll be surprised at how many experiences don't support it now that you're clued in. A good undo/redo scheme supports an appropriate amount of each capability based on the tasks at hand and should be as descriptive as possible. Figure 11-8 shows the Adobe InDesign undo and redo capabilities, which supports a large number of each capability, as well as providing context for what can be undone or redone.

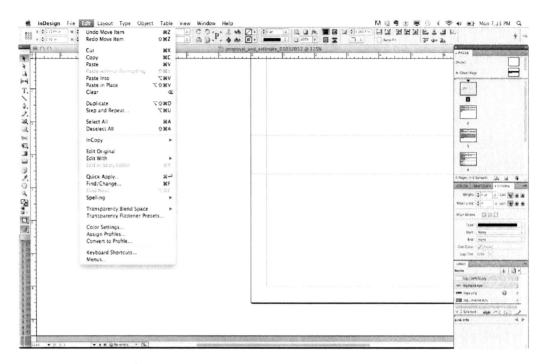

Figure 11-8. The Adobe InDesign Undo and Redo functions provide valuable freedom of movement to their users

How to build it

1. Identify opportunities for users to produce results they might not have intended in your experience. In this case, you are designing an experience for small clinics to manage their information. Search will be a primary way to locate information. From talking to the administrators at the clinic, you know that:

   - Admins don't always know whether they are searching for general patient information or information related to a specific transaction.

   - Admins will perform hundreds of different searches each day

   - Choose controls that allow flexibility and movement around the identified areas of risk. In this example, instead of creating an experience where admins must first choose what type of information to search and then enter search terms, we've added a "type" drop-down menu to our search field to help admins filter results before or after terms are entered. (See Figure 11-9.)

Figure 11-9. Example of a Search box with an attached filter, allowing for flexible searches and quick error recovery

Expert tips

Avoiding modal states (views in which Close or Back are the only actions available to your user) is a good way to increase the flexibility of your experience. Unless you can justify a specific situation or need where you should not do this, choose controls that allow your user to move from one area of your experience to another without closing the interface or application.

Solution 11-4: Establishing error prevention

Even better than providing good error messages is creating a careful design that prevents a problem from occurring in the first place. Either eliminate error-prone conditions or check for them and present users with a confirmation option before they commit to an action.

I hope you're beginning to see that it's the little things that make great experiences. Error handling is probably one of the least sexy and most overlooked tasks. Even so, as a UX designer, your job is to not only handle the errors gracefully, but to prevent users from making as many of them as possible. On the error-handling side, good form validation is one of the easiest ways you can guarantee getting the data you need in the format you need it to be in. Figure 11-10 shows the Mint.com account registration form. Not only does it validate each field once it loses focus (which you should do whenever you can), it also promotes successful error recovery (which I'll say more about later).

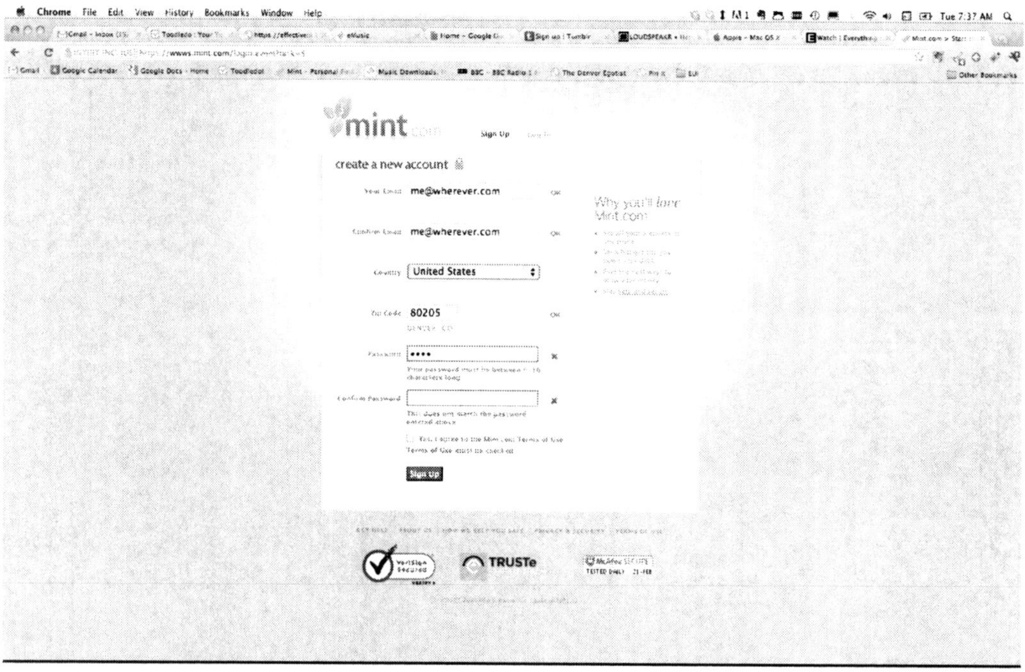

Figure 11-10. Mint.com form validation

What's involved

Although it might seem to be less efficient, breaking lengthy data-entry tasks into multiple steps, or simplifying them to gather only the most critical information, helps users to digest the task and pay attention to the rules of the data entry process. Figure 11-11 shows the tumblr blog registration page. With only three fields for the user to complete, it doesn't get much simpler than that! All of the other settings and preferences that might normally appear on a registration page are populated with intelligent defaults and left for the user to peruse once he's familiar with the application.

Figure 11-11. tumblr's blog registration—as simple as it gets

How to build it

1. Identify locations in your experience that will require user input, and specify what the elements of that input are. In this case, we're designing a bookmark manager that requires users to create an account. We'll need them to create the following:

    ■   User Name

    ■   Password

2. For each input required, define the exact format of the data you want to get from users and design messages that let users know whether they've entered the data correctly or not. In this case, the User Name text box can contain any characters the user wants to use at any length the user prefers. The Password text box, however, needs to contain at least six characters. (That's what our security guy told us.) We've included an upfront note letting users know this so that they can avoid errors. (See Figure 11-12.)

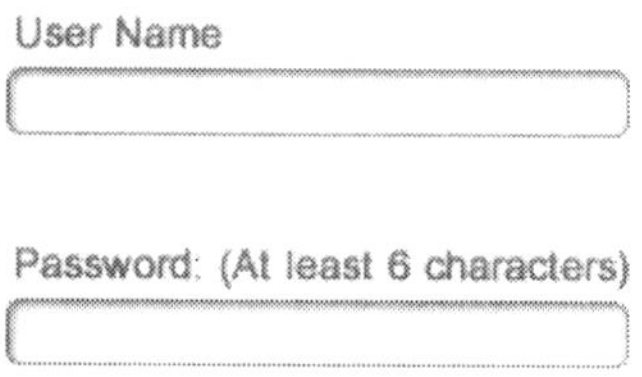

User Name

Password: (At least 6 characters)

Figure 11-12. An example of an account creation form, indicating the rules for creating a password

3. For each required input, design short, clear messages to reinforce the formatting requirements in case your user's entries are poorly formatted. Display these messages as quickly as possible after your user enters the data (on submission of the form is good, and on loss of focus from the specific field is even better). In this case, our user has entered a password containing only five characters and we display the error message immediately after the user clicks outside of the field. (See Figure 11-13.) You could also use Cascading Style Sheets (CSS) here to style the field differently if there was an error.

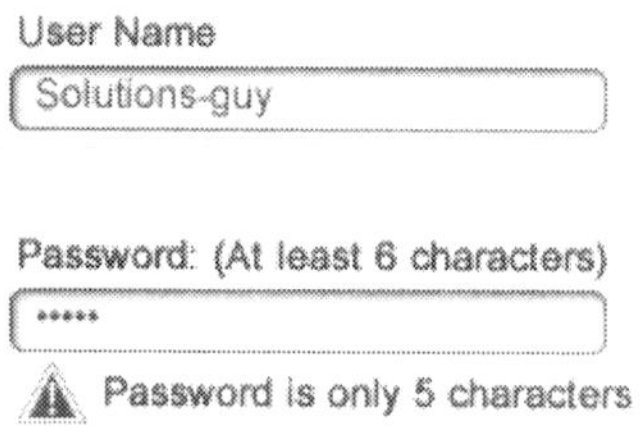

User Name

Solutions-guy

Password: (At least 6 characters)

•••••

⚠ Password is only 5 characters

Figure 11-13. An example of an account creation form with a clear, contextual error message

Expert tips

Determining what defines an error is almost as important as handling the errors themselves. It's easy to determine an error on the system side (for example, a dollar amount that's entered in a format the database isn't expecting or a failure to connect to a web service), but determining what constitutes an error to your users is more nuanced. An error from your user's perspective could be an improperly displayed layout or an errant piece of reference data that's been truncated strangely. Reviewing, and re-reviewing your experience with an eye toward these smallest of details (even if they're "being worked on") will help you prevent errors before they occur.

Solution 11-5: Promoting recognition over recall

Minimize the user's memory load by making objects, actions, and options visible. The user should not have to remember information from one part of a dialog box to another. Instructions for using the system should be visible or easily retrievable whenever appropriate.

Your users have enough to remember without having to store information that your experience could just as easily hold on to. It's commonly understood that most users have a cognitive load (the number of items they can be expected to remember at any given time) of five to seven pieces of information. With this fact in mind, the best experiences are designed to request information from users that can be easily recalled based on cues. Figure 11-14 shows the inline Attributes menu from Adobe Dreamweaver. As the user

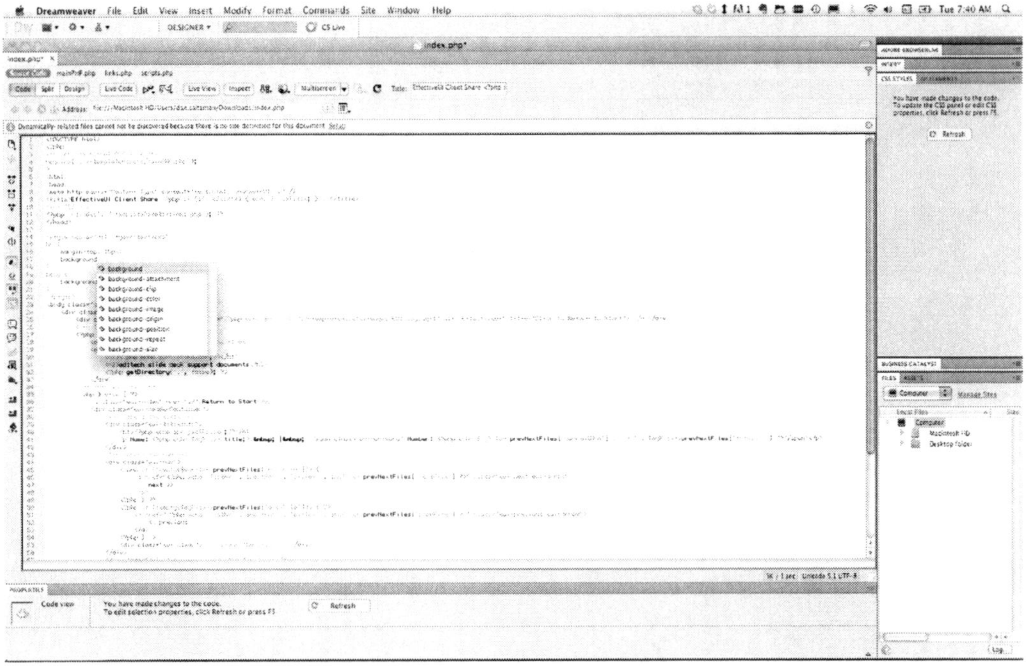

Figure 11-14. The Adobe Dreamweaver inline Attributes menu suggests attributes for the selected tag

writes code, the interface recognizes the tags being edited and suggests attributes that are pre-validated (which is a good error-prevention practice), without the user having to mentally catalog and locate the proper attribute and determine whether it has well-formed syntax.

What's involved

Recognition does not need to be limited to textual cues. In many cases, the best uses of recognition rely on nontextual cues, such as images or sounds. Consider all the ways a user might interact with your experience and how you might engage them with textual and nontextual cues. An excellent example of this is the WYSIWYG styles incorporated into recent versions of the Microsoft Office Suite. Figure 11-15 shows the Microsoft Word Home Ribbon and the Styles palette within it. Instead of describing each text style via its font attributes, the palette displays a representative example of each style, allowing the user to bypass the step of mentally building an image based on a list of attributes, as was common in the past.

Figure 11-15. The Microsoft Word Styles palette displays representative examples of each available text style

How to build it

1. Look for opportunities to show your users what you want them to do, even after the first time they walk through your experience. In this case, we're designing a travel experience where users can search for vacation packages. There are two places in particular we've identified as opportunities to demonstrate the data entry process we're looking for:

   ■ Departure Date

   ■ Return Date

2. For each opportunity, choose controls that mimic the expected data or demonstrate it in easily recognizable ways. Instead of hoping that the user can recall the departure date format that the system prefers, we've included a calendar widget in this example that can be used to auto-populate the Departure field. (See Figure 11-16.)

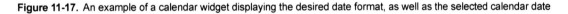

Figure 11-16. An example of a calendar widget that aids users in entering the correct date format

Whenever possible, draw a connection for the user between the control you offer them and the result that it delivers. In this example, the selected departure date on the calendar is displayed, as well as the well-formatted numeric date in the Departure field. (See Figure 11-17.)

Figure 11-17. An example of a calendar widget displaying the desired date format, as well as the selected calendar date

Expert tips

Let's talk about icons. Arguably, icons live and die by the principle of "recognition over recall." Good icons are universally recognized by your user base, while bad ones are just…weird. Many of the best icons—the classics—take their recognition cues directly from the real world. The best example of this is the classic "cut" icon with its offset, open-scissors imagery. But this isn't the only way to create a good icon. The classic refresh icon, with its semi-circular arrows has no basis in the physical world. However, after years of use, it is commonly recognized as "refresh." So what should you stay away from?

The best advice I can give is to steer clear of modifying something users already strongly associate with another action. For example, if your menu browser experience shows a steak for the meat options on a menu and a carrot for vegetarian options, you're probably better off choosing something totally new for vegan options rather than showing a purple carrot or something of that nature. As always, let common sense be your guide.

Solution 11-6: Designing for efficiency of use

Accelerators—unseen by the novice user—often speed up the interaction for the expert user such that the system can cater to both inexperienced and experienced users. Allow users to tailor frequent actions.

Determining (and sticking to) a closely defined set of target users for your experience is one of the more difficult tasks for any designer. There will always be pressure to include additional subtargets and, generally, to design for everybody. Although part of your job certainly is to help mitigate this onslaught of requests, another part involves designing for various skill levels. In the book *About Face: The Essentials of Interaction Design* (Wiley, 2007), Alan Cooper states the following:

> *Most users are neither beginners nor experts: instead they are intermediates. The experience level of people performing an activity tends, like most population distributions, to follow the classic statistical bell curve. For almost any activity requiring knowledge or skill, if we graph number of people against skill level, a relativity small number of beginners are on the left side, a few experts on the right, and the majority—intermediate users—are in the center...*
>
> *Although everybody spends some minimum time as a beginner, nobody remains in that state for long. People don't like to be incompetent, and beginners, by definition, are incompetent.*
>
> *–Alan Cooper*

What's involved

The concept encapsulated in the preceding quote is often referred to as "designing for the perpetual intermediates." In practice, this theory can be applied in several ways. One of the simplest and most often employed approaches is known as progressive disclosure. By hiding more advanced functionality until a user explicitly requests it, the experience can be kept simple for beginners but scale up for intermediate and advanced users looking for efficiencies. Figure 11-18 shows the Adobe Photoshop Actions palette. This palette is hidden by default and must be explicitly invoked by the user. When it is, the powerful capabilities of keystroke recording are exposed, and the user can repeat complex actions again and again on an unlimited number of files.

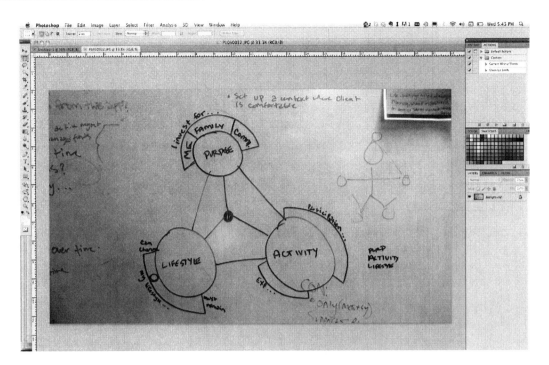

Figure 11-18. The Adobe Photoshop Actions palette

Power users can also be accommodated through thoughtful, contextual cues to more advanced functionality. Mint.com's budgeting view achieves this well, by introducing functionality for power users into an interface that is already targeted toward intermediate users. Figure 11-19 shows Mint.com's budgeting view. When the user rolls over a budget item, arrows appear preceding and following the budgeted total. These arrows allow advanced users to quickly increase or decrease the amount budgeted for that item without having to enter a dialog box.

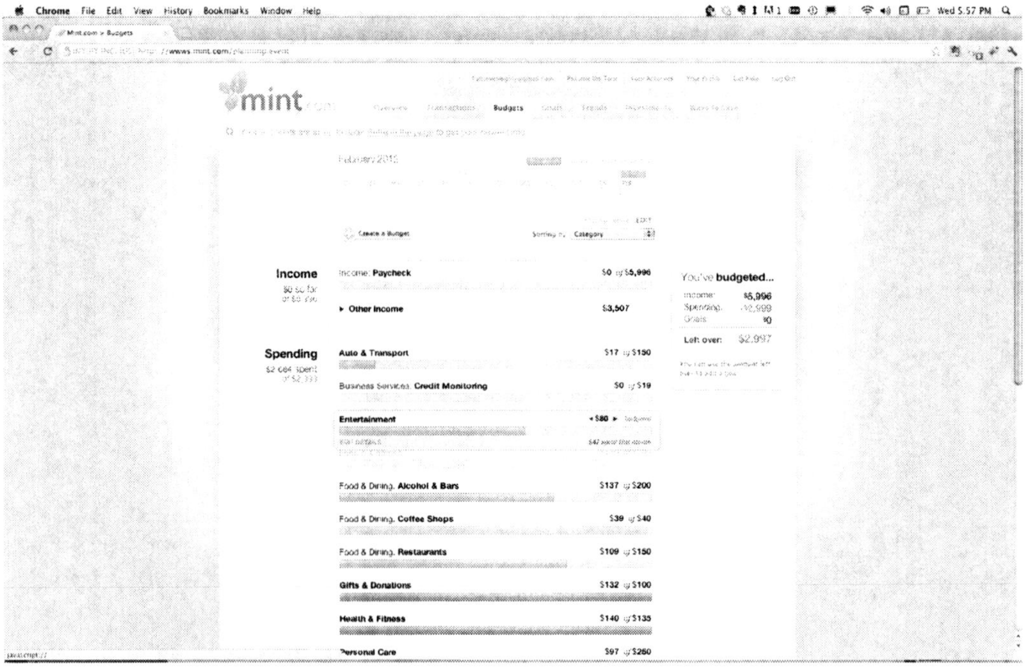

Figure 11-19. Mint.com's budgeting view provides intermediate and advanced functionality together

How to build it

1. Simplify, simplify, simplify. This might seems like an odd approach to accommodating advanced users, but it's truly the key. With your feature list in hand, rank each feature on its frequency of use and its criticality to completing the core tasks of your experience—for both your novice and advanced users. In this case, we're designing a photo-taking experience and have ranked the feature set accordingly. (See Table 11-1.)

Table 11-1. An example Frequency/Criticality Matrix for a photo experience

Task	Novice User Frequency	Criticality	Advanced User Frequency	Criticality
Take Photos	High	High	High	High
Adjust Aperture	Low	Low	Medium	Medium
Zoom In/Out	Medium	Low	High	High
Adjust Exposure	Low	Low	Medium	High
Take Several Photos at Once	Low	Low	Medium	Medium
Edit Photos	Medium	Low	High	High
Share Photos	High	Medium	High	Medium
Delete Photos	High	Low	High	Low
Organize Photos into Albums	Low	Low	High	High

2. Analyze the key differences for each feature between novice and advanced users. Where there is a large discrepancy between the two, consider placing small cues in the basic interface to the more advanced functionality. In this example, exposure adjustment appears to be a feature that is important solely for the advanced user. With this in mind, you could place a small icon in the upper left corner of the interface to access exposure controls, out of sight of novices but discoverable for advanced users who are looking for it.

Expert tips

Don't fear the V2. Remember that adding to a wildly successful app is much easier than scaling back one that is performing poorly because of users' confusion with the interface. All too often, experiences are delayed in their release because, even though they're good enough, someone has decided they need to be absolutely perfect. If you're confident that your experience is satisfying the core of your users' needs, send it out. This will give them time to respond to your hard work, and it will give you more time to refine the next set of features.

Solution 11-7: Helping users recognize, diagnose, and recover from errors

Error messages should be expressed in plain language (no codes), precisely indicate the problem, and constructively suggest a solution.

Although we've already spent a good deal of time talking about errors, it's time to get down to the business of actually presenting them. Although your goal, no doubt, is to build error-free software, the reality is that the system will fail sometimes. This familiar inevitability, when properly handled, can be turned from a user-experience dead-end into a learning opportunity and a chance to connect with your users. Error handling, in this sense, is a powerful way to let your user know that the experience will be there to support her tasks not only when they are successful, but also when the system fails. Figure 11-20 shows one of Twitter's famous error messages. Real-time feature deployment is a reality for Twitter, so in those few minutes in which code is being updated and the service is inaccessible, the interface provides the user with a proper explanation, takes responsibility for the error, and provides instructions and actions to help resolve the issue.

Figure 11-20. Twitter provides well-formed error messages when its service goes down

What's involved

Sometimes, an error can also be an opportunity to present core functionality to the user, allowing him to completely bypass the error state itself. Google Chrome's Page Not Found error page not only displays the hallmarks of a well-handled error, it also provides the ability to execute another search without having to return to the home page. Figure 11-21 shows this best-case scenario, which helps to minimize the fact that an error was even encountered in the first place.

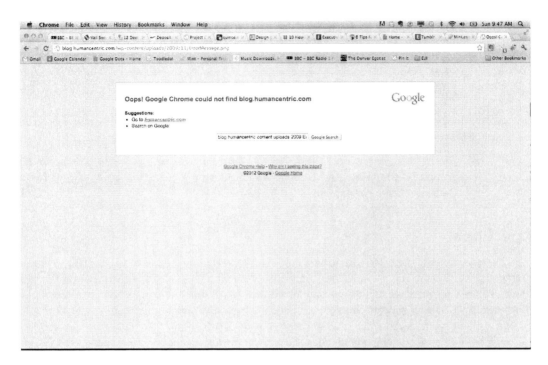

Figure 11-21. Google Chrome's Page Not Found error page helps users continue searching

How to build it

1. Clearly identify what error the user has encountered. Remember that, even though error states can be powerful tools to help developers debug and improve experiences, your user is still the primary target for your error messages. State the problem in language users will understand. In this case, we're designing an e-reader experience that produces an error when the user attempts to open a book whose file has been corrupted. The problem statement is as follows:

    ■ "Something went wrong! Bram Stoker's Dracula can't be opened."

    > Note: Use personal, conversational language as appropriate for your audience. A puzzle game's users might appreciate a snarky "OMG…We've got a problem!" at the beginning of an error message, while a legal-document browser would likely benefit from something a bit more terse.

2. Help your user diagnose the problem, if possible. In this example, the error could be related to an actual corrupt file or a file type that wasn't expected. The diagnosis is stated as follows:

    "This may be due to a corrupt file or unexpected file type."

The last part of an error message is the most important—provide a clear, direct course of action for addressing the problem. In this case, re-downloading the file is the easiest, most likely way to resolve the issues. The resolution is stated as follows:

> "Re-download the book by clicking <u>here</u>. If the problem persists, please call support at 1-888-xxx-xxxx."

3. Combine each of the three components to create a clear, cohesive error message that helps your user recover from the error state. The error message is:

    ■   "Something went wrong! Bram Stoker's Dracula can't be opened. This may be due to a corrupt file or unexpected file type. Re-download the book by clicking <u>here</u>. If the problem persists, please call support at 1-888-xxx-xxxx."

Expert tips

Providing guidance to direct the user toward the action most likely to resolve the error state he has encountered is good, and providing a secondary option is even better. In the error message shown in step 3 the final sentence provides a catch-all solution for the rare cases that the primary solution does not work for the user. By providing support contact information (where appropriate), you can ensure that all of your users will be covered even when your experience is throwing errors. Oftentimes, a user who is able to recover from an error state quickly and easily will become your number one fan.

Solution 11-8: Help and documentation

Even though it is better if the system can be used without documentation, you might need to provide help and documentation. Any such information you provide should be easy to search, focused on the user's task, include a list of concrete steps to be carried out, and not be too large.

Gone are the days of installation disks and several-hundred-page software manuals to accompany them. And I say, "Good riddance." This doesn't mean, however, that help is dead. If anything, providing guidance and assistance throughout your experience has become a more nuanced challenge to tackle.

What's involved

Your user expects to find an answer to her question immediately, in the same place on the interface where she finds herself stuck. The moment she moves to her search engine of choice for the answer is a chance for you to lose her. Help should strive to be contextual and, as stated, not too long. To meet this criteria, video is an excellent option. Figure 11-22 shows the Apple OS X Trackpad Preferences. Because multiple trackpad gestures were added to the operating system, the ability to describe each one with text alone decreased. So Apple chose to include small, looping videos to accompany each gestural preference.

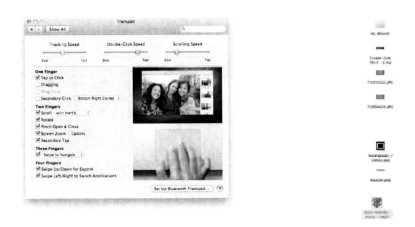

Figure 11-22. Apple OS X Trackpad Preferences—A picture's worth a thousand words

How to build it

1. Provide help for your users before they even ask. Identify tasks for which this might be appropriate. In this example, we're designing a retirement-planning experience. The design is well executed, but it covers a wide range of functionality. We've identified one area where most users are likely to benefit from some upfront help:

   ■ Getting started for the first time

   With the tasks/areas identified provide concise tips and help, in as many ways as appropriate. In this case, we have step-by-step instructions, walkthrough videos, and forums to offer our user. (See Figure 11-23.)

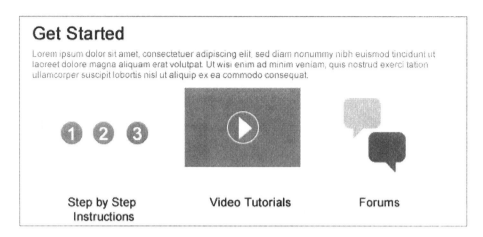

Figure 11-23. An example message providing upfront help to users getting started in the system

Note: This particular example of providing help when getting started is one place where modal dialogs and windows can be beneficial. By forcing your user to slow down and, at the very least, close the window, you can create greater probability that more users will pause to read the tips.

2. Providing contextual help for your users along the way is also a crucial component of a good support system. Identify terms, concepts, and controls that might not be immediately familiar to your target users. In this case, we've identified several terms that might require further explanation:

- Roth IRA

  SEP

  Money Market Account

  Annuity

  As the terms, concepts, and controls are displayed, provide nondestructive, nonmodal opportunities for your user to learn more. In this case, an overlay window appears when the user hovers over the help icon. (See Figure 11-24.)

Figure 11-24. An example contextual help message for an unfamiliar term

Expert tips

Don't feel like you have to build your own help and support system from the ground up for your new experience. Online tools such as GetSatisfaction (www.getsatisfaction.com) provide help, support, and knowledge-base service platforms for reasonable fees. By combining interfaces that allow users to engage in self-service help, as well as to get support if problems persist, these platforms can provide you with a virtual helpdesk without adding to your organization's headcount.

Summary

Creating a great user experience is not achieved by blindly implementing an idea that sounds great on paper. It is achieved by careful, methodical attention to detail at each design decision along the way. The rules of thumb we reviewed in this chapter can direct many of your design decisions. As you've seen, some of the biggest names in creating online user experiences present excellent examples of how to follow these guidelines. Following these guidelines and developing a thorough knowledge of who your users are and how they work will help to make your experience stand out.

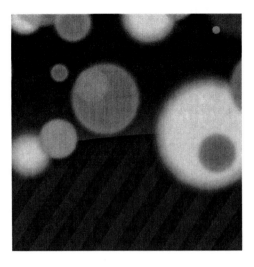

Chapter 12

Mobile UX Patterns

"We need a mobile app. Yesterday!" If I had a dollar for every client call that started out with that phrase, I'd definitely be on a beach somewhere sipping cold drinks for the rest of my days. While there's no doubt that much of the competition in developing applications that enrich the user experience has moved away from desktop apps, there's certainly no worse reason to build a mobile experience than to simply achieve parity. The emerging, as well as the established, mobile channels provide us, as designers, with unparalleled access to our users in their chosen contexts rather than one dictated by technology (i.e., a desk to accommodate a desktop computer and monitor). With this access, though, comes a host of additional considerations and approaches to explore.

Considering mobile

I once had the opportunity to work on a project whose basis was ideally suited to the mobile context: exercise. My client, let's call them Sweat, had a successful online presence from which they distributed proprietary audio and video based workouts for users to follow at home or on the road. As expected, the online presence also included articles on fitness and nutrition, a workout tracker, calorie calculator, and host of other peripheral support tools. When it came time to create a mobile experience, I couldn't wait. It seemed so right to port this core functionality to a platform where users could be much more mobile than when tied to a laptop or desktop computer.

When we first met to discuss the project, my client eagerly passed across the table a full set of design comps that Sweat's in-house designer had produced. He thought that after a simple UX review and signoff we would be done. The comps looked great, with an unobtrusive visual design and access to all of the workout content Sweat had online. All of it: the calculators, the articles, the About Us content, and background on the owners, trainers, and investors. We had a miniature version of the web experience in front of us—all of the content that any user of any kind could ever want, and so much that none of them would ever find any of it on their phones.

Solution 12-1: Scope. Cut. Repeat.

As discussed in Chapter 11, scoping to user needs is critical to designing the best user experience for your product. The mobile context amplifies this even further. Because attention spans are getting shorter online, you can bank on about half of the normal online attention span in the use of your mobile app. You have one chance to grab your user, and that's it.

What's involved

As I found with Sweat, presenting all of your functionality in the mobile context actually dilutes your message and overall brand value rather than bolstering it. Presenting a focused, targeted, and yes, limited set of functionality can greatly increase your users' satisfaction with their experience. So, how do you do this? As with UX design in general, you need to trust your gut.

How to build it

The following two exercises will help to create a conceptual framework for your experience. Identifying the most critical and highest frequency tasks for your users will create the focus that will help make your experience successful. Further grooming of this list will ensure that scope will not hold your experience back from your users any longer than necessary, and can help guide an on-going product roadmap.

1. Assuming you've identified your target users, list the major tasks those users will want to complete in your mobile experience. You can do this for an online experience that is being reimagined for mobile or a brand new product that will go to mobile first. For Sweat, the list was as follows:

    ■ Find a workout.

    ■ Listen to or view a workout.

    ■ Track your progress.

    ■ Track your calorie intake or diet.

2. If your list contains more than three or four items, consider removing one or moving the items into groups. Use your instincts here, and carefully consider and vet each area of focus. It's good to consult a friend or colleague here and justify to them each of the task areas you want to keep in the mobile experience. In the case of Sweat, we couldn't come up with a compelling enough case to keep the diet-tracking functionality. It didn't seem critical to the success of completing a workout, and the functionality quickly got complicated even as we tried to pare it down for mobile. We ended up with a small, targeted scope, which was ideal for our mobile audience:

- Find a workout.

- Listen to or view a workout.

- Track your progress.

- ~~Track calorie intake/diet~~

Expert tips

Chances are good that you'll be approaching mobile with an original scope that contains at least 10–20 items rather than an ideal 3–4. If you find yourself with a larger scope to start from, consider removing 4–6 items, scaling up as necessary to accommodate the size of the original scope. You might also have the opportunity to create multiple apps. Try card-sorting your features into two or three groups if you have a larger scope. You just might find that there's a lot more opportunity for great mobile experiences than you initially expected. Figure 12-1 shows the SoundCloud iPhone app, which trades in a long list of functionality for a direct focus on the things its users do most: listen and record.

Figure 12-1. The SoundCloud iPhone app focuses on the listening experience

Solution 12-2: Design for context

As you saw in Solution 12-1, reducing scope and being hyper vigilant about the included functionality in your mobile experience helps to create a great foundation to build upon. The most critical tool, by far, to help determine scope and to answer almost any mobile design question you might have down the road is an intimate knowledge of your user's context for use.

What's involved

Although we can reasonably assume that Sweat's online users interact with the website while seated at a desk, table, or couch while looking at their laptop, the context for mobile use has many more possibilities. Are users at the gym, standing on a treadmill? At the grocery store, standing in line? Or are they in bed, planning how to fit in tomorrow morning's cardio session before the kids wake up? Knowing what these possible contexts are and designing specifically for them increases the probability of success for your mobile experience, in the form of continued engagement and usage. Figure 12-2 shows Mint.com's iPhone app. The powerful Mint.com interface has been reimagined to provide just those things that users on the go would be most interested in—like checking the details of a recent transaction.

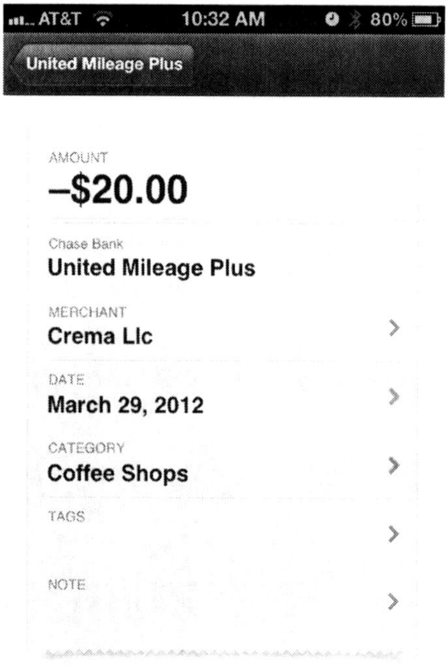

Figure 12-2. The Mint.com iPhone app promotes the information that users on the go want to see

How to build it

Imagination is key to the process of identifying triggers and distractions. While you have, hopefully, had some contact with your users, you'll still need to paint yourself a cinematic view of what their daily lives look and feel like. Don't be afraid to literally sketch the pictures that come to mind, or even to cover a spare wall in photos or magazine clippings that help to bring to life the real-world scenarios in which your users find themselves.

1. Determine the triggers that cause your users to open your experience on their mobile device. Take your best, educated guess if you haven't had direct access to your users yet. If you've interviewed a few, you have this information in hand already. Maybe your users saw a print or

online ad. Or they could be responding to an environmental cue (i.e., wanting to know the name of a song that's playing on the car radio). In our case, we determined Sweat users would most often think to launch the app in the following scenarios:

■ Once they are dressed and ready to work out

■ When they finish work for the day

■ When their kids are eating dinner

2. Determine where your users are when they use your experience. Keep in mind the same rules as before—guess if you need to. For Sweat, our users told us that they most often used the app in the following situations:

■ At home

■ On the bus or subway

3. Based on your determinations in the previous steps, identify environmental distractions that pose a threat to completing the task, as well as benefits that support task completion. Because you're designing for a handheld device where, literally, you can expect your users to be mobile, all of the distractions we encounter every day when we're not planted in front of our computers are fair game for planning around. Deliberately identifying and designing your app to combat these distractions is a must if you want to create lasting, meaningful user engagement. In the case of Sweat, the list looked something like this:

■ Waking up too late to work out in the morning [distraction]

■ Working late [distraction]

■ Kids need help with school project [distraction]

■ Fixed amount of personal time on bus or subway [benefit]

■ No need to travel to gym when working out at home [benefit]

■ Familiar equipment/space at home [benefit]

4. As your designs come together through implementation, use the list created in step 3 as a point of validation. Ensure that the functionality and overall experience specifically mitigate each distraction and amplify each benefit.

Expert tips

Take as much advantage as you can of the hardware that your selected mobile platform provides. Mobile doesn't simply mean that your users can interact with your experience from new places. It means that they can do new things in those places. One of the most interesting options available to designers and developers is the possibility of augmented-reality views. Apps that provide augmented-reality features take advantage of the hardware's camera as an input device.

Escapist Games' Star Chart is a great example of this. By not only taking advantage of the fact that users are outdoors with their mobile device, but also that the camera can be used as an input device, Star Chart can decode and display complex constellations for anyone looking to identify formations in the night sky.

(See Figure 12-3.) Other standout augmented-reality views overlay additional, relevant information, such as restaurants, reviews, and directions over cityscapes for travelers and locals alike.

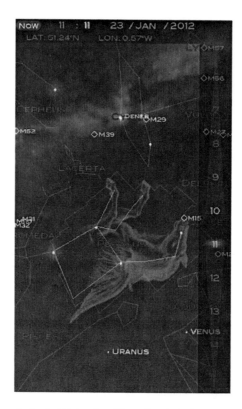

Figure 12-3. The Star Chart app for Android takes input from the device's camera and displays an overlay of the constellations the user can currently view

Solution 12-3: Craft the right approach

With your thoughts on scope and context in hand, the next phase of the design process you want to consider (before you get to the nuts and bolts of laying out views) is how best to approach your users. This is the time to start considering the actual devices your users will use to interact with your designed experience. Will it be iPhone-only? What about tablets? How much Android adoption is expected?

What's involved

Even though the decision about which platforms to support might have already been made by the time you begin designing and developing your experience, you still have an opportunity to influence future versions and, maybe, with the right information, the current approach. If these decisions are not yet set in stone, your platform approach should be heavily based on the responses from your users about the contexts in which they will use your app. (Much of this will be contained in the information you gathered for Solution 12-2.) You need to decide whether to build native applications for each platform, to go with an HTML5/CSS3 approach that many different platforms can adapt to, or a hybrid that sits somewhere in between. Armed with user-derived information, you can make a decision that accommodates the greatest number of users and user needs while keeping a close eye on efficient spending for development.

How to build it

The father of modern industrial design and a great influence on 20th century product design, Raymond Loewy, once proclaimed that

> *Ugliness does not sell.*

The thing is, he's right. Without question, many of your users will react more negatively to a bad experience than to no experience at all. With this fact in mind consider, as EffectiveUI's Shane Church suggests, that your options for determining a proper mobile approach represent a continuum rather than a discrete set of choices. (See Figure 12-4.)

Figure 12-4. The options for a mobile approach are best represented as a continuum

Ultimately, the following considerations need to be addressed to determine where on the continuum your mobile experience approach falls:

- Determine whether your experience requires access to specific hardware that is not universally available on all devices/platforms. In the case of Sweat, we did not need access to anything special like the iPhone's accelerometer. If any of the core features identified in Solutions 12-1 and 12-2 require specific hardware, you'll likely need to build a native mobile solution. If not, consider the rest of the following questions.

- Does the app need to be functional offline? To what degree?

  If yes, some sort of hybrid approach—such as using an app shell to house offline functions—will be needed.

- How sensitive is the app to variances in network performance?

  If it is moderately to highly sensitive, a hybrid approach might need to be considered.

- Does the app need to perform any processor or graphics-intensive operations like 3D graphics or real-time calculations (i.e., most games)?

  The more processor-intensive requirements that exist, the closer to native you will likely need to skew for your experience approach.

301

- What is your tolerance for supporting multiple applications and operating systems?

  Keep in mind that building multiple experiences is only one side of the coin. Make sure to consider maintenance and support costs. A mobile web approach can help cut down on the costs of maintaining several platforms.

- Do you need a presence in the app stores (Google Play, iTunes, Windows Phone Marketplace)?

  If yes, a native or hybrid approach is required.

- Do the majority of your users favor a single device or platform currently? Do you expect this to change?

  The more platforms you find necessary to support, the more attractive a mobile web solution may be.

Expert tips

Tablets are not giant mobile phones. (See Figure 12-5.) That's an overstatement of the obvious, of course, but it's critical to keep in mind that designing for tablets is a very different context from that of mobile phones. Trying to take your mobile phone experience directly to tablet, or vice versa, often results in a subpar experience. If you do need to rapidly deploy to both sets of form factors, strongly consider getting periodic user feedback during the design stages using a rapid prototyping tool such as Field Test (http://fieldtestapp.com/). Field Test allows you to take your wireframes and quickly link them together. With the mobile-friendly links it provides, you can deploy test interfaces directly onto the target device, complete with hotspots to simulate button actions.

Figure 12-5. Four iPhones does not an iPad make

Solution 12-4: Respond to the target view

Designing a miniature version of your website should not be your guiding principle for mobile development. And although we've reviewed some of the best techniques to help determine what content and functionality should flow from your online experience into your mobile experience, it does not mean that the two can't be harmonious, or even based on the same front-end codebase. In his landmark 2010 article, Ethan Marcotte makes the case for "Responsive Web Design" based on the principles of building "flexible foundations" and executing in a way that aims to "Adapt, respond, and overcome." Just as in the transition from print to web, where old layout constraints were broken and new ones introduced, he argues, the inclusion of mobile and other non-desktop viewing contexts in the mix of potential endpoints for your online experiences introduces an opportunity and a need to adapt. While a number of core UX design concepts predate the coining of "Responsive Web Design" as a term, the emergence of this approach is greatly tied to the rising popularity of HTML5 and, especially, CSS3 as viable languages for creating dynamic user experiences across digital channels.

What's involved

In theory, responsive design embraces architecture that accommodates the lowest common denominator in your multichannel approach (i.e., smartphone) and then progressively enhances the experience as it scales up to more robust channels (i.e., desktop browsers). In practice, this often means that content, in addition to straight functionality, must be prioritized. The Boston Globe, as shown in Figure 12-6, has embodied the principles of responsive design beautifully on Bostonglobe.com. As the size of the viewport changes, the content shifts, disappears, and reorders itself in an intelligent manner, with the most important articles and headlines remaining in primary view.

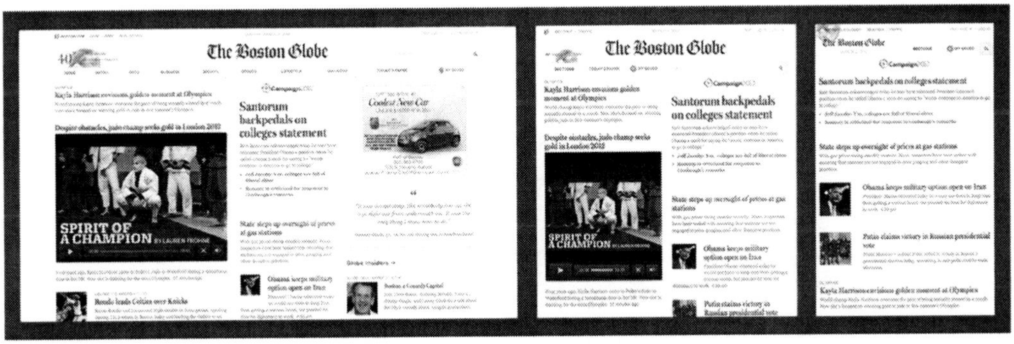

Figure 12-6. Bostonglobe.com's responsive design accommodates a variety of desktop browser viewport sizes

The beauty of this approach, however, becomes apparent when viewing the mobile version of the site. Navigate your smartphone to www.bostonglobe.com and you'll quickly see that there is no branched, mobile-specific version of the site at all. Your smartphone will resolve directly to www.Bostonglobe.com, as shown in Figure 12-7, and you'll notice that the layout looks very similar to the one shown at the right in Figure 12-6. This is the holy grail of responsive design. The design, with its content properly prioritized, accommodates viewports of any size, not just on the desktop, but for mobile and tablet as well. The consistency in experience that is established through this type of approach adds serious value to all channels of your user's experience.

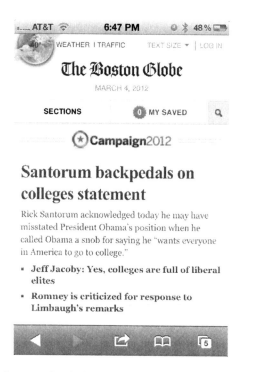

Figure 12-7. Bostonglobe.com's responsive design responds to any viewport size, even those of smartphones

How to build it

The media query can be used to support style sheets created for different device expressions. By using the media query, a whole range of device expressions can be supported with compatible css files.

In this example, the media query is written to link the "smartphone.css" file with any device that expresses that it is screen based and has a maximum device width of 480 pixels:

```
<link rel="stylesheet" type="text/css"
  media="screen and (max-device-width: 480px)"
  href="smartphone.css" />
```

Also, the media query can be used directly in the CSS. This could prove useful if minor tweaks to the layout are desired:

```
@media screen and (max-device-width: 480px) {
 .content-body {
   width: 100%;
 }
}
```

The media query uses media features to define the expressions of output device. Media features like device-width, device-height, orientation, aspect-ratio, and so on can be used to link to the correct style information for a device that expresses the values that are defined in the media query. For more information, visit http://www.w3.org/TR/css3-mediaqueries.

Expert tips

Identify the devices that will be supported prior to the design phase. By identifying the devices and their screen requirements, this will drive design and define how the media queries are implemented. For instance, if a device is orientation aware, a design that takes that into account can be created and a media query can be set up to direct the device to CSS that will support that design.

Solution 12-5: Go mobile first

Perhaps the best way to harness the power of a responsive-design approach is to adopt one of its related principles, Mobile First. Popularized by Luke Wroblewski, this foundational approach flips the traditional mobile/desktop design workflow on its head and calls for designing and deploying on mobile first, and then considering your traditional web presence—as an extension of the mobile rather than vice versa. If your application is new and you anticipate heavy mobile usage, consider this approach.

Don't assume usage on the desktop just out of habit. Try making the case for a desktop version in the same way you might have to today for a mobile version. You might be surprised at how difficult it can be. Conversely, if you're looking to bring an existing desktop web experience to mobile, think about continuing to innovate and push the product and design forward through the mobile experience, rather than just creating a stripped-down version of the original. In this way, you can offset the balance of power between desktop and mobile, setting up the potential to begin leading future design efforts with mobile, and then extending back to the desktop.

What's involved

Figure 12-8 shows the up-and-coming social network, Path. Though the functional nuances of Path differ from Facebook and the like, its true differentiator is its mobile-first (and only) approach. Rather than launch mobile and desktop web experiences together, the Path team chose to pare down the social feature set to only those things that matter in a mobile context (check-in, photos, comments, music the user is listening to). The more robust features like planning events, sharing articles, and playing Farmville are left out completely.

Figure 12-8. Path embraces a mobile-only approach

Path also provides a great example of light desktop web integration, while maintaining a mobile foundation. Figure 12-9 shows the web view for a Path "moment." This is the primary web view for Path, created in part to support its e-mail-notification functionality. Where, in the past, mobile might have been adopted only as a way to see read-only content from a desktop experience, Path has relegated the desktop to read-only status as a pathway to drive traffic back to the more robust mobile experience.

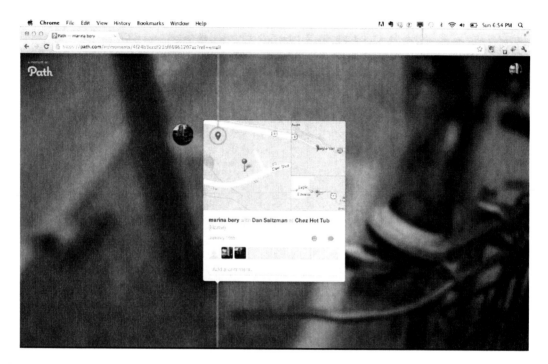

Figure 12-9. Path's desktop experience drives traffic back to the mobile experience

How to build it

Many of the new mobile-only sites are using fluid layouts that can accommodate various screen widths. Elements like buttons and form fields are built to expand and contract using simple CSS layouts. Fluid layouts will only go so far. Many of the new devices have much greater resolutions that can contain as much as 326-ppi screens. In many cases, just simply viewing a site with one of these screens forces the screen to either vertically scroll or display very small.

Mobile Safari introduced the viewport `meta` tag to allow control of the viewport's scale and size. Technically, the `meta` tag is not a part of the web standard, although many mobile browsers have begun to use it. The following `meta` tag is a typical example:

```
<meta name="viewport" content="width=device-width, initial-scale=1, maximum-scale=1">
```

The width if the viewport is set to `"device-width"`, which sets the width to the width of the screen in CSS at a scale of 100%.

The "initial-scale" sets the view port to the zoom level of 1, and the "maximum-scale" locks the zoom level to 1. This setting displays on mobile devices like iPhone and Android at about the correct physical pixel dimensions despite the higher dots-per-inch (dpi) values of the device.

Expert tips

To capitalize on the increased resolution of these new devices, designers have been designing comps at twice the resolution of the traditional design compositions. Icons and other image-based elements are sliced and kept at that higher resolution. Maintaining the higher resolution gives the images a much smoother and less pixelated look on these higher resolution screens.

If an image is going to be used as a background the background-size attribute can prove useful.

```
.my-icon-button{
    background: url('myicon.png') left top norepeat;
    background-size: 10px 20px;
}
```

In the preceding code, the image myicon.png is used as a background image. The original size of this image was 20 pixels by 40 pixels. The background-size attribute is used to reduce the image to work on devices with less screen resolution while giving the higher-display-density screens enough visual information to display the higher quality of the image without it looking pixelated.

Summary

As you've seen, designing for mobile presents much more than just another opportunity to get your brand in front of your users. It has the potential to encourage user engagement with your experience in meaningful ways that aren't possible on the desktop. Knowing that mobile devices are highly personal, you can see how designing experiences that fit this personal context will help your experience win. By presenting a tightly focused scope that speaks intelligently to the contexts on which your users will engage with your experience, you increase your opportunity to delight them. As you approach your mobile experience, consider it a first-class citizen alongside the desktop experience and strive to create harmony between the two. In some cases, you might decide that mobile-only is the strongest move for your brand.

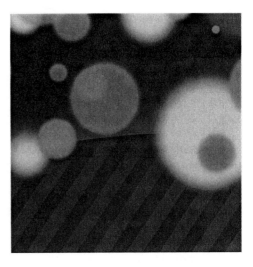

Index

O

P, Q

U

User interface
    CSS3 pseudo-classes, 261–262
    HTML5 specifications, 262

V

Video player design, 253
    browser support, 254
    jQuery plug-in, 255
        hover effect, 256
        Mute/Unmute button, animation, 257
        parent container style, 255–256
        set float, 256
        sleek style, 256
        video and volume navigation bars for
          sliders, 256
        volume slider, hide/unhide, 257–258

    markup, 254–255
    native browser video controls, 254
    themes creation, 258

W, X

Web forms. *See* Form accessiblity
World Wide Web Consortium
    (W3C), 2

Y

YUI library page, Get method, 17

Z

Zebra striping, 99

CPSIA information can be obtained at www.ICGtesting.com
Printed in the USA
LVOW110743101112

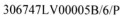

306747LV00005B/6/P

9 781430 243359